高中英语
阅读教学实践

冯喜红 冯译萱◎著

武汉理工大学出版社
·武汉·

内 容 提 要

本书是作者基于理论学习和教学实践归纳出的如何解决教学过程中实际问题的总结与思考。根据新课标提出的英语学习活动观，英语教学应以主题意义为引领，以语篇为依托，并整合语言知识、文化知识、语言技能和学习策略等学习内容，以培养学生的英语核心素养为目标。针对教材和高考题型中频率最高的记叙文、说明文和议论文，通过判断语篇类型、分析语篇的结构特征，以高考真题和教材中的语篇为例进行实践，给一线教师的教学实践带来启发，是一本值得学习研究的著作。

图书在版编目 (CIP) 数据

高中英语阅读教学实践 / 冯喜红 , 冯译萱著 .
武汉 : 武汉理工大学出版社 , 2024. 10. -- ISBN 978-7-5629-7280-8

Ⅰ . G633.412

中国国家版本馆 CIP 数据核字第 2024U1J967 号

责任编辑：尹珊珊
责任校对：严　曾　　　**排　　版**：任盼盼
出版发行：武汉理工大学出版社
社　　址：武汉市洪山区珞狮路 122 号
邮　　编：430070
网　　址：http://www.wutp.com.cn
经　　销：各地新华书店
印　　刷：北京亚吉飞数码科技有限公司
开　　本：710×1000　1/16
印　　张：18
字　　数：285 千字
版　　次：2025 年 3 月第 1 版
印　　次：2025 年 3 月第 1 次印刷
定　　价：98.00 元

凡购本书, 如有缺页、倒页、脱页等印装质量问题, 请向出版社发行部调换。
本社购书热线电话：027-87391631　87664138　87523148

·版权所有, 盗版必究·

前　言

阅读对学生的发展至关重要。正如苏霍姆林斯基在《给教师的建议》中所说,不会阅读的学生是潜在的差生。阅读能力是最基础、最关键的能力,直接决定着学生的学习效率和学习效果。阅读是进行一切英语学习活动的基础,阅读教学是高中英语教学的基础和前提。

《普通高中英语课程标准》是高中英语教学的指导性文件,它提出了六个要素构成的课程内容,并指向学科核心素养的发展。课程标准强调对学生语言能力、文化意识、思维品质和学习能力的综合培养,最终的评价也重点考查学生的英语理解能力和表达能力。虽然师生都理解阅读的重要性,但在实际教学中,很多学生的阅读能力还不能达到高考水平要求的二级学科素养水平划分标准。当学生无法理解或阅读困难时,语言能力就无从谈起,而文化意识、思维水平和学习能力更难以提升。

对一线教师而言,每天的备课、上课、批改和辅导占据了大部分的工作时间。在疲于应付每天的教学常规时,笔者也曾对专业理论知识比较排斥,认为那些阳春白雪离我们的教学非常遥远,我们有来自实践的经验,这些就足以让我们的工作得心应手。但教学中总有些困惑常常是难以解决的,当经验不足以支撑教学水平的提升时,笔者开始了研读专业领域理论书籍的历程,并总能在思考之后在教学实践中验证效果。自身理论水平的提升,伴随着教学理念的改变,在解决自身实践中大部分的困惑和问题的同时,笔者的课堂教学也产生了变化。在这个过程中,受益的不仅仅是教师,学生也能站在一个更高的平台理解英语,学习效率的提升自然水到渠成。

本书的语篇分析方法是功能语言学的语篇分析理论,语言素材主要来源于近五年的高考真题和笔者在用的外研版(2019)新教材。笔者通过梳理相关文献,包括理论专著、学术期刊论文、教材等,了解高中阅读教学的最新研究动态和教学现状,结合自己的教学实践,提出适合高中师生进行语篇分析及阅读学习的方法和策略。

本书遵循"提出问题—分析问题—解决问题"的思路,有对高中阅读教学问题的剖析,有理论知识的介绍,更多的是笔者针对高考常考语篇类型、对教材和高考语篇进行的分析和教学实践。利用功能语言学理论对记叙文、说明文、议论文等高考真题进行解题技巧的探索,以此提升教与学的效率,解决阅读中的问题。借此帮助学生形成语篇分析的结构图式,进而创建不同文体的阅读图式,提升语篇分析和解题能力,培养学生的文化意识和思维品质,全面提升学生的综合语言运用能力。同时希望能对高中一线教师有所启发。本书共分七个章节。

第一章重点阐述高中英语阅读教学的重要性和挑战。从《普通高中英语课程标准》(简称《课程标准》)和《中国高考评价体系》(简称《高考评价体系》)对高中英语阅读教学的相关要求和标准,到高中学生在英语阅读中的困难与挑战及应对措施。阐明教材和高考真题对高中英语教学的价值,在把握课程标准的基本要求的基础上,二者结合使用,达到教考衔接。

第二章通过对专业领域中的理论学习,结合课程标准的要求,重点介绍基于语篇分析理论的语篇教学,并从宏观和微观两个层面分析语篇的结构以及语篇的衔接与连贯,这是进行高中英语阅读的核心指导理论。

第三章围绕记叙文的特点、模式、判定方法以及拉波夫叙事分析等方面展开,探讨记叙文在课程标准中的篇章分析结构框架,并深入分析高考试题中的完形填空和读后续写题型的解题策略。

第四章主要从说明文的类型、语篇结构和说明方法等重点介绍说明文的阅读与分析。针对高考阅读理解对说明文的考查及七选五的语篇特点,介绍解题策略与技巧。

第五章重点关注议论文的阅读与分析。从议论文的特点及语篇结构,到高考议论文的语篇特征及考查要点,落点到教材中议论文的教学实践。

第六章重点介绍阅读中的词汇教学。从词汇学习的挑战与策略到针对高考中的猜测词义题目,分析语篇学习过程中的猜词策略与技巧。根据介词的功能,介绍教材中最活跃的几个介词及其在教材中的用法。

第七章重点介绍阅读中的语法学习。从标点符号的准确运用,到实践中的语法学习。真正落实课标要求的"形式—意义—运用"一体的语法学习要求。

在本书写作过程中,冯喜红承担了整本书的架构及大部分的写作任务。冯译萱完成了第六章第三节和第七章第一节的内容,并做了大量的素材收集和整理工作。

由于笔者的理论和实践水平有限,书中呈现的主要是笔者在教学中的实践和思考,难免存在一些谬误,敬请语言教学前辈、专家以及广大同仁不吝赐教。

冯喜红

2024 年 5 月

目 录

第一章　高中英语阅读的重要性及挑战 ······················ 1
　第一节　课程标准和高考评价体系对英语阅读教学的要求 ······ 1
　第二节　高中英语阅读中学生的挑战与应对 ···················· 6
　第三节　教师阅读教学中的困扰及改进措施 ··················· 16
　第四节　教材和高考真题对高中英语教学的价值 ··············· 27

第二章　语篇及语篇分析 ···································· 32
　第一节　语篇及语境 ·· 32
　第二节　语篇组织结构 ······································ 37
　第三节　语篇分析的 What, Why 和 How ······················ 58

第三章　记叙类文体 ·· 68
　第一节　记叙文的特点及判断要点 ···························· 68
　第二节　记叙文的语篇结构及分析 ···························· 74
　第三节　记叙文语篇中的语言学习 ···························· 87
　第四节　高考记叙文的考查形式及重点 ······················· 101

第四章　说明文文体 ······································· 112
　第一节　说明文语篇类型及结构 ····························· 112
　第二节　高考说明文阅读及解题技巧 ························· 125
　第三节　高考七选五解题策略 ······························· 145

- 第五章　议论文文体 ································· 168
  - 第一节　课程标准对议论文语篇要求及其结构特征 ········ 168
  - 第二节　高考议论文考查点及教材议论文分析 ············ 174
- 第六章　阅读中的词汇教学 ··························· 182
  - 第一节　高中学生英语词汇学习的挑战与应对 ············ 182
  - 第二节　利用高考真题探求阅读猜词技巧 ················ 194
  - 第三节　教材中常见介词的用法介绍 ···················· 214
- 第七章　阅读中的语法学习 ··························· 253
  - 第一节　小标点，大用途 ······························ 253
  - 第二节　阅读中的语法学习 ···························· 262
- 参考文献 ··· 275

第一章 高中英语阅读的重要性及挑战

英语学习需要沉浸式的学习以及大量地道语料的输入,从而确保大脑对语言的建模,建立语言学习的心理表征,为语言实践应用奠定基础。本章重点从课程标准和高考评价体系对英语教学的要求、学生在阅读中的挑战、教师的困惑及教材和高考真题对于阅读教学的价值几个角度展开。

第一节 课程标准和高考评价体系对英语阅读教学的要求

本节重点介绍高中英语教学指导性文件课程标准和高考评价体系对高中英语阅读教学的相关要求和标准,以及分析高考真题的考查侧重点。

一、课程标准对英语阅读教学的要求

《高中英语课程标准》在教育体系中具有重要地位。它是制定和规范高中英语教学内容、目标和评价体系的文件和指南,在高中阶段的英语教育中具有重要的地位和作用。其主要作用体现在以下几个方面。

指导教学内容和目标。《高中英语课程标准》提供了具体的教学目标和内容框架,明确学生需要学习的知识、技能和能力要求,帮助教师确定教学内容和教学进度。通过规范课程内容、教学目标和教学方法,

为教师提供教学指导和参考，帮助教师设计和实施教学计划；明确了学生需要掌握的知识、技能和能力要求，确保学生得到全面发展。

引导教材编写和选用。各个版本的教材可以有各自的编排体系和特色，但必须满足课程标准基本要求，以课程标准规定的课程目标、课程内容和学业质量为标准，落实学科核心素养目标。

促进教学质量提升。课程标准的制定和实施对于提升教学质量起着重要作用。通过统一的标准和要求，为教师提供规范和引导，确保不同学校、不同地区的教学水平基本一致，减少教学差异，促进了教学质量的统一性。

评价学生学习成果。课程标准明确了学生需要掌握的知识、技能和能力要求，并规定了相应的评价方式和指标，为教师提供了评价学生学习成果的依据和标准。此外，课程标准提出的能力要求和评价指标指导试题的命制，也为学生准备相关考试提供了参考。通过评估学生的学习成果，有助于促进学生的全面发展，为升学、就业提供指导。

促进教育改革。课程标准的更新和完善反映了教育改革的方向和目标。通过适应社会和时代的需求，促进学科观念和教育理念的更新，推动教育教学的转变和创新，鼓励教师运用多种教学方法和资源，培养学生的综合语言运用能力和自主学习能力。

《高中英语课程标准》对于指导教学、提升教学质量、评价学生学习成果和保障教育公平性起着至关重要的作用。

课程标准对于英语学习活动的要求，是我们教学中的圭臬。教学活动中要兼顾不同学习层次的需求，在教学中设置不同层次的活动，引导学生逐步提升自己的语言能力、思维能力和文化意识。通过活动设计，激发学生的学习兴趣，培养他们独立思考和解决问题的能力。比较文化异同、评析语篇意义等，并引导学生在新的语境中运用所学语言和文化知识，表达个人观点、情感和态度，培养学生积极主动的学习态度和正确的价值观。

语言离不开语篇，真正的语言是以语篇形式存在的，语言学习的对象是语篇。在真实生活中，语言学习者直接面对的是各式各样、长短不一的语篇，包括书面语篇和口语语篇。语言学习离不开语篇，只有将语言构成要素置于语篇之中，才能构成表达意义的语言。

"语篇不仅要有内容，而且其内容要围绕一定的主题。语言离不开语篇，语篇离不开内容，内容离不开主题和语境。"（程晓堂，2018）

教师可以根据课程标准的要求,设计多样化的活动,在语篇阅读与分析的过程中,帮助学生发展英语学科核心素养,并培养学生的语言能力、思维能力、文化意识以及积极的情感态度。

二、高考评价体系对高考阅读教学的要求

高考评价体系明确了高考的核心功能、考查内容、考查要求和考查载体,是制定高考命题标准和指导命题工作的重要依据。

结合国家课程标准修订及吸收中外教育发展和评价研究新成果,高考评价体系创造性地提出"价值引领、素养导向、能力为重、知识为基"的高考评价新理念,构建了"一核""四层""四翼"的评价体系。

近几年的高考真题,无论什么来源,都呈现出"无价值,不入题;无思维,不命题;无情境,不成题"的典型特征,这是高考评价体系在高考命题实践中的具体体现。

"高考评价体系将'引导教学'纳入核心功能,有利于理顺教考关系,增强'以考促学'的主动意识。通过考试改革,紧密对接高中育人方式改革,进一步健全立德树人落实机制,完善德、智、体、美、劳全面培养的育人体系,着力扭转教育的功利化倾向,提升教育评价水平并发挥正向积极的导向作用;通过高考改革与基础教育、高等教育改革的协调推进,在实现高校人才选拔目标的同时,高度契合高中课程改革的培养目标和评价目标,从而达到理顺教考关系、实现'以考促教、以考促学'的目的,促进立德树人根本任务的落实,共同形成更高水平的全面培养体系。"(中华人民共和国教育部考试中心,2019:11-12)

高考评价体系以充分体现核心价值的问题情境,包括"生活实践情境或学习探索情境,来承载考查内容"。学生对问题的回答必须以正确的思想观念为指导,回答也必将反映出其核心价值及心理素质。恰当而丰富的情境设置使核心价值可感可测,确保价值取向对命题实践的引领作用。这一点对于英语学科来说,所有题型都体现了核心价值引领,特别是在读后续写题型中,学生的三观及心理健康程度可以得到充分体现。高考的选拔不仅包括对知识和能力的要求,还包括对情感态度与价值观的要求,更包括以德育为主的五育并举的要求。

三、英语科高考命题特点及对高中阅读教学的启示

高考英语试题在命制过程中,注重贯彻落实高考评价体系和高中英语课程标准,进一步探索核心素养考查路径。以情景任务为重要依托,以语言能力考查为主要驱动,兼顾考查文化意识、思维品质和学习能力等要素,深度考查高考英语科的交际素养、学习素养和思辨素养,促进学生核心素养的发展。

高考命题总体保持结构稳定,稳中求变,充分体现"方向是核心,平稳是关键"的原则。试题结合高中英语教学和复习备考实际,深化基础知识,着力考查关键能力。同时,突出时代主题,强化对学生的核心价值引领,注重关键能力的评估,引导教学回归教材,稳步推进高考内容改革,并充分发挥高考的育人功能和高中英语教学的积极引导作用。

全面考查学生对英语语言的综合运用能力,加强对关键能力的考查,充分体现时代性。试题以立德树人为原则,以核心素养为目标,所选语篇全面关注人与自我、人与社会、人与自然三大主题语境,充分体现高考评价体系"一核、四层、四翼"的相关要求,难度和区分度控制较好。试卷题型稳定,在合理范围内设置适当难度,试题质量稳步提升。选材丰富多样,渗透中外文化,助力文化品格培养,培育学生的中国情怀和国际视野。同时,试题的选材符合时代性强、真实性强、体裁多样化、语篇典型及难度适合的原则。

高考题均基于语篇进行考查,加大关键能力的考查力度,提示中学英语教学要认真研究、实施新课程标准,提高课堂教学效率,有意识地渗透语篇知识,帮助学生形成语篇意识,提高语篇理解能力,以达到提高综合运用语言能力的目的,考查学生方法掌握及思维方法等高阶思维能力。

英语科的考查内容,主要体现在学科素养(包括交际素养、学习素养和思辨素养)、关键能力和必备知识三个方面。"高考英语科评价体系把高中英语科的关键能力提炼为理解和表达两大方面,四项能力(听力理解、阅读理解、书面表达和口语表达)。其中听力理解能力归纳为五项具体能力,即获取具体信息、理解主旨要义、理解说话人的观点和态度、理解说话人的目的和推断说话人的意图。阅读理解能力归纳为七项具体能力,即理解词汇、理解具体信息、理解主旨要义、理解观点和态度、

理解目的、推断、理解文章结构和类型。"(中国高考报告学术委员会，2021：71）

近几年高考英语试卷要求学生在不太熟悉的语境中使用语言，考查对语言的理解和运用及对语篇概念的准确把握。从主题角度分析意义，考查学生对语篇意图、情感态度和内涵的把握，同时重点考查学生对关键信息的识别与加工、逻辑推理与论证、语言理解与表达、批判性思维与创新思维等高阶思维能力。

高考对基础教育具有反拨作用。二者统一在立德树人这一教育根本任务之下，彼此又相对独立，遵循的规律、呈现的方式和实施的路径都存在较大差异。在这一对统一对立的矛盾中，高考虽属次要矛盾，但对教学发挥着重要的反拨作用，在特定条件下，会成为矛盾的主要方面，甚至成为基础教育的指挥棒，"考什么、教什么、学什么"，造成"不考便不教不学"的弊端。

通过对近几年高考试题的分析可以发现，"阅读理解题目的设置都旨在考查语篇的关键因素，题目的设计以帮助学生进一步理解语篇为目的，题目以考查学生对语篇的基本信息理解为主，同时加大对学生高阶思维能力的考查。对关键能力的考查并非都是难题，而是呈现出合理布局。主要体现在语篇材料的难度、试题本身的难度、题目类型的搭配、考点的呈现顺序等方面。因此，今后对阅读理解能力的考查可能会有如下趋势：一是主题语篇继续围绕三大主题选择；二是语篇类型继续呈现多样化；三是不同难度的试题比例将相对稳定；四是问题的设问方式将更加巧妙，干扰项的设置方式将更加优化（语义替换与问题突破）；五是各个具体题目的命题质量将持续提升，不断创新。"（中国高考报告学术委员会，2022：89）

以上对高考题的分析和对未来高考阅读理解能力的考查预测，对高中教学的启示主要表现在以下几方面。

多样化的语篇类型训练。考题呈现出多样化的语篇类型，学生需要具备面对不同类型文本的阅读能力。教学中引入多样化的语篇材料，强化学生对文体及其结构的理解，从全局到细节提升解读能力，着重基础信息掌握。

重视基本信息，特别是复杂信息提取。题目设计的目的是帮助学生进一步理解语篇，主要考查学生对语篇的基本信息理解。因此，在教学中适时引导学生进行深入思考和分析，加强对学生的基本信息理解能力的培养,提升他们分析、推理、判断等高阶思维能力。

设计合适的题目难度。试题的难度应该合理布局,包括语篇材料的难度、试题本身的难度、题目类型的搭配以及考点的呈现顺序等方面。在教学中根据学生的水平,逐步引入更复杂的阅读材料,尝试设计新颖的题目形式和策略,帮助学生逐渐提升阅读能力。同时,关注教材和教学方法的创新,以适应阅读理解考查的新趋势。

巧妙的问题设计与干扰项设置。问题设计可以更加巧妙,使学生需要深入思考和分析才能选出正确答案,以增加对学生高阶思维能力的考查。同时,优化干扰项的设置,增加干扰项的难度,以提高学生的应对能力和选项判断能力。例如,通过语义替换和问题突破等方式,调整试题的难度和挑战性。

通过以上启示,我们可以了解到高中英语阅读教学可能出现的趋势。教师可以根据这些趋势进行相应的教学设计和教学改进,调整教学策略和教学内容,以提高学生的阅读理解能力,更好地应对未来阅读理解考查的变化和挑战。

第二节　高中英语阅读中学生的挑战与应对

经过义务教育阶段的学习,升入高中的学生带着曾经的学习经历而来。大部分的学生为高中学习打下了坚实的基础,但也有部分学生学习中存在着漏洞,适应高中的学习有困难。本节重点从阅读动机、文化意识等几个方面,探讨高中学生在英语阅读中的困难与挑战及应对措施。

一、阅读动机不足

"所谓阅读动机,就是直接推动人进行阅读活动的内部动因,它与阅读需要密切相关,是在阅读需要的基础上产生的"。(龙群力,2012)阅读动机与阅读能力关系密切。动机不同、阅读方式不同,阅读的效果也就不同。目前高中阶段的英语学习,不少学生是为了高考而读,主要想要从阅读中获得阅读技能、提高考试分数,阅读主要是属于工具型阅读,内生动力不足。造成的后果就是阅读积极性不高,阅读层次较浅,获取的信息主要停留在课程标准中语篇分析框架中的 what 层面,很少关注 why 和 how 层面的要求,这样训练出来的学生难以适应高考对语篇深度理解的要求。

（一）影响学生阅读动机的因素

要激发学生的阅读动机,首先需要了解影响其动机的因素。学界普遍认为,影响阅读动机的因素包括个人、阅读材料和教学几个方面。

1. 学生自身因素

对于高中学生而言,经过义务阶段的英语学习,他们虽然具备一定的基础,但水平千差万别。有些学生因为英语启蒙阶段努力程度不够,英语基础知识掌握不牢固,甚至基本语音都没有掌握,不敢开口说和读。当面对高中陡然增加的课程难度时,由于初高中学习方式和侧重点存在差异,这些人仅仅跟上基本要求都很困难。许多学生无法体会到学习的成就感,陷入自我怀疑,自我效能感低,导致他们感到无助。面对学习任务时紧张、焦虑,甚至想要放弃或逃避。

2. 阅读材料因素

合适的教材能激发学生对阅读的兴趣,并促进他们内在的阅读动机。特别是渐进式的教材,在每个阶段都略微比前一个阶段更具挑战性。正如语言学家克拉申所提出的理论,学习者在自然语言环境中通过接触到稍超过他们现有语言水平的可理解内容,自然而然地掌握语言,并按照自然语言习得的顺序进行学习。语言学家克拉申的输入假说认为,"最佳的语言输入量应为 i+1,其中 i 代表学习者当前的语言水平,而 i+1 则表示语言发展的下一个阶段。只要提供足够的可理解输入,学习者的语言水平就能从 i 发展到 i+1 的阶段"（克拉申,1985,转引自文秋芳,2010：54）。

尽管现如今的教材编写已经包含了多种文体和多模态语篇，内容也贴近学生的生活，但仍不可能满足每个人的兴趣需要。教师在确保主题语境的学习的同时，还需在其他版本的教材或其他来源中寻找更好的资源进行替换、补充。学生只有在学习内容和他们自身建立更强的关联性，明确学习该内容的长远意义时，才能激发他们内在的学习动机。

教师还应通过课后拓展阅读为学生提供更多选择。学业水平和学习兴趣等因素会影响学生选择阅读材料的倾向，教师可以给学生一定的自由度，允许他们自主选择阅读的书目或内容。对学生而言，拥有选择的自主权会让他们具有更强的学习动力，学习效果也会更好。兴趣驱使是继续阅读的保证，阅读中获得的成就感会进一步增强他们的学习动机。

3. 教学因素

任何技能的掌握，既是认知性的也是非认知性的，情绪因素都起到关键作用，中学生的学习受情绪影响尤其大。他们"亲其师，信其道"，对老师的喜欢程度在很大程度上会影响他们的学习动机。当然，具备一定判断能力的高中生，是否喜欢一个老师很大程度上取决于教师的专业水平。教师需要不断提高自身的专业化水平，以灵活多样的形式践行英语课程活动观的要求，让学生从课堂学习中获得满足感，并激发其内在的阅读动机。

学生的学习活动需要指导，更需要教师精神上的支持和鼓励，这也是作为教师的价值所在。优秀的教师会督促学生积极思考，同时提供激励和支持，帮助学生主动发现学习内容对自身发展的意义。

（二）教学中可以采取的应对措施

1. 尊重学生差异、实施分层教学

在阅读教学中，尊重学生差异、实施分层教学，让每个学生都能在原有基础上提升。

（1）诊断评价。采用多样化的评价方式，进行阶段性或定期的评价，了解学生的阅读水平和能力差异。关注学生的阅读理解能力、语言

运用、思维品质和表达能力等方面。根据评价结果划分学生群体,确保每个学生都在适合自己水平的教学环境中学习,并针对性地提供反馈和指导。

诊断评价的主体应包括教师和学生。越是学生积极主动参与的学习活动,其学习效果会越好。实际上,自我诊断或测试才是更有效的学习方法。

(2)积极反馈和鼓励,提供个别指导。重点关注学生的学习过程,以便及时发现学生的进步和优点,并提供具体的建议和指导,激励学生保持持续动力。反馈不仅要对学生的结果进行评判,还应对学习过程、学习习惯等给出指导意见。如有必要,还可根据学生的个性化学习需求,提供有针对性的个别指导。在与学生一对一的交流和互动中,帮助他们解决阅读中遇到的难题,适时提供精神支持。

(3)分组活动,鼓励合作。根据学生的阅读水平和需求划分小组,在小组内开展针对不同能力水平的阅读活动,提供各自稍具挑战性的阅读材料和任务,激发他们的思维能力和分析能力。在阅读反馈环节,在小组内实行费曼学习法,较高水平的学生可以充当小组讲师,与其他学生分享自己的经验和知识。

2. 为学生的阅读搭建支架,提供策略指导

(1)根据学生兴趣和水平,提供适宜难度的阅读材料,以成就感驱动持续阅读。辅以词汇表和解析注释,帮助学生攻克生词和文化障碍。鼓励学生分享阅读体验和喜好书籍,加强互动,深化阅读理解。习得效果受情绪影响,放松愉悦促进学习,紧张焦虑则阻碍进步。

学生对英语所持有的态度和他们的英语学习经历有关,教师过多的评价和纠错会让学生感到紧张和焦虑。当他们掌握的语言和实际的语言还存在偏差时,最需要的是更多的时间和更丰富的输入。

设置合理的目标,及时给予正向反馈。教师课堂教学目标设定得 SMART 原则[①]同样适合给学生设立个性化的阅读目标。及时认可学生的努力和成果会激励他们更加投入到阅读学习中。只有当学生跨出舒适区一点点,稍稍努力就能达到要求,学习效果才会发生进步。

---

① SMART 是指要让目标明确(Specific)、可测(Measurable)、可实现(Achievable)、相关性(Relevant),并且要有时限(Time-bound)。

3. 加强语篇分析，帮助学生创建语言学习的图式和心理表征

（1）语言学习的图式。认知心理学家认为，人们在认知过程中，通过对同类事物的基本结构的信息进行抽象概括，在大脑中形成的框架结构图便是图式。有心理学家认为，图式在英语阅读的心理过程中起着一种关联的作用，是将背景知识存入脑中的一种方法，也是人类利用现有的结构对新信息进行存储加工的方法。阅读理解是读者运用头脑中的图式去理解新文本信息的过程。学习者在接触新信息时，原有的图式会被激活，新知识的学习更便捷、有效。根据图式理论，阅读能力受语言图式、内容图式和形式图式的影响。简言之，阅读能力受到大脑对基本语言知识、背景知识和语篇知识等方面的心理表征的影响。

语言知识的积累便于读者在面对新的语言材料时，能够准确理解。而背景知识和话题知识越丰富，越能帮助读者整体理解语篇。高考阅读理解中的 C 篇和 D 篇均为说明文，很多内容超出学生认知，即使具备了足够的语言知识，他们也可能会读不懂语篇内容，这对学生的阅读广度和认知水平提出了更高的要求。不同体裁的语篇其框架和组织结构各不相同，但同一题材的语篇往往有类似的结构框架。语篇知识的掌握能帮学生提高阅读速度，加深对新语篇的理解。

体裁不同，表达方式和写作手法也不相同，高中生应该重点掌握记叙文、说明文和议论文体裁的基本图式。阅读中，要明确体裁，激活形式图式，理解文章结构；结合文章主题，激活内容图式和语言图式。

本书重点要根据形式图式进行语篇分析，基本可以遵循以下几个步骤进行：

A. 确定语篇类型。首先需要确定语篇的类型，因为不同类型的语篇具有不同的形式图式。

B. 分析语篇结构。在确定语篇类型后，需要进一步分析其结构。通常，英语语篇的结构包括开头、主体和结尾三个部分。开头部分包括标题、导语等，主体部分是文章的主体内容，结尾部分是对全文的总结或评论等。

C. 识别语篇的组成部分。在分析语篇结构的基础上，需要识别语篇的各个组成部分。每个部分都有其特定的功能和作用。例如，标题用来概括文章主题，导语用来简述文章要点，段落用来组织文章内容，句

子用来表达完整意思。

　　D. 分析语篇的组织方式。英语语篇的组织方式通常包括逻辑关系、时间顺序、空间顺序等，要根据组织方式的不同对文章进行分析和理解。

　　E. 判断语篇的形式图式。形式图式通常包括文本格式、结构、语义关系等。例如，新闻报道通常采用"倒金字塔"结构，即最重要的信息放在开头，而较次要的信息依次放在后面；议论文通常包括论点、论据和结论三个部分。根据这些特点，可以判断该英语语篇的形式图式属于哪一种类型。

　　（2）心理表征。作为认知心理学的核心概念之一，心理表征是外部事物在心理活动中的内部再现，是信息预先存在的模式或概念式结构，用于快速有效地处理特定问题。几乎在每个行业或领域，杰出表现的关键是在一系列事物中发现规律，并利用这些规律来预测未来可能的问题，并迅速作出优秀的决策。学生之间的差别在很大程度上取决于他们能多敏锐地察觉自己所犯的错误。技能与心理表征之间的关系是一个良性循环：技能越娴熟，创建的心理表征就越好；心理表征越好，就越能有效地练习，磨炼技能。

　　语言学习的心理表征是指学习者在语言学习过程中对语言知识和语言使用情况的抽象表达和认知建构，是一种内在的心理结构，它涉及到对语言的理解、分析和记忆等方面。在语言学习中，心理表征的建立与学习者的认知和情感因素密切相关，是提高语言能力和语言交际效果的重要基础。

　　浸润式学习在英语教育中至关重要。它创造了一个全方位的语言环境，使学生能够广泛接触英语材料，通过听、说、读、看、写等多种方式实践，逐步构建英语内在认知，掌握语言技能。这种学习方式强调语言的自然与流畅，培养英语语感，构建心理表征。同时，它促进深度理解和认知加工，提升英语语言能力。总之，浸润式学习对英语语感和心理表征的建立具有显著提高作用。

　　心理表征是语篇解读的重要基础。对于篇章结构，心理表征可以帮助读者理解和记忆各个段落之间的关系，以及文章的主题和组织结构，识别和理解文章中的关键信息，以及如何将这些信息整合在一起。在阅读英语语篇时，读者需要将文本信息转化为心理表征，即在自己的脑海中形成对文本的内部表征。心理表征的建立有助于读者更好地理解和记忆语篇的内容。

通过建立心理表征，读者可以更好地理解语篇的内容信息，同时也可以根据形式图式对信息进行组织和预测。反过来，形式图式的运用可以促进心理表征的建立和发展，帮助读者更好地理解和记忆语篇的内容。

二、文化意识

语言是文化的载体，文化是语言的内容或内涵。通过语言可以传递和表达文化的各种概念、价值观、习俗和信仰等。语言不仅仅是一种交流工具，同时也反映了所属文化的特色。通过语言的使用和学习，人们可以获得文化知识，理解和体验不同文化的思维方式、行为规范、社会关系等方面的差异。两者紧密相连，相互影响、相互塑造。"文化和语言一体两面，互为镜像，如鸟之双翼，车之双轮，币之两面，二者相互依存，不可分离。"（武银强，武和平，2023）从词汇到语法中的时、体、态，到句子的展开模式，到语篇的图式等都能看到明显的文化差异。

文化意识作为英语学科核心素养之一，课程标准的阐释是："获得文化知识，理解文化内涵，比较文化异同，汲取文化精华，形成正确的价值观，坚定文化自信，形成自尊、自信、自强的良好品格，具备一定的跨文化沟通和传播中华文化的能力。"（中华人民共和国教育部，2020：6）

学生在语篇学习过程中，被干扰理解的有时不是词汇和语法，而是因为缺乏文化背景知识导致的。语言学习甚至可以理解成文化学习，但英语阅读教学中，教师往往偏重于语言知识，对文化背景知识重视不足，导致文化教学常常被忽视或缺乏规划。结果是学生对英语国家的文化背景缺乏了解，即便能准确掌握词汇和语法结构，却难以深入理解文章的核心和作者的意图，无法探究主题意义。

要培养文化意识，首先要了解什么是文化？英语中"culture"一词源自拉丁语，原指耕作和栽培，后引申为脱离蒙昧、走向文明的过程，强调个体实现自我价值。最早也是最经典的定义是英国人类学家泰勒（E. B. Tylor，1871）对文化的界定："文化或文明……是一个复合整体，包括知识、信仰、艺术、道德、法律、习俗以及作为一个社会成员的人所习得的其他一切能力和习惯。"从文化的本义上来讲，文化就是一个"以文化人"的动态过程。（转引自武银强、武和平，2023）

"从这个意义上来理解外语课程中的文化教学，……通过'化人'来实现'育人'和'树人'的课程目标，……'内化'为个人的文化品德、文化自觉和内在气质,'外化'为对多元文化差异的尊重和理解以及对跨文化交流能力的获得。"(武和平,2017)。

我们对于文化教学涵盖的内容、范围、课程育人目标都发生了巨大的变化。"曾经,文化在外语教学中的作用是培养了解英美文化的'外语人';现在,文化教学的作用则表现在培养具有家国情怀和全球视野、具有跨文化交际能力的'国际人'。"(武和平,2023)

语言既是文化的载体,也是思维的工具。语言能力的提高应与思维品质的发展和文化意识的形成同步。

根据功能主义语言学的观点,语言的意义是由使用语言的语境来决定的。"语言使用的语境可从内到外分为语言语境(或称为上下文)、情景语境和文化语境。(1)语言语境,即篇章内部的环境或称上下文;(2)情境语境,即篇章产生时的周围情况、事件的性质、参与者的关系、时间、地点、方式等;(3)文化语境,即说话人或作者所在的语言社团的历史、文化和风俗人情。这三种语境都有助于理解篇章的意义和交际意图。"(胡壮麟,1994:181-188)

即使在最常见的语言学习和应用场景下,也能看到"文化"的影子。单纯的一个颜色词也蕴含着文化的差异。例如,蓝色,汉语中,蓝色代表宁静、祥和,而英语中 blue 的引申义较多,常用来表示忧郁、哀伤之义,如 in a blue mood(情绪低落抑郁)。布鲁斯(Blues)更是起源于美国南部的黑人民歌乐曲,音乐节奏缓慢忧伤。此外,西方文化中 blue 还可以表示"贵族血统",blue blood 表示血统高贵。once in a blue moon(罕见的事情;难得一次),由于历法不同造成一个月中出现两个满月的情况,第二个满月被称为 blue moon,其背后也有文化的原因。

另外,生活中常见的打招呼和对人的称呼、命名也能看到非常明显的文化差异。中国人跟老师见面打招呼,一般直接称呼"老师好",所以英语课堂组织教学过程中,不少学生以"Good morning, teacher"这样的方式问候老师,其实不符合英语习惯。词典中对 teacher 的解释是:someone whose job is to teach, esp. in a school。从这个解释中,可以明显看出 teacher 是职业,不是称呼。课上对女老师的称呼最简单的方式是以"Ms + 老师的姓"来称呼,既可以避免讨论老师的婚姻状况,也可以避免 Mrs 之后需要冠夫姓的非必要性。

在我们的汉文化中,不会以长辈、位尊者的名字给自己的孩子命名,哪怕只是发音相似都要避免,但西方人经常以这种方式,来表达对这些人的尊重或纪念。外研版教材必修一 Unit 4 Friends Forever 单元中的第二篇文章 *After twenty years*，Jimmy 作为警察把成为罪犯的朋友 Bob 投入监狱。出狱后，来接 Bob 出狱的是 Jimmy 的儿子 Bob。这里可以明显看出，Jimmy 仍把 Bob 当作自己的好朋友，而且也一直怀念着他。

另一个著名的例子是马尔克斯的《百年孤独》，书里描述了布恩迪家族至少五代人，每一代都有多个人拥有相同的名字，给初读者造成混淆和极大困惑。这种重复的名字是作者马尔克斯用来展现家族血脉的连续性和重复性的一种手法。西方人有时候区分父子只在名字最后加上 Jr. 和 Sr.，如著名的 Martin Luther King, Jr. 的父亲一定是 Martin Luther King, Sr.。

2019 年全国高考 Ⅱ 卷 C 篇中 "He likes that he can sit and check his phone in peace or chat up the barkeeper with whom he's on a first-name basis if he wants to have a little interaction. 'I reflect on how my day's gone and think about the rest of the week,' he said. 'It's a chance for self-reflection. You return to work recharged and with a plan.'"

针对这段文字的设题是：

30. What do we know about Mazoleny?

A. He makes videos for the bar.

B. He's fond of the food at the bar.

C. He interviews customers at the bar.

D. He's familiar with the barkeeper.

这个题目属于文化意识方面的问题，当年出错较多。原文中 "on a first-name basis" 主要用于描述人们之间的亲密关系，通常指的是彼此直呼对方的名字而不使用姓氏。这种情况适用于朋友和熟人、家庭成员间，主要应用于非正式场合。在正式场合或与陌生人交往时，还是更适合使用姓氏或敬称来表示尊重和礼貌。

我们曾写过一篇关于圣诞节的读后续写，不少学生也因为文化背景知识的缺失造成写作情节的续写出现偏差。原文给定的信息是作者的姐姐告诉他世界上没有圣诞老人，奶奶否认了这个说法。并给了作者钱让他去买一件礼物送给最需要的人。作者买了一件外套，要送给买不起外套的同学。续写的两段分别要写的是祖孙俩把礼物送到了同学家，同学收到礼物后的感动。

中国人通常当面送礼物，所以我们的文化背景对这个续写产生了负面影响。特别是第二段的续写,给的段首句是"Grandma and I waited breathlessly for..."一方面,学生不了解这个续写语篇的故事走向是奶奶为了让孙子感悟圣诞老人的存在;另一方面,很多学生不了解圣诞老人送礼物的方式,写成了祖孙俩当面把礼物交给了 Bobby Decker,而这样就破了 Christmas 本身的魔力。其实,在外研版教材必修二 Unit 2 *The Real Father Christmas* 语篇中,对这种文化现象有说明:

"Many people still remember the magic of Father Christmas from when they were children. As parents, they try to keep that magic alive for their children for as long as they can.

That is why Letters from Father Christmas could be the perfect book for those who regard Christmas as a special time of year."

这篇文章是对 J.R.R. Tolkien 的书信集 Letters from Father Christmas 的书评。为了使孩子们相信圣诞老人的存在,在长达二十多年时间里,作者每年都以圣诞老人的口吻给家中的四个孩子写信,甚至盖上北极的邮戳。如果在处理教材语篇的时候,能够读懂读透这个文化背景,学生续写时就不太容易跑偏。

在培养学生文化意识的过程中,应深入挖掘教材语篇中的文化现象,以拓宽学生视野并提升其跨文化交际能力。现行高中英语教材版本多样,虽各有特色但均涵盖不同文化背景和价值观的语篇。在主题语境群文阅读中,我们可以跨版本选取语篇进行拓展,借助不同教材中的案例和场景,引导学生减少文化误解与偏见,并发展他们的批判思维和解决问题的能力。同时,通过对比不同文化间的差异,鼓励学生尊重和接纳多元文化。

除了教材,还可以利用多种多样的学习资源,如文学作品、音乐、电影等,拓宽学生对不同文化的认识。组织学生参观文化机构、参加文化交流活动或者举办跨文化体验活动,让学生亲身感受和体验不同文化。践行英语学习活动观的过程既是语言知识与语言技能整合发展的过程,也是文化意识不断增强、思维品质不断提升、学习能力不断提高的过程。

"文化知识的教学应以促进学生文化意识的形成和发展为目标。……这是一个内化于心、外化于行的过程,涉及几个步骤的演进和融合:感知中外文化知识——分析与比较;认同优秀文化——赏析与汲取;加深文化理解——认知与内化;形成文明素养——行为与表征。"

（中华人民共和国教育部，2020：33）

教师在进行文化教学的过程中，首先需要将语言的工具性和人文性结合起来，敏锐地观察和感知不同语言间的文化差异，发掘语言教学中的文化内容。在尊重和理解异域文化的基础上进行语言学习，同时要引导学生认知、认同本土文化，涵育文化素养、文化自信。二者相辅相成，互相促进跨文化能力培养和文化品格培育的过程。

跨文化交际能力的获得是文化教学的重点。文化知识学习主要靠记诵和理解，能力获得则主要靠体验与实践。在教学活动中，多创造一些融语言学习与文化体验为一体的实践活动，学生可以逐渐形成相互尊重、理解、包容的文化意识，感悟文化的精神内涵。

三、词汇量不足

一个人的词汇量直接影响着他的交流能力和语言表达能力。有些学生在词汇学习中存在困难，其主要原因可以归结为学生因素和教师因素。

本节内容较多，放在后面第六章，单独成章。

第三节　教师阅读教学中的困扰及改进措施

阅读课是高中英语教学中最重要的课型。在高中英语教学过程中，在充分关注语篇解读的基础上，教师要培养学生的语感，提升学生阅读技能，通过阅读教学全面提升学生英语素养和综合语言运用能力。但是限于主客观方面的多重因素，阅读课目前还存在着一些可以改进的地方。本节主要基于笔者的教学实践、理论学习和行动研究，针对目前高中阅读课中存在的问题进行分析，并基于笔者的学习与教学实践提出了一些可能的改进措施。

一、英语教师阅读教学中的困扰

(一)客观因素

1. 学生个体差异的客观存在

进入高中的学生,带着自己过去的学习经历和烙印,包括他们的学习方法、学习策略,以及知识的掌握情况等。对于理科的学习来说,学生的学科成绩跟总成绩匹配度较高,但对于英语学科来说,情况有很大不同。

首先,初高中英语教和学存在着很大的差异。初中英语学习更注重基础知识的掌握,包括词汇、语法和基本阅读理解能力。高中英语学习无论在学习目标、学习内容、思维方式、学习策略等方面的要求陡升,更注重语篇深层次的理解和分析,要求全面提升学生的综合语言运用能力。其次,高中英语学习的评价标准不同。初中英语考试更侧重于基础知识的记忆和简单应用,但高中更加强调学生的阅读理解能力、写作技巧和批判性思维。这需要学生在学习方法、策略上进行相应的调整。此外,英语学科的个体差异在学习过程中表现得尤为明显。每个学生的学习进度、对英语的兴趣,以及他们的语言天赋都不同。男女生在语言学习方面存在着先天的差异,大量理科学习优秀的男生,更喜欢抽象思维,对记忆要求较高的学科本身兴趣不高,在英语学习上存在着更大的差异。

进入高中的学生不仅需要适应新的学习内容和评价标准,还需要找到适合自己的学习方法和策略,保持学习的热情和耐心。面对班级中比较明显的个体差异,如何为学生提供有针对性的指导和支持,对英语教师提出了更高的要求。

2. 大班教学带来的挑战

高中的班额普遍较大,这对于需要很多互动和语言实践活动的英语学习不利。人数过多,学生的平均练习时间将减少,学生之间的差异性表现也更加明显。这使教师在教学起点、材料的选择和应用、讲解的深度和广度等方面很难根据学生的具体情况进行有针对性的教学。为了提高英语教学的质量和效果,在班额不变的情况下,如何增加学生实践机会,并根据学生的实际情况进行个性化教学,对教师的教学水平和教学经验提出了更高的要求。

(二)教师的主观因素

Richards(1998:1)认为,外语教师的核心知识体系包括六大领域,即教学理论、教学技巧、交流技巧、学科知识、教育推理与决策能力和情境知识。这些领域的学习需要大量的时间和精力,以及外在的支持。反思笔者个人的教学实践,曾经体现在教学中的一些突出问题主要有以下几个方面。

1. 缺乏对学生主体地位的认识

在新课程改革的大环境下,英语阅读教学环节应紧密围绕学生的需求来设计。但实践中,会更关注教学内容的完成,有时难免忽略学生的主体地位,甚至忽视学生的心智特点和思维特点,无法完全基于学生的实际问题进行教学。教学中不自信,也不信任学生能自主思考和解决问题,经常采用满堂灌的教学方式,学习以被动接受为主,课堂活动思维含量不高,学生被动和机械学习的特点突出。往往采用一刀切的教学方法,没有针对不同学生的特点进行教学,无法兼顾分层次教学,影响学习效果。

富兰克林有一句名言: Tell me, I may forget; teach me, I may remember; involve me, I will learn. (告诉我,我可能会忘记;教我,我可能会记得;让我参与,我会学习。)这句话强调了通过亲身参与和体验来学习的重要性。仅仅告诉或教授知识给他人可能不足以让他们真正理解和记住,而真正的学习发生在亲身实践、参与和探索的过程中。只有当个体参与其中并主动学习,才能真正掌握和应用所学的知识和技能。但实际教学中,因为各种因素,包括大班的因素、赶进度的要求、学生个体差异大,以及课堂掌控力的问题等,多数高中英语课堂还是教师主导,学生更多是被动听讲,难以全身心参与课堂的全过程。

没有留白意识,课堂上有时为了赶进度,没有给学生留下思考和消化的时间,给学生造成压力和焦虑,同时也无法保证他们真正理解和掌握课程内容。给学生提供的自助餐项目和内容较少,造成了部分学生吃不饱,还有部分学生掌握不好的情况。

2. 对英语阅读教学缺乏清晰的目标

教师在解读阅读材料时缺乏深入理解,教学目标不明确。教学活动形式单一,未能针对不同语篇内容实施目标导向的教学。课堂设问主线模糊,缺乏整体性和对语篇主题的凸显。教学过分聚焦在语言点和语法知识上,未能与语篇主题有效融合。缺乏多元解读能力,教学思路不清晰,未利用问题链串联课堂,活动设计模式化,常将词汇、语法与语篇割裂。这种模式过度关注文本细节,导致学生难以把握文章整体意义,忽视整体视角。

3. 评价方式过于单一,无法充分激发学生的学习积极性

教育教学中的评价方式以终结性评价为主导,如考试、测验和作业,但这种方式无法全面、客观地反映学生的真实学习情况,也无法有效激发学生主动投入学习。其局限性在于过分关注学习结果,忽视了学习过程和个体差异。为调动学生的积极性并促进全面发展,教师应探索多元化评价方式,如形成性评价、过程性评价和自我评价,并及时给予学生正面的鼓励和反馈。

4. 语言处理缺乏语境意识

首先,语法教学过于系统化,往往通过演绎法讲解语法规则,学生首先需要背记大量语法规则,配以单句强化训练,导致学生在实际语境中难以准确运用。其次,词汇处理常常脱离语境集中讲解,看似拓展了知识面、增大了容量,实则学习效果一般。集中识词或大量拓展词汇用法,反而干扰对文章本身的透彻理解,偏离主题。另外,由于缺乏语境,学生在交际中难以做到准确、达意和得体,语用知识相对匮乏。

5. 脱离语境的语言学习，学生难以进行思维训练

思维和语言紧密相连，思维是语言的先导，语言是思维的载体。通过词汇、语法等符号系统，我们传达思维的内容和形式。没有语言，思维无法完整表达；没有思维，语言将失去意义。没有基础的语言知识，就不可能有高深的分析、综合与创造性思维的发生。然而，实际教学中语言学习与思维训练常常被割裂，学生缺乏多元思维和批判性思维，无法进行深度阅读和思考。

在阅读教学中，无论文体难易，都要求学生划分文章结构并确定中心观点。尤其限制学生思维的是，提前告知学生文章的总体结构，再根据主旨大意划分段落。教学节奏看起来很快，内容充实，但多体现在知识的重复和变换角度操练上，学生难以形成个性化地分析和研究问题的思路和方法。

另外，阅读时间往往不够，老师的问题太多，干扰了学生的静心阅读时间。还没有读完、读懂，老师的提问环节就开始了，整个课堂还是教师的独角戏或者是少部分学生的展示课，其他的学生都沦为看客，影响长久的学习效果。

教学中，有时会忽视对教材语篇的学习，用大量的时间去做一些与语篇无关或者关系甚微的练习，导致学生英语阅读理解能力普遍较弱，学习效果不佳。将阅读教学等同于语言技能训练也是影响阅读教学成效的重要因素。忽视学生的语篇理解能力的培养，阅读课堂中缺乏主动思考、表达和解决问题的训练。

6. 课后作业缺乏足够的设计和关注，无法与课堂内容进行有效匹配

作业是课堂教学的延伸，是落实和巩固课堂所学、发展学生英语学科核心素养的重要手段。但实践中，作业设计中常常存在以下几个方面的问题："作业设计往往更关注语言知识的巩固和练习，忽视语言运用实践，……作业形式单一、设计碎片化，未能依托不同类型的语篇引导学生在完成作业的过程中探究主题意义、在生活情境中解决真实问题；普遍较少考虑学生的差异性，教师统一布置的作业难以满足不同学生的发展需要。"（李兴勇，2023）

二、英语阅读教学中的改进措施

高耗低效的教与学的状况,在笔者自身不断学习、实践的过程中,逐渐得到了改善。针对上面提到的问题,采取的改善措施主要包括以下几点。

(一)始终把学生放在课堂的中心位置,尊重他们的主体地位

为了提高课堂教学的效果,教师需要树立正确的学生主体意识,尊重学生的心智特点和思维特点,采用灵活多样的教学方法和手段,激发学生的学习积极性和主动性,提高他们的学习效果和综合素质。

核心素养引领下的课堂教学,突出了教育的育人功能,强调以学生为中心,教学应由知识的简单传递转向知识的构建。学科教学在尊重学科知识和发展规律的同时,更应聚焦于人的全面发展,服务于国家的人才选拔。为适应这一变革,教师需增强学习,深入研究学科专业及学生学习机制、心理学等,确保知识结构覆盖核心领域,以更好地实施素养为本的教学。

教师需要尊重学生的个体差异,并采取措施确保每个学生都能在课堂中得到纵向的发展和提升。"没有差异就没有对话;没有对话就没有教学。差异是客观存在的,是推进课堂教学的正能量。教师上课的本质恰恰在于:如何尽可能调动儿童活跃的思维,发现不同的思路,激发认知冲突,展开集体思维。"(钟启泉,2018:21)学生带着先前的认知和经验进入学习,并在学习过程中建构自己的意义。教师要重视和关注学生的需求和已有知识,将其作为学习新知识的基础和桥梁,引导他们探索新知识,促进学生的学习。

在处理学习问题时,我们鼓励学生通过合作学习,相互学习、取长补短。但为确保学习的深度和效果,教师的角色不可或缺。正如于漪老师所言,"教要教在学生不知道的地方,教在他似懂非懂之处。"学生能自己解决的问题,教师应给予空间,同时持续监控他们的学习进展。对于学生无法自行解决的难点和困惑,教师应根据学生的具体情况和能力,提供清晰、透彻的讲解,确保学生充分理解和掌握知识。教师还需根据教学目标灵活调整讲解与学生练习的时间分配,关注学生学习能力的提升、学习策略的优化,并通过课堂教学培养学生的高阶思维能力。

在课堂教学中,教师需要以学生学习为中心,主要关注"学生的情绪状态、参与状态、交往状态、思维状态和生成状态。"(余文森,2017:108—109)高度关注他们的学习状态,因为学生的状态直接影响教学的质量和效果。尊重学生的个体差异,适应学生的发展需求,关注学生的最近发展区,采用多样化的教学方法,设计适切而适度的教学。通过刻意练习,给予学生必要的引导、支持和帮助,推动他们走出舒适区,将潜在的发展区转化为实际的发展区,从而促进学生的成长。

(二)创建以学生为中心的学习共同体

学生在课堂中应该是最活跃、最重要的个体,但高中师生关系常常是单向交流,教师控制课堂,导致学生对教师保持距离。学生很少积极回应老师的问题,也不愿向老师请教自己不懂的问题,导致师生关系消极,课堂的生态失衡,教学效果不理想。

佐藤学把学习比喻为从已知世界到未知世界之旅,学习的实践是对话的实践。语言实践是培养学生综合语言运用能力的前提和基础。创建师生学习共同体,能够有效解决大班教学中学生实践机会比较少的问题。

美国学习专家埃德加·戴尔于1946年提出学习金字塔模型。他用数字形象地呈现了采用不同学习方式,学习者在两周后还能记住的内容有多少。学习金字塔显示,学习内容平均留存率在30%及以下的几种学习方式,都是个人学习或被动学习,而学习内容平均留存率在50%及以上的,是主动学习或互动学习,费曼学习法的效率尤其高。教育神经科学表明,人类是通过社会交互作用而展开学习,个人的知识建构通过交互和协同产生。知识的社会属性决定了学习组织需要保持高度的社会性。

钟启泉教授认为,人不可能一个人成长。课堂中倘若不能同他人分享,那么理解教学内容本身是难以成立的。在个体千差万别的课堂中,学生之间需要彼此取长补短:"同等学力的伙伴之间的互补,不同学力水准之间的互补——高学力的教低学力的、低学力的向高学力的学习,等等。"(钟启泉,2018:33)学生间的相互学习,彼此从同伴身上得到的学习影响力甚至大于教师。

有效地构建学生之间的学习互助,是改进教学的重要手段。首先,同伴互动可以增强学生的学习动力,提高学习效果。其次,同伴互助有利于提升学生的思维和解决问题的能力,培养他们从多个角度思考问题的习惯。此外,同伴互助能培养学生的沟通和表达能力,促进知识的应用和拓展。最后,同伴互助能增强学生的自信心和自尊心,促进情感和社会发展,建立良好的人际关系,培养合作精神和社会责任感。给予学生充分的展示机会,分享个体思维过程,使差异可视化,促进所有学生的反思,并进一步深化问题、激发新的疑问,形成可持续的学习问题,成为真正掌控自己学习的自主学习者。

(三)根据教学内容,制订可行的学习目标

学习对于学习者而言,是设定适当的目标,参照目标制订妥当的学习计划,并根据自身的具体情况进行必要的修正的过程。教学活动必须遵循"目标先行"的原则,要以终为始,在开展教学活动之前,首先需要明确活动能够达到的目标。

课程标准对英语整体学习目标有如下要求:"树立正确的英语学习观,保持对英语学习的兴趣,具有明确的学习目标,能够多渠道获取英语学习资源,有效规划学习时间和学习任务,选择恰当的策略与方法,监控、评价、反思和调整自己的学习内容和进程,逐步提高使用英语学习其他学科知识的意识和能力。"(中华人民共和国教育部,2020:6)

目前实施的大单元教学中,教师需要对单元整体教学内容和语言两方面制定学习目标。具体到每一堂课,在兼顾单元整体目标的同时,根据教学语篇的内容,在认真研读课程标准的前提下,关注学生差异,制定每堂课的教学目标。

目标制定的过程中,仍然要牢记 SMART 原则,也就是五个具体方面。分别是:

具体(Specific):目标应该明确、具体,能够清晰地描述所要实现的结果或行动。它需要回答以下问题:什么、为什么、谁、何时、在哪里等。

可测(Measurable):可以通过具体的标准评估目标的达成程度,使目标的实现进程可追踪和监控。

可实现(Achievable):目标需要考虑资源、时间、能力和现实情况等因素,是可实现的,具备合理性和可行性。

相关(Relevant):目标应该与整体目标或个人价值相一致和相关,以确保达成目标的意义和重要性。

时限（Time-bound）：目标应该设定明确的截止时间或时间范围，以推动行动和保证目标的及时性。

教师在教学活动开始之前就应该对教学活动结束后所产生的效果以及在教学过程中应该呈现的样态有清晰的预测，为教学评价的实施做好准备。

（四）采用多元评价方式，推动教、学、评一体化实施

目前，高中教学采用多元化的学业质量评价机制，主要有终结性评价和过程性评价。高中阶段的终结性评价主要包括期中/末考试、学业水平考试和高考，评价主体以教育主管部门为主，评价主体单一，评价的目的主要是为学校、教师、家长和学生提供学业质量报告，忽视学习过程，尤其重视结果。形成性评价主要以促学为目的，为教学决策提供依据，"教师要以英语学科核心素养为导向，根据活动内容，与学生共同设计形式多样的评价活动，如演讲、描述、展示、对话、游戏、陈述、讨论、制作思维导图等非纸笔测试活动。对于专项能力的评价，教师可以采用档案袋、网络学习状态数据收集和分析等途径和方式。"（中华人民共和国教育部，2020：87）

教学永远包括教和学。教和学是相辅相成的两个方面，它们彼此独立却又互相依存。教是教师的教学设计，必须明确指向具体的素养要求，好的设计会有效促进学生的学习，使学习活动中的素养培养得以在有意义的学习过程中自然形成。学是动态的语言实践活动，评是教学活动中不可或缺的部分，目的在于让学生在真实情境中展现素养，以便进行恰当的评价。

学习是语言实践的动态过程，评价是其不可或缺的组成，无评价则教学不完备。教学中的评价应该反映学习目标达成的程度，并贯穿于整个学习过程，凸显其目的性和自觉性。

学习的真实发生是评价的前提，有重点地选择学习内容进行学习与评价是教学的重要特点。评价的重点应是教学内容的重点。对于不能评或不值得评的内容，可以不评。就日常教学评价而言，只有简便易行的方式，才能持续进行。"当前改进英语课程评价方式至关重要的一点在于，要将那些需要专门纸笔测验或通过考试才能得到的指标，转化为可以在课堂上用简便易行的方式即可获取的指标。"（郭华，徐广华，2023）

课程标准中关于评价的内容非常完备,教师需要加强学习,并在教学中推动教、学、评一体化实施。

"完整的教学活动包括教、学、评三个方面。'教'是教师把握英语学科核心素养的培养方向,通过有效组织和实施课内外教与学的活动,达成学科育人的目标;'学'是学生在教师的指导下,通过主动参与各种语言实践活动,将学科知识和技能转化为自身的学科核心素养;'评'是教师依据教学目标确定评价内容和评价标准,通过组织和引导学生完成以评价目标为导向的多种评价活动,以此监控学生的学习过程,检测教与学的效果,实现以评促学,以评促教。"(中华人民共和国教育部,2020:77)

(五)合理设计作业,发挥其巩固、拓展课堂内容的功能

作业是贯彻课标理念、培养学生学科核心素养的关键手段。课后作业应该是课堂内容的延伸和拓展,旨在巩固和加深对课堂所学内容的理解和内化吸收,同时鼓励有所创造。有人形象地指出,高中的学习,课堂上老师教给学生包饺子,课后作业是包包子,考试要求包馅饼。这句话表明,老师在课堂上教授的主要是基础知识和方法,就像包饺子的方法和技巧一样,为学生构建知识的框架,课后作业则要求学生在此基础上进行实践和应用,而考试则进一步要求学生对课堂所学进行掌握和运用,并具备创新思维,能够灵活运用所学知识解决实际问题。

"高中英语作业设计应该在实践中坚持英语学科核心素养导向,将课程内容统一于作业设计中,体现主题意义探究、语言实践运用、学生分层发展和学习能力培养等理念。"(李兴勇,2023)《课程标准》明确了学生在高中必修阶段的课外阅读量平均每周不少于1500个词,在选择性必修阶段平均每周不少于2500个词。教师可以根据单元主题设计形式多样的课外阅读作业,包括单篇阅读、整本书阅读和全文阅读。多模态语篇可以帮助学生积累主题词汇,更深入地探索课程主题意义。

笔者在外研版教材 Book 1, Unit 4 *After Twenty Years* 语篇分析之后,给学生提供了另外两篇 O.Henry 的著名短篇小说,*The Gift of the Magi* 和 *The Last Leaf* 作补充阅读。这两篇文章主题积极向上,语言很美,适合高一学生阅读。给学生布置的阅读任务,首先是借助词典准确领悟语篇内容和情感表达,其次是自己组队,表演这两篇小说中的一个

片段。各组根据队员的语言能力，分配了角色，实现了分层作业和全员参与。经过一段时间的课下练习，最终在课堂上呈现了非常棒的表演，加深了对 O. Henry 小说结尾的感悟，练习了口语，赏析了语言，体会了人物的情感，自身情感也得到了升华。

（六）关爱、关心学生的心理，调动其主动学习的积极性

在学习过程中，学习的情感、认知维度交织在一起。除了学习者的认知发展之外，其动机与情感特征也同样重要。教师应该了解学生的学习情况和心理状态，给予他们适当的支持和鼓励。

首先，教师要为全体学生创建积极的课堂氛围。"教师的移情是指教师将自己的情绪或情感投射到学生身上，感受学生的情感体验，引起与学生相似的情绪性反应。移情的教师会使学生更多地参与课堂活动，获得较高的成就，形成更高水平的自我意识，学生之间的交往也会增多。教师对学生的期望和焦虑适中的时候，才会推动教师不断努力以谋求最佳的课堂气氛。"（皮连生，2009：305-308）

其次，教师要满足各层次学生需要关注的心理需求，关爱他们。通过与学生沟通、关注他们的情感变化、提供个性化的辅导等方式来解决他们的问题。同时，鼓励学生在学习中保持积极的心态和自信的态度，实现自我成长和进步。

（七）加强语篇解读，提升学生语篇阅读能力

语言能力是英语学科素养的核心，而语篇阅读能力是语言能力的核心。英语教师的专业能力，特别是语篇解读能力，对学生的阅读能力有重要影响。在某种程度上甚至可以说，教师的专业能力差异造成学生阅读能力的差异。教师首先准确把握语篇的结构、主题和信息组织方式，才能清晰地向学生介绍文章的主旨和要点及内涵。教师自身的解读策略和技巧，也会助力学生的阅读策略和技巧的提升。

语篇结构有清晰的，也有模糊的。老师划分方法只能是一种参考，未必就是最好的。结构是为主题建构服务的，如果学生能明白语篇的核心问题，明确写作手法，就可以更多地浸润在语言学习上，加强对文本的赏析与解读。

针对不同学生的需求和特点，教师可以采用归纳法、演绎法、任务型教学法等不同的教学方法，或多种教学方法相结合的方式进行教学。注重语境的创设，引导学生理解语法和词汇在实际语境中的运用。注重培养学生的语用能力，强调在不同语境中语言的准确性和得体性，使学生有更多的机会在实际语境中运用所学知识。

第四节　教材和高考真题对高中英语教学的价值

课程标准是教学和考试命题的基本依据，是学业质量标准和考试评价共同的重要性指导文件。2020年修订的课程标准清晰界定了本学科的学业质量标准，阐明了学业质量标准与考试评价的关系，并提出了学业水平考试与高考命题建议。课程标准中不仅为教材编写和教学提供了方向，也涵盖了考试命题的指导。教学和考试命题都必须服从于课程标准，确保"以标为纲，教学相宜"及"以标为准，考核有据"。

国家课程标准是教材编写、教学、评估和考试命题的依据。教材和高考题的出发点都是课程标准，是课程标准在教学与评价两个方面的具体应用。研透课程标准，也就抓住了教材的编写理念、高考题的考查方向。"依标施教"是根据课程标准进行教学活动。教材是对课标的细化落实，由课标生发而来，虽然有版本的差异，但是所有教材都是基于课标要求编写的，涵盖所有"应教"的内容（课标规定的内容），具体到学校和教师，就是依标教学。"英语教材是学生接触和学习英语语言的重要材料，也是学生了解世界，认识社会，形成正确的价值观念，培养积极的情感态度的重要途径。"（中华人民共和国教育部，2020：110）

作为大规模考试，高考客观上对高中教学起到重要的引导作用。高考评价体系界定了高考的核心功能，以高考命题改革促进教学方式改革，紧紧围绕教育的根本问题，全方位、系统化地阐释"为什么考"的问题。以新的素养考查方式引领新的学习方式，促进高中育人方式转变。"高考评价体系将'引导教学'纳入核心功能，有利于理顺教考关系，增强'以考促学'的主动意识。"（中华人民共和国教育部考试中心，

2019: 9-11)

汪瑞林在《教考衔接 破旧立新——对高考改革中两个热点问题的思考》的文章中提到"教学与考试二者是同向同行且相互影响的,加强'教考衔接'是处理二者关系的一个基本原则。考试要反映教学实践的变化发展,与教学改革的节奏与进程相协调,适度体现引领性,以考改促教改;教学要接受考试的检验,主动适应基于核心素养的考查方式的变化,摒弃过去填鸭式、满堂灌的课堂,注重培养学生的高阶思维能力和知识迁移应用能力。"(王瑞林,2022)

随着英语教学和考试改革的推进,主题意义对于语篇理解的重要性愈发凸显。选择优质的阅读素材对落实学生英语学科核心素养的培养非常重要,教材和高考题是高中英语教学最好的教与学素材。

一、教材分析与利用

要合理利用教材内容,教师首先要正确认识教材的作用。"英语教材是学生接触和学习英语语言的重要材料,也是学生了解世界,认识社会,形成正确的价值观念,培养积极的情感态度的重要途径。"(中华人民共和国教育部,2020:110)作为学生学习和教师教学的重要内容和手段,教材为学科育人提供语境和语用的范本。著名的美国作家舒伯特曾说过:"教科书中编著的阅读文章都是写作素材的集散地,也是语言现象的展示厅,是文章体裁的示范本,是语法规则的解剖室。"教材提供大量值得借鉴的语言形式、语言风格、语言表达等内容,对学生而言,教材中的文本是进行书面表达训练最方便、直接可用的素材。

教师应确立教材的核心地位,认识到其对学生学习和教学质量提升的基础性和工具性作用。创造性地使用教材的前提是对教材的精准解读,分析其篇章结构、主题思想、文化情感、文体特点、写作手法等。"教材是教师开展教学的载体和依据。教师合理分析教材,对教材提供的素材的利用价值进行正确判断,能够确保教学目标的准确定位,进而有效设计课堂活动。高效的课堂教学始于准确、合理、有效的教材分析。"(李宝荣,2016:8)

教材是教学内容的载体而不是目标,在阅读教学中,要充分利用教材,但又不能局限于教材内容。教材中涉及的文章体裁多样,涵盖但不限于高考题中的应用文、记叙文、说明文和议论文。不同文体的特征和结构、写作目的、表现手法及语言特点各不相同,不同体裁阅读文本的教学重点也各有侧重。教师可以根据语篇体裁,设计有针对性的阅读要求,给予学生必要的阅读指导,建立学生针对不同文体的阅读图式,使学生轻松掌握不同文体的阅读方法。

教材中的阅读语篇都有标题。文章的标题体现了语篇的主旨和作者的写作意图,是文章主题的高度概括。在阅读文本之前,先引导学生从标题理解入手,利用其已有的知识背景对即将学习的文本内容进行预测,充分激活学生的格式意识。另外,教材中为每一篇文章都配有精美的插图,直观、形象地呈现了教学语篇的情境,能够帮助学生更好地理解教材内容。教材中还有其他的一些文本特征,如不同字形、字号、图表、提示框等,可以为教材语篇分析提供依据。

教材除了文本材料之外,还为文本解读提供了相应的练习、活动等素材,为文本语篇的理解提供了重要的手段。以笔者所用的外研版高中教材中25篇记叙文的配套练习为例:配套练习涉及不同类型,从文章主旨大意角度,要求给文章另起题目、主旨大意、写作目的等;故事情节中有事件排序题、时间线、图表题等;最多的是体现人物性格和情感变化的;还有语篇结构和写作手法的练习。

教材中练习数量不多,但质量都非常高,涵盖了同一类语篇的重点知识点,为教和学提供了重要的参考。教师可以在阅读同类语篇时,根据语篇特点,补充其他语篇中的练习形式,对教材内容多元分析和利用,而不能简单地照搬教材内容,只实施教材中的教学任务。语言学习的目标和评价要一致,输出要跟输入匹配,确保学生的输出任务要基于足够的支架搭建。

在目前主题引领下的大单元教学情境下,教师可以适当调整教材内容顺序,特别是高三复习阶段,可以按照主题重新设计教学单元。在"一标多本"背景下,借鉴不同版本教材同一主题内容来作拓展阅读材料,帮助学生整理并积累主题词汇。大量的主题语篇阅读,词句的反复接触使学生在丰富的语境中创建心理表征,对掌握语言极有帮助,既能提高学生阅读理解能力,又能培养学生表达技能。

二、高考真题的分析与利用

语言输出的质量在很大程度上与学习材料的质量相关。教师要"选择语言地道的文本,选择让学生在阅读的过程中能有新的信息、新的收获的文本"(陈新忠、汤青等,2019)。高考真题以其独特优势,在高中英语阅读教学中占据重要地位,成为重要取材来源。"高考真题阅读材料内容积极向上,对立德树人有很好的引导作用;语言地道,能提供原汁原味的语言情境;为专家精心命制,权威性高;难度适中,生词量控制在 3% 以内,符合高中生的阅读水平。为教学内容增加语言地道、语境真实、内容丰富的语言材料。"(王来民,2020)

高考英语语篇材料来源权威,语言地道,内容紧贴时代发展,主题涵盖"人与自然、人与社会、人与自我"。体裁多样,既强调语言运用能力的综合考查,又注重学科的育人价值,充分体现了英语的工具性和人文性。经过改编和处理,突出对综合语言运用能力的考查,落实了对英语学科核心素养的考查,实现英语学科课程总目标。

在高考试题中,所有题型都以语篇为载体进行考查。简单来说,就是通过 19 个语篇考查考生的听力和阅读语篇的理解能力、综合语言运用能力和书面语篇表达能力。从语用视角整合形式、意义与应用,全面考查语用能力及思维。试题重基础,强语境,必备知识为核心。难易搭配,考点覆盖面广,布局合理,既考查学生对语篇主干信息的理解,又考查学生归纳整合信息的能力。在试题情境中,更加注重传承和发扬中华民族的优秀文明成果,增强文化自信。此外,语篇还引导学生关注和提高审美情趣,以培养其全面的素质。

教学中要充分发挥高考题对教学的导向作用。教师应认真研究高考真题,面对多年高考积累下来大量的经典真题,选择与教材单元主题语境相同的阅读材料。结合单元课文的主题语境与文章结构的分析,构建学生对同类语篇的图式,并迁移到对高考真题阅读材料的解读上。

总之,高考真题阅读材料品质卓越,不仅传递了积极向上的价值观,而且结构完整、语言地道,为教学提供了真实的语境。将这样的材料引入高中英语阅读教学,是对传统教材的突破,赋予了学生更多的学习资源。兼顾多元文体和主题语境,教学中可以按需对阅读材料进行必要的处理和二次开发,通过改变试题的提问角度、改变试题形式等改编试题,更好地适应教学目标。教师还需要了解考试要求,熟悉命题技术和规律,训练学生考试要求的核心技能。学生既可以从高考真题中获得实践经验,也能将这些经验运用到课本学习中,形成语言学习的良性循环。

除了教材和高考真题,教师还可以选择其他语言地道的阅读材料进行教学补充。例如,英文报刊、英美名著的简写本、英美文学名著等,引导学生拓展阅读范围,体验更丰富的主题语境,理解特定主题所承载的文化信息,在增加学生语言知识储备的同时,也增加他们的文化背景知识储备。

本书后面章节中用到的语言材料主要取材于近几年高考真题和外研版高中教材。

第二章　语篇及语篇分析

语篇分析是对整体语言环境下的连贯方式、逻辑思维的内在联系以及语言形式方面的分析。它将语言放在更大的语言环境中研究,使学生能够统领全篇,掌握文本的主题和句子在表达篇章整体意义上的作用,这是对传统阅读理论的发展。本章通过对专业领域中的理论学习,结合课程标准的要求,重点介绍基于语篇分析理论的语篇教学,并从宏观和微观两个角度分析语篇的结构以及语篇的衔接与连贯。

第一节　语篇及语境

本节重点介绍语篇的概念、课程标准对于语篇的定义演化、语境对语篇的意义及课程标准中提到的主题语境。

一、语篇的含义

英国人很早就注意到语篇研究在语言研究中的重要性,但语言学界对语篇研究进入迅猛发展阶段是从20世纪60年代开始的。20世纪70年代韩礼德(Halliday)提出的系统功能语言学是从语言的整体系统研究语言及其使用的语境,为语篇分析的发展奠定了基础。我国学者50多年来在语篇分析方面作出了很大的成就。

语篇的概念进入高中英语教学是21世纪的事,历经2001年版《英语课程标准(实验稿)》、2003年版《高中英语课程标准》和2017年版

《普通高中英语课程标准》。从这三版课程标准中关于语篇的界定，我们可以看到，对语篇这个概念的理解是动态的、发展的，涵盖内容越来越全面、清晰。原来的定义中，语篇是大于句子的语言单位，2017年版课程标准如此定义：语篇是表达意义的语言单位，包括口头语篇和书面语篇，是人们运用语言的常见形式。

语篇可长可短，长到一本甚至几本书，短至一句话甚至一个单词，抑或一个字母。比如，人在遇险时喊出的"help"就可以是一个独立的语篇；国际通用的无线电通话遇难求救信号，也是飞行员最高级别的求救信号，由重复的三个"Mayday"构成。陈力博士曾提到，教师给学生作业的等级评价中，一个字母也可以是一个语篇，比如A、B等。他认为判断一个单位是不是语篇的关键要素，是看它有没有语境意义、情境意义、交际意义和主题意义四种意义。对语篇知识的把握有助于学生理解语篇，也有助于他们把这些语篇知识迁移到自己的语言表达中。

人们交际时采用的语篇形式，无论是口头的还是书面的，无论长短，都是根据要表达的意义和交际的功能决定的。我国著名系统功能语言学家黄国文指出，语篇必须满足如下的条件：

"语篇应有一个论题结构或者逻辑结构，句子之间有一定的逻辑联系。语篇中的语段或句子都是在这一结构基础上组合起来的。……韩礼德和哈桑认为，最好把语篇看作语义单位，即不是形式单位，而是意义单位。"（黄国文，1988：7）

从上文可以看出，语篇是合乎语法且语义连贯的语义单位。在多模态的语篇中，本书要讨论的是教材和高考题中呈现的书面语篇样式。"韩礼德认为，语篇连贯的第一个标准是语篇内部必须一致，即内部各个部分彼此衔接；第二个标准便是语篇与语境保持一致，即符合语域要求。"（转引自胡壮麟等，2008：284-285）胡壮麟也认为，"语篇在交际功能上的连贯有赖于语篇产生时的语境知识和语篇使用者的语用知识"（胡壮麟，1994：181）。几位语言大家都提到了语境对于语篇功能体现的重要作用。

二、语境

课程标准中学科核心素养的语言能力目标要求学生："具有一定的语言意识和英语语感，在常见的具体语境中整合性地运用已有语言知识,理解口头和书面语篇所表达的意义,识别其恰当表意所采用的手段,有效地使用口语和书面语表达意义和进行人际交流。"(中华人民共和国教育部,2020:6)还提出了六要素构成的课程内容以及指向学科核心素养发展的英语学习活动观,要求"所有的语言学习活动都应该在一定的主题语境下进行,即学生围绕某一具体的主题语境,基于不同类型的语篇,在解决问题的过程中,运用语言技能获取、梳理、整合语言知识和文化知识,深化对语言的理解,重视对语篇的赏析,比较和探究文化内涵,汲取文化精华。"(中华人民共和国教育部,2020:12—13)

语境对于英语学习如此重要,那么什么是语境?语境都包含哪些内容?它们彼此的关系如何?这是本小节要重点介绍的内容。

作为社会现象的语言,其意义就在于它的社会功能和交际目的。同一个语篇在不同的语境下会传递完全不同的意义和效果。"语境是指言语活动在一定的时间和空间里所处的境况。语言是人们交流的工具,离不开交际的参与者、交际的主题、时间、地点等情景。因此,言语活动总是在一定的语境中。语篇的含义主要依赖于语境:语篇与语境相互依存、相辅相成。语篇产生于语境,又是语境的组成部分。要准确地理解语言结构所传达的意义,通常是离不开语境的。"(黄国文,1988:42)

语境可以分为语篇的内部环境,即上下文语境或语言性语境和非语言性语境,包括情景语境和文化语境。情景语境指语篇产生时的周围情况、事件的性质、参与者的关系、时间、地点、方式等;文化语境指语言参与者的文化背景,如历史文化和风土人情等,有时还指说话人的经验、知识等。

在阅读时,读者根据作者信息、自身语言及认知能力构建语篇语境。语境是语言学习的关键,帮助读者增强语感、扩大词汇、提升语言运用能力。这种构建依赖于读者的语言水平。后续章节将分析语篇结构,但主要聚焦文化与情景语境。

(一)文化语境和情境语境

每个人都属于特定的言语社团,都有其独特的历史、文化、风俗习惯、思维方式、道德观念和价值观,属于同一个特定社会文化环境中的人通常可以理解产生于该文化环境的语篇所涉及的问题,要呈现的交际功能,甚至交际双方的关系。有些情况下,对语篇的真正理解还得联系最高层次的语境,即文化语境。在中国,熟人见面常说"吃了吗?"或"去哪儿?"这是常见问候。但对不了解中国文化的西方人,他们可能误解为邀请或隐私窥探,展现了文化差异。

在跨文化交际中,本族语者能容忍语言差错,因能力可提升。但无视文化差异、言辞不当的行为难以被接受,易致交际失误和严重后果。如随意询问年龄、收入,或提出中国式的问候"去哪儿?"可能引起不快甚至冒犯。

在语篇阅读过程中,如果不了解语篇发生的社会文化背景,就可能影响学生的理解。例如,外研版高中教材 Book 3 Unit 3 *Developing ideas* 中的语篇标题是 The power of good,副标题是"The British Schindler": the life of Nicholas Winton。开课前的简单调查,发现学生不了解二战中德国对犹太人的屠杀,且大多数人没读过《辛德勒的名单》这本书或看过同名电影,很有可能理解不了副标题中加引号的部分。于是,在开始学习语篇之前,给学生播放了《辛德勒的名单》的电影简介,让学生对辛德勒从纳粹手中解救犹太人的事迹有了直观的感知,补充语篇的文化语境。在读语篇题目预测语篇内容的时候,重点关注的是副标题中"英国辛德勒",问题是"What did Schindler do during World War II? Predict what 'the British Schindler' did."学生因为有了文化背景知识的铺垫,加上教材配图,非常容易地就猜到了语篇中人物最伟大的贡献,后续的语篇理解活动就进展得非常顺利。

有学者把语篇体裁看作文化语境的内容,因为它涉及的是在一定的社会文化范围内有目的的交往。黄国文认为,"从文化语境角度看,每个语篇都可看作属于特定的语篇体裁。语篇体裁通过两种方式呈现:一是'纲要式结构';二是'体现样式'"(黄国文,2001:126)。纲要式结构指的是特定结构表明语篇的体裁,比如信件结构;语篇体裁的体现样式指从特定的结构可以判断语篇类型。例如,一个以 Once upon a time... 开头的英语语篇表明是关于童话或神话的叙事。

如果说文化语境是无形的、抽象的、根植于文化环境下每个人的内心,情景语境则需要考虑的是在什么时间、什么地点、什么人之间说过什么话、做过什么事。情景语境是生成语篇的直接因素。

情境对核心素养的形成与考查至关重要,与高考命题紧密相关,强调实际英语运用和文化意识。复杂开放情境促进学生核心素养的培养,成为评价其发展水平的依据。高考命题不断创新情境,注重考查考生在具体情境中的信息处理能力。在教授外语时，须确保学生运用语言恰当、得体且易于接受，这要求教师引导学生了解并熟悉所学语言的社会和文化背景知识。

（二）文化语境与情境语境的关系

根据 Eggins（1994，转引自黄国文 2001：130-131）的观点，"文化语境（语篇体裁）比情景语境（语域）要抽象得多，文化语境位于情景语境的层面上。情景语境决定了语域的实现，它包括了语场、基调和方式三个语域变体。文化语境比情景语境的覆盖面要广得多，但它和情景语境都是通过语言来体现的。"

概括黄国文和胡壮麟等语言大家关于韩礼德（Halliday）的观点如下："语域是一个意义概念，从语言的使用角度看，语域（情景语境）中有三个重要的影响因素影响语言使用，分别是：语场、语旨或基调和语式或方式，共同构成了语域变体。语场指的是正在发生什么事，所进行的社会活动的性质、语言所谈及或描述的内容。语旨指的是交际双方的身份、特点、地位、角色以及彼此间的关系。语式指的是语言在交际中所起的作用，包括交际采用的媒介或渠道，它可能是口头的，可能是书面的，也可能是介于两者之间的。这三个语境因素共同作用，决定了交际的内容以及对词语和语义结构的选择、交际双方的关系和交际的方式。"

要研究语篇的文体，需要从语域特征的三个语境变体着手，即从语篇所表达的内容和题材、参与者的角色及其关系，以及产生语篇的渠道和媒介。由于语境的目的决定篇章的语法和结构，因此，从语场、语旨、语式三要素着手，引导学生掌握文章所传递的主要信息，并进一步探索这些因素在语言形式上的体现，帮助学生弄清语篇文体特征，了解语篇的体裁及框架结构，并准确应用于实际交际中。

（三）主题语境

英语学习活动观由六要素整合而成，其中第一个就是主题语境。"主题为语言学习提供了主题范围或主题语境。主题语境涵盖了人与自我、人与社会和人与自然三大主题语境，涉及人文社会科学和自然科学领域等内容。学生对主题意义的探究应是学生学习语言的最重要内容，直接

影响学生语篇理解的程度、思维发展的水平和语言学习的成效。"(中华人民共和国教育部,2017:14)

主题语境的教学提示环节要求教师以主题意义为中心设计课堂活动和教学内容,紧密联系生活,鼓励学生学习和运用语言,培养他们的批判性思维和多元文化视角。正如德国一位学者比喻的那样,"将 15 克盐放在你的面前,无论如何你都难以下咽,但将 15 克盐放入一碗美味可口的汤中,你就会在享用佳肴时,不知不觉地将 15 克盐全部吸收",说明知识只有融入情境才能更好地被理解和吸收。同时,激发学生学习兴趣,培养他们的语言理解和表达能力,树立正确的三观。这样的教学可以帮助学生更好地理解和应用英语知识,提高学习效果和语言表达能力,促进他们全面发展和实现知行合一的目标。

就如何发展学生根据不同语境运用语言的能力,胡壮麟、朱永生、张德禄和李战子合著的《系统功能语言学概论》里这样说:"语言教学的主要目标是发展学生的'意义潜势'。其中主要的任务之一是发展学生根据不同的语境运用语言的能力,因此在语言教学的各个步骤中都需要注重语域特征。例如,在语篇分析中,老师可以通过各种方式把语篇的语域特征作为重要的学习内容来处理,首先要阐明语篇的语域特征是什么:讲的什么事儿(语篇的主要内容);语篇是针对什么人说或者写的,是语篇交流的对象(读者)是什么人,作者的目的是什么,用的什么口气和态度;是以什么方式组织的,如口语还是书面语;是面对面的或者是通过电话、书信、电子邮件等传过来的;是单向交流或是对话性的等等。这对语篇的分析和理解十分有益。"(胡壮麟等,2008:346)

这里面就蕴含了课程标准中语篇分析的三要素:what,why 和 how 的问题,后面会有详细的分析。

第二节 语篇组织结构

2017 年版的课程标准中,语篇类型作为课程内容被首次提出,这不仅突出了语言的整体性特征和语篇具有传递意义的重要功能,也为教师处理不同类型的语篇提出了要求。"规定了语篇类型后,学生将有机会接触和学习更加丰富多样的语篇类型,包括生活中常见的语篇和多模态形式下的各种语篇,从而有利于学生把握不同类型的语篇的特定结构、文体特征和表达方式,有助于学生加深对语篇意义的理解,也有助于他们学会使用不同类型的语篇进行有效地表达与交流。因此,在开展对主题意义探究的活动中,教师要认真研读和分析语篇,包括语篇的文体类型、篇章结构和语言特点等,引导学生在挖掘主题意义的活动中,整合语言知识学习、语言技能发展、文化意识形成和学习策略运用,落实培养学生学科核心素养的目标。"(梅德明,王蔷,2018:98)

语篇教学强调的不只是内容,更侧重其结构,尤其是信息与结构的和谐统一。在实际语言运用中,我们不仅要学习语言知识,更需要掌握不同功能的语篇如何谋篇布局、表达意义。特定的语篇体裁要求特定的语篇结构,即语篇结构中各个部分的出现与体裁有关。属于同一语篇体裁的语篇应该有相同的必要成分。

黄国文认为,系统功能语法是一种可操作性强、实用性强的语篇分析理论。在语篇分析中,本书主要以系统功能语法作为语篇分析的理论框架,并根据语篇特征进行语言学习活动,努力践行课程标准的英语学习活动观要求。

本节重点从宏观和微观两个角度介绍语篇内部各要素之间的关系。

一、语篇的组织结构

语篇的存在总是为了实现特定的交际目标,并发挥特定的功能。语篇中的每一个元素都必须直接或间接地支持这一功能的实现。语言作为社会交际的工具,具有多种功能:信息功能,用于传递信息和交流思想;表情功能,用于表达情感;劝说功能,用于说服或影响听者支持或反对某种观点;社交功能,用于在特定社交场合进行交际和应酬。为了发挥这些功能,必须采用适当的语言形式。语篇结构是作者对主题和材料深刻理解的外在体现,是体现作者构思的手段。换言之,是为文本功能的表达服务的。

篇章结构可以从宏观或微观角度分析。课标明确地阐释了宏观和微观组织结构的界定:"语篇中各要素之间存在复杂的关系,如句与句、段与段、标题与正文、文字与图表之间的关系。……句子内部的语法结构、词语搭配、指代关系、句子的信息展开方式等,属于语篇的微观组织结构。语篇中段与段的关系以及语篇各部分与语篇主题之间的关系,则属于语篇的宏观组织结构。语篇宏观组织结构还包括语篇类型、语言格式等。"(中华人民共和国教育部,2020:26-27)

语篇的宏观结构指的是总主题和语义结构,由次级话题共同蕴含。而微观结构连贯则是句子或一系列句子之间的线性或顺序性连贯,表达的命题意义相互联系。宏观组织结构涉及语篇意义的连贯性,微观组织结构则涉及语言形式的衔接性。语篇的连贯性意义或者语义,是通过语言形式的衔接手段而体现的。

同时,课程标准认为学习语篇知识是发展语言运用能力的基础:"……语篇知识有助于语言使用者有效理解听到或读到的语篇……在口头和书面表达过程中,语篇知识有助于语言使用者根据交流的需要选择恰当的语篇类型、设计合理的语篇结构、规划语篇的组成部分、保持语篇的衔接性和连贯性。"(中华人民共和国教育部,2020:27)

关于语篇的衔接与连贯之间的联系与区别,黄国文在《语篇分析概要》中曾作了非常清晰的表述:"衔接是语篇特征的重要内容,它体现在语篇的表层结构上。语法手段(如照应、替代、省略等)和词汇手段(如复现关系、同现关系)的使用,都可以表现结构上的粘着性,即结构上的衔接。衔接是语篇的有形网络。连贯指的是语篇中语义的关联。连贯存在于语篇的底层,通过逻辑推理来达到语义的连接,它是语篇的无形网络。"(黄国文,1988:10-11)

黄国文在《语篇分析的理论与实践——广告语篇研究》中有如此表述:"连贯可以通过语篇模型、语法、词汇手段等有形网络来建立。事实上,连贯也可以依靠交际双方的共有知识和逻辑推理等手段来达到。"(黄国文,2001:12-13)

在上面的讨论中,我们已看到衔接在形成语篇连贯中所起的作用。"……衔接是一种语义关系,这种语义关系可以通过各种语言手段来实现。常见的衔接手段有照应、替代、省略、词汇衔接、连接、时和体形式、语篇模型等等。"(黄国文,2001:14)

在比较研究中,我们可以发现,语篇的连贯和衔接在本质上是关于语义逻辑的关系。连贯作为语篇的隐形脉络,常常处于语篇的核心地位,拥有整体性的宏观视角,因此不容易被直接察觉,需要深入的逻辑推理来揭示;衔接则是语篇的可见脉络,常常出现在语篇的表面层次,表现出局部性的微观特性,其识别有助于确保语篇的语言意义和逻辑关系的连贯性。正如赖朝晖老师所说的,概念简化后的衔接是一种手段,连贯是最终达成的效果。连贯和衔接不可分割,互为关联。

课程标准中英语学科核心素养水平划分表中关于语篇的能力要求如表2-1所示(中华人民共和国教育部,2020:117)

表2-1 课程标准中英语学科核心素养水平划分表中关于语篇的能力要求

素养级别	语言能力
一级	在熟悉的语境中,较为熟练地使用已有的英语语言知识,理解多模态语篇传递的要义、主要信息和意图,辨识语篇的整体结构和文体,根据上下文推断意义
二级	在常见语境中,较为熟练地整合性运用已有的英语语言知识,理解多模态语篇传递的要义和具体信息,推断作者的意图、情感、态度和价值取向,提炼主题意义,分析语篇的组织结构、文体特征和语篇的连贯性,厘清主要观点和事实之间的逻辑关系,了解语篇恰当表意所采用的手段

为了培养具备高考二级水平的学生,教师的日常教学必须精准地围绕这一能力标准展开。

通过梳理课标中所列的语篇组织结构内容,宏观和微观组织结构及它们各自包含的四个方面如表2-2所示。

表2-2 语篇的组织结构

语篇的宏观组织结构(连贯)	语篇的微观组织结构(衔接)
语篇标题与正文、文字与图表之间的关系,如画龙点睛、辅助解释等	语篇中的显性衔接和连贯手段,如通过使用代词、连接词、省略句、替代等手段来实现的指代、连接、省略、替代等衔接手段
语篇类型、语篇格式,如记叙文、说明文等体裁	词语搭配,如名词短语、动词短语、形容词短语、副词短语和介词短语等
语篇各部分与语篇主题之间的关系,如"问题—解决""一般—特殊""叙事""主张—反主张""假设—真实"等语篇模式	句子内部的语法结构,句子之间的关系,如主谓宾,主从复合句所体现的递进、转折、因果关系等
语篇中段与段的关系,如体现时间和空间顺序、逻辑关系等	句子的信息展开方式,如新旧信息的布局及承接关系等

宏观结构连贯是从语篇的角度看待句子意义的总体关联,判断标准是语段或语篇必须有一个主题。语篇中的其他部分都是这个主题的组

成部分，是为主题服务的。微观结构连贯是从句子的角度看其内部的线性关联，可以通过语法、词汇、逻辑等手段来实现，是语篇的表层结构。一个语篇必须同时满足这两方面的连贯性才能被称为连贯的语篇。

因此，高中语篇教学应着眼于语篇的完整思想意义和交际内容，重点培养学生利用词汇和语法衔接手段，从宏观和微观结构入手，整体把握语篇，围绕主题，分析作者所要传达的信息及其信息构建方式，提高学生的英语阅读能力，形成英语思维能力。

在本章后续进行语篇分析时，以笔者所用的外研版 Book 1 Unit 6 中的语篇 *Longji Rice Terraces* 为例，尝试运用所学的理论进行实践应用。

二、语篇的宏观组织结构

本小节将从语篇的宏观组织结构的四个方面对语篇教学进行探讨。

（一）语篇标题与正文、文字与图表之间的关系

教材中的每个语篇除了正文，都会有一些特殊的视觉特征和文本特征。前者包括语篇正文中的一些黑体字、下划线、斜体字、不同字形字号、插图、提示框、表格、图案及不同颜色等，后者包括标题、小标题、说明、标点符号以及活动指令。它们蕴含了与语篇相关的丰富信息，不容忽视。

其实"标题如同题眼，给读者提供了一个观察和分析主题的视角或者工具，如果教师有意识地引导学生关注语篇主题与标题之间的联系，或者图片与主题之间的联系，常常会收获意外之喜。标题的文字通常比较简短，字数偏少，它与正文的关系包括：(1)提示语篇的核心概念；(2)概括整个语篇的主题内容；(3)提炼语篇的主题意义。总之，标题要体现'文字短、抓眼球快'的特点，对读者有一定程度的吸引力。标题是对正文画龙点睛的神来之笔或者独具匠心的体现。"（朱晓燕，2023：143-144）

标题与正文密不可分，相互呼应。正文需要标题引导和启发，而标题则需要通过正文的详细阐述来深化和拓展。文字作为语篇的主要表达方式，与图表等辅助手段共同构成了语篇的完整性。

图表通常指文章中附带的插图、照片和表格，不是随意配置的，也不

单纯为了版面美观,而是与课文内容相呼应,且承载了大量的知识和思想,能够使文章更加直观、形象,内容更加丰富。作为文字的补充,对正文内容起着直接或间接、明显或隐性的支持作用,有助于读者更快地梳理语篇结构,理解语篇内容,尤其对于专业性强、学生不太熟悉的话题更能提供直观的解释和帮助。语篇配图和头脑中形成的意向都可以促进学习者对语篇内容的理解和记忆。

课程标准要求,学生不仅要理解这些视觉特征和文本特征,而且还要能在自己的表达中运用。教师在语篇分析时,必须重视视觉和文本特征,并且培养、引导学生对这些信息的重视和解读。

Longji Rice Terraces 这篇文章的整体配图是大幅笼罩在云雾中的龙脊梯田春耕图(如图 2-1 所示截取的部分图片),加上题目的编排也很有特色,顺着梯田的地势排版,读者马上就能抓住文章的主要内容和文体(关于梯田的说明文)。另外,还配有两幅壮族和瑶族人的图片,跟语篇第二段中的内容匹配:"These terraces were built by the local Zhuang and Yao people, to whom Guangxi is home." 点明梯田的建造者和所在地,介绍梯田建造的历史。

图 2-1　Longji Rice Terraces 文章配图

在课后的练习 5 中,要求学生在文章中找到龙脊梯田的工作原理,利用所给图片(如图 2-2 所示)用自己的话复述。这个图片非常直观地展现了龙脊梯田局部地区的水循环,帮助学生理解第四段中提及的通过建造梯田,达到人与自然和谐相处,回应单元主题。

图 2-2　龙脊梯田局部地区的水循环

（二）语篇类型和语篇格式

概括课程标准对语篇类型的说明，语篇类型包括一切口头的、书面的；连续性的、非连续性的听、说、读、看、写多模态的形式。语篇类型主要有记叙文、议论文、说明文和应用文等。对文体的选择基于交际的目的，不同的语篇类型对应不同的表达需求：描述人物经历和事件发展，会选择记叙文；如果要说明事实、解释现象等，就会选择说明文；如果要表达观点、说服他人，就要选择议论文；如果是广告、通知等，就会选择应用文。

根据课程标准中关于语篇类型的内容要求和知识内容要求，四种常见的语篇类型的写作目的和表现形式归纳如表 2-3 所示。

表 2-3　不同语篇体裁的写作目的和表现形式

语篇体裁	语篇目的	语篇表现形式
记叙文	叙述人物经历，描述事件的发生过程	个人故事、人物介绍、短篇小说、童话、剧本、科幻故事、幽默故事、文学名著等
说明文	说明客观事物，阐释抽象事理，介绍操作步骤	地点、事物、产品介绍、现象说明、事理阐释、科技成果介绍、操作指南等
议论文	表达立场观点，阐明情感偏向及理由	论说文、评论、报刊社论、专栏文章、书评、影评等
应用文	传递信息，处理事务，解决问题	日程表、菜单、操作指令、天气预报、书信、提议、建议、工作计划、议事日程等

不同交际功能导致语篇主题和内容各异,进而形成多样化的语篇结构,每种体裁都有其特定的结构。这些结构揭示了语篇的主要思想及脉络,确保了整体语义的连贯性,并控制了语言内部各部分的关联。体裁分析有助于学生理解语篇的组织架构,掌握其特有特征,把握主旨,理解作者的写作意图和篇章结构,进而提升阅读能力。体裁教学法起源于20世纪初,旨在通过教授不同文体和体裁的写作技巧,帮助学生提升写作能力。它强调学生对文体特点、结构和语言运用的理解,使他们能在不同场景下灵活运用,提升沟通技巧。

"因体读文"教学法能够迅速指引学生捕捉文章要点,深刻理解作者的立场、态度和创作目的,从而高效解答问题。图式理论是分析不同语篇类型和格式的有力工具。在理解语篇时,读者会同时运用形式图式和内容图式,基于上下文和篇章结构来预测或推断内容,确保对语篇的全面理解。图式的构建是逐步进行的,它贯穿人的认知发展过程。每当遇到新知识,与现有图式的连接有助于理解,同时这种理解也促进了图式的完善,形成更为精细的心理表征。在教学中,形式图式,即学生对不同文章体裁和篇章结构的熟悉度有助于深化对语篇的理解。教学的本质就是在学生脑海中逐步构建和丰富这些图式。

连淑能在《英汉对比研究》中对英语语篇的基本结构模式作了阐述:"演绎式是英语语篇结构的基本模式。在谋篇的过程中,英人偏重直线式思维,偏爱演绎推理,注重追溯因果;英人习惯开门见山,一落笔就点明主题、交代要点,然后再逐层细叙、分析推理,较常按照从一般到细节、从概况到具体、从整体到个体的原则。"(连淑能,2010:39)

不同文体的语篇特征不同,不同文体又对语篇的内容和形式起着制约作用。"不同的语篇通常用不同的结构形式表示开头、中间、结尾等部分。如故事的开头部分往往对时间、地点、人物等方面作出交代,中间部分主要是描述故事的发展,结尾是描写人物和事态的结局或给人的启示。议论性的语篇的开头往往指出问题,说明该文章要议论什么问题,中间部分是对开头所提出的问题加以分析,对论点加以论证,结尾部分则提出解决问题的办法或得出一个结论。书信的开头是称呼,中间是正文,结尾是结束语和落款。"(黄国文,1988:25)

不同体裁的文章各自遵循一定的结构,甚至相同体裁的文章也会采用不同的结构。记叙文主要是直线式的语言模式,以事件发生的时间、地点、人物和情感的变化为线,叙述发展事件发生的始末,还有顺叙、倒叙、插叙等方式；说明文的结构通常包括总分式、总分总式、分总式、并列式、递进式等；议论文的基本结构形式包括总分式、并列式、递进式、正反式、对比式、归纳式等。文本结构体现了作者的行文思路以及观点表达的技巧，有助于达成其写作目的。

Longji Rice Terraces 这个语篇是典型的说明文语篇，采用了总分式的结构。首先，描绘春夏秋冬四季的景象，引发读者的兴趣和好奇心；第二段介绍建造者及建造历史；第三段从两个方面阐述了建造梯田的原因；第四段介绍人与自然和谐共生的意义；最后一段强调传统和价值。这种结构使整个语篇内容紧凑、逻辑清晰、语言生动。

解读文本结构、理清脉络，有助于学生掌握篇章知识，提升语言运用能力。"接触和学习不同类型的语篇，熟悉生活中常见的语篇形式，把握不同语篇的特定结构、文体特征和表达方式，不仅有助于学生加深对语篇意义的理解，还有助于他们使用不同类型的语篇进行有效地表达与交流。"（中华人民共和国教育部，2020：17）语篇阅读教学强调完整性，促进学生从语义出发，培养分析、归纳、推理的思维模式。

（三）语篇各部分与语篇主题之间的关系

语言学家拉波夫认为，"作者使用语篇可以实现三种功能：人际功能，指参与社会互动的过程；篇章功能，指形式完美，适宜的文章创作；概念功能，即作者以连贯的方式表达思想和经历。"（Labov，1966，转引自李宝荣，2016：118）就篇章结构而言，语篇分析的重点是语篇中的句子如何通过显性连接手段形成连贯，以及篇章的组织要素和组织形式如何表达作者的意图。

李宝荣在《中学英语教学设计优化策略》中提到了语篇的五种组织模式。

"语篇组织模式种类一般有：叙述模式；提问—回答模式；问题—解决模式；主张—反主张模式；概括—具体模式等。每一类别的语篇组织模式又有一定的结构规律可循。

（1）叙事结构：拉波夫叙事结构。

（2）提问—回答模式：一般在篇章开头设置一个明显的问题，并通过寻找对这一问题令人满意的答案来构建篇章的发展。

（3）问题—解决模式：一般在语篇的开始向读者描述一个事件或社

会现象作为文章的背景,接着由此事件或社会现象引出一个难以解决的问题,然后陈述人们对这一问题的反应,最后提出对这一反应的肯定评价或结论。该模式与提问回答模式有很多相似之处。

(4)在主张—反主张模式中,作者首先提出一种普遍认可的主张、观点,然后进行澄清,说明自己的主张、观点,或者提出反主张或真实情况。

例如,Joe's an old friend of mine(situation). People say Joe's stupid(claim). That's because he's always forgetting things(reason for claim). He's not stupid, though(denial). He's actually very bright(correction). For a start, he's got a degree in Psychology(reason for correction).(Hoey, 2001)

(5)概括—具体模式的宏观结构大致有两种:

第一,概括陈述→具体陈述1→具体陈述2→具体陈述3……→概况陈述;

第二,概括陈述→具体陈述→更具体陈述→……→概况陈述。"(李宝荣,2016:118-119)

Longji Rice Terraces 这篇文章各段与主题之间的关系,可以归为第五种宏观结构中的第一类。在后续的分体裁说明章节中会详细分析每种体裁对应的结构类型。

(四)语篇中段与段的关系

句子和段落构成语篇,其内部关系共同塑造其结构和意义。句子是段落基础,部分段落仅一句,多数则由句组组成。句际关系主要通过句子的逻辑关系和语义关系来建立,黄国文在《语篇分析概要》中提到,"从逻辑意义来看,语篇中有9种不同的句际关系类型,分别是:并列关系、对应关系、顺序关系、分解关系、分指关系、重复关系、转折关系、解释关系、因果关系。"(黄国文,1988:19-24)通过这些关系,句子之间形成了有机的联系,共同表达了整个段落的意思。

在语篇分析中,要特别关注语篇的立论句、段落主题句、话语标记词,帮助学生把握文章脉络,提高阅读效果。"有逻辑的段落结构往往条理清晰,内容连贯。清晰的段落都有一个主题,所有的句子均围绕该主题展开,主题往往以主题句呈现,段落内部其他句子为支撑句。教学时布置学生寻找段落主题句、关键词或者概括段落大意,有助于加深学生

对文本的理解,同时训练学生的抽象、概括能力。"(李杰、李若菲,2012)

段落间的逻辑关系主要通过主题、语境和逻辑关系建立,不仅使段落间形成有机联系,还共同构建了整个语篇的主题和深层意义。教师应指导学生理解这些关系,以准确把握语篇内容和作者意图。教学中,教师要引导学生概括段意、绘制篇章结构图,以提高他们的阅读理解能力,帮助他们有效组织和整合信息,形成清晰的语篇格式图式。自主学习时,学生就能迅速识别段落间的逻辑联系,深入理解作者的布局意图和写作技巧,从而训练和提升逻辑思维能力。

根据上面对 *Longji Rice Terraces* 的段落主旨的分析,这个语篇结构是概括—具体结构,语篇中各段围绕龙脊梯田这个话题,分别从不同的角度进行介绍。

三、语篇的微观组织结构

本小节从语篇的微观组织结构的四个方面介绍各种语篇的衔接手段,以及句子内的信息展开方式。

(一)语篇中的显性衔接和连贯手段

语篇作为一个语义连贯的整体,其内部句子通过多样化的衔接方法紧密结合,共同传达完整的语境意义。学生需从宏观上把握语篇的行文特征,并深入分析其组织结构,以识别衔接手法并准确理解其连贯性。此外,课程标准对显性衔接和连贯手段有具体要求,包括代词的指代、连接词的使用、省略句的省略以及替代关系的运用。

这些都是显性衔接和连贯的主要方式,但是衔接与连贯的定义和手段都有哪些?语言学家们有不同的阐释:"衔接与连贯是篇章语言学中的一对核心概念,也是语篇研究能否站得住脚的关键。"(胡壮麟,2018:7)"它指的是语篇中语言成分之间的语义联系,或者说是语篇中一个成分与另一个可以与之相互解释的成分之间的关系。当语篇中一个成分的含义依赖于另一个成分的解释时,便产生了衔接关系。"(胡壮麟等,2008:179)"衔接纽带的距离、形式和重要性决定衔接力的大小,从而影响语义关系的传递效果"(张德禄、刘汝山,2003:125-161)。

衔接主要关注的是语篇如何通过特定的形式和手段将词汇组合成

完整的篇章,而连贯更注重于分析语篇意义的内在关联性。意义上的连续与形式上的衔接是语篇最重要的两个要素,所以对语篇的分析能力也就涉及语言的衔接与连贯。"语篇连贯评价的标准就是各个部分是否支持主题、为主题服务"(张德禄、刘汝山,2003:75)

王全智对连贯总结了七种解释:"(1)连贯表现为语篇的主题;(2)连贯是形式、语义和语用上的相关性;(3)连贯由统一的修辞结构来体现;(4)连贯是语用上的相关性;(5)连贯是推理的结果;(6)连贯是参与、谈判、合作的结果;(7)连贯反映经验或常识。"(王全智,2002:29,转引自张德禄、刘汝山,2003,Ⅸ)

衔接对语篇连贯起到关键作用,分为显性衔接和隐性衔接,二者共同作用于语篇的连贯性。显性衔接具有明显的语篇标记,体现在语法和词汇两个层面。其中,语法衔接涉及照应、替代、省略和连接等手段,而词汇衔接包括词的复现和同现关系。词的复现又可细分为原词复现、同义词/近义词复现、上下义词复现和概括词复现;词汇同现涵盖反义关系和互补关系等。

根据连淑能教授在《英汉对比研究》中的表述:"总的来说,英语比较忌讳重复,因而常用替代、省略和变换的表达手法。"(连淑能,2010:236)"一般说来,除非有意强调或出于修辞的需要,英语总的倾向是尽量避免重复。讲英语的人对于随意重复相同的音节、词语或句式往往感到厌烦。"(连淑能,2010:221)上述的显性衔接手段,除了连接,其他主要是为了避免重复所采用的语篇衔接手段。

1. 语法衔接手段

除了前面提到的四种,语法衔接手段还可以用表示时间和地点的词语,以及时和体形式的配合和排比结构等多种手段。这里重点介绍上面提到的四种。

(1)照应

"照应指用代词等语法手段来表示语义关系。照应关系可分为两大类:一类是可以在语篇中找到所指对象的,另一类是在语言中找不到所指对象的。前一种称为内照应,后一类称为外照应。内照应指语篇内的语言项目之间的照应关系;外照应指语言项目的意义解释直接依存于语篇外客观环境中的某个事物。内照应可分为两种情况,一种是前照应,所指对象位于上文;另一种是后照应,所指对象位于下文。

照应分三类:人称照应;指示照应;比较照应。"(黄国文,1988:90-91)

①人称照应

"人称照应指通过人称代词(如 I, you, he, she, they, her, them 等),所属限定词(如 your, his, her, their 等)和所属代词(如 mine, his, hers, theirs 等)来实现的。从语言的使用来看,用作人称照应的常常是第三人称代词。"(黄国文,1988:91-92)

The Longji Rice Terraces 第三段中"Building the terraces therefore meant that they could increase the areas in which they could grow rice"里的两个 they 都用来回指第二段中的 the local Zhuang and Yao people。

②指示照应

"用于指示照应的词可分为三类:指示代词如 this, that, these, those;定冠词 the; 指示副词 here, there, now, then 等"。(黄国文,1988:93-94)

一般说来,this 和 these 既可用于前照应用法,也可用于后照应;但 that 和 those 通常只用于前照应。定冠词 the 常用于前照应。here 可以表示前照应和后照应,there 通常只表示前照应。

第二段开头"These terraces were built by the local Zhuang and Yao people, to whom Guangxi is home"中的 these terraces 回指第一段中 the Longji Rice Terraces。最后一句话"Today, the Longji Rice Terraces attract thousands of visitors who come to admire this great wonder created..."中 this great wonder 回指前面的 the Longji Rice Terraces。

③比较照应

"比较照应指的是通过形容词和副词的比较等级形式以及其他一些有比较意义的词语(如 same, so, as, equal, such, similar(ly), different(ly), other, otherwise, likewise 等)表示的照应关系。一般说来,表示异同、相似、差别、量与质的优劣等词语都有照应作用。"(黄国文,1988:99)

第四段开头"But perhaps what is most significant is the way in which people have worked in harmony with nature..."中的最高级照应

了上一段中的两条，分别由 Firstly 和 Secondly 引出的理由。最后一段开头 "Although modern technology could help produce more crops..." 中 produce more crops 回应上文中多次提到的 rice。

（2）替代

"替代就是用替代词去取代某一个成分。替代词只是形式，它的语义要从所替代的成分中去寻找。替代有名词性替代、动词性替代和小句替代三种。其中，名词性替代常用的替代词是 one 及其复数形式 ones，还有 the same 等；动词性替代的替代词是 do 及其变化形式，如 does 等；小句替代词是常用的替代词 so 和 not。使用替代既可以避免重复，也可以达到衔接。"（黄国文，1988：104-109）

最后一段 "This knowledge is passed down through families, which means that..." 定语从句引导词 which 用来替代前面的句子。语篇中还有许多定语从句的引导词替代其前面的先行词的例子。

（3）省略

"省略是把语篇中的某个成分省去，是避免重复，突出新信息，并使语篇上下紧凑的一种语法手段。省略有三种，名词性省略、动词性省略和小句省略。被省略的成分与它的对应成分在结构上应当是一致的，否则一般不能省略，另外还应当出现在句中的同一层次上。"（黄国文，1988：109-114）

第四段 "During the rainy season, it is along these waterways that rainwater moves down the mountains and (moves) into the terrace" 中介词 into 前省略了同一个谓语动词 moves。

"替代和省略十分相似，主要的不同在于前者有替代词语，后者没有（或者说零替代）。替代与省略是一种语法关系，照应是一种语义关系。在替代和省略中，读者需要在上下文中寻找他们所替代省略的词语；而在照应中，读者需要在上下文中寻找的往往是意思和解释。"（黄国文，1988：113）

下面的例子可以作些比较：

This is a fine hall you have here. I'm proud to be lecturing in it.（it 指的是 a fine hall，属于照应中的回指）

This is a fine hall you have here. I've never lectured in a finer one.（one 替代 hall，属于替代关系）

This is a fine hall you have here. I've never lectured in a finer.

（finer 后面省略了 hall 或 one，属于省略）

（4）连接

"连接是通过连接成分体现语篇中各种逻辑关系的手段。连接成分往往是一些过渡性的词语，表示时间、因果、条件等逻辑上的联系。"（胡壮麟等，2008：184）例如，then, meanwhile 表示时间关系；consequently, for 表示因果关系；in that case 表示条件关系；but, however 表示转折关系；also 表示递进关系；for example 表示例证关系。

The Longji Rice Terraces 语篇中的连接关系较多，仅以第三、四段为例。

Para. 3 "① So why did these people go to so much trouble to turn the entire mountains into terraces? ② Firstly, there are few large, flat areas of land in the region. ③ Building the terraces therefore meant that they could increase the areas in which they could grow rice. ④ Secondly, although the region has plenty of rain, the mountains are steep and the soil is shallow. ⑤ The flat terraces catch the rainwater and prevent the soil from being washed away."

Para. 4 "① But perhaps what is most significant is the way in which people have worked in harmony with nature to make these terraces and grow rice. ② The terraces are cleverly designed, with hundreds of waterways that connect with each other. ③ During the rainy season, it is along these waterways that rainwater moves down the mountains and into the terraces. ④ The sun heats the water and turns it into vapour. ⑤ This forms clouds from which rain falls down onto the mountain terraces once again. ⑥ These terraces also provide a perfect environment for birds and fish, some of which feed on insects that can harm the rice crops."

这两段涉及以下的一些句间逻辑关系：

并列关系。第三段中②和④两句话分别说的是可用来种水稻的平地少和山陡峭、土层浅，二者是并列关系，共同说明一个话题，谁前谁后没有影响。

对应关系。第四段中③④⑤主要依靠词语衔接关系中的复现关系，即通过 rainwater, the water, it 和 rain 建立对应关系。

顺序关系。第四段中的③④⑤句呈现了雨水的循环过程，顺序不能调整。

分指关系。第四段中③④⑤通过 rainwater, the water, it 和 rain 指代相同。

转折关系。第四段的①跟上文的内容构成了转折。

解释关系。第三段的②③和④⑤两个句组构成了对①的介绍。

因果关系。第三段中的②和③,④和⑤分别构成了因果关系。

2. 词汇衔接手段

词汇衔接在语义层面黏合语篇,保障连贯性。"英语的词汇衔接手段包括复现和同现。训练学生掌握词汇衔接手段能够促使学生围绕主题,根据上下文语境,通过推理、判断等思维活动来解读文本,有助于形成语篇衔接的意识,掌握语篇衔接的手段,发展逻辑思维。"(黄国文,1988:122-128)

Longji Rice Terraces 语篇中运用了多种词汇衔接手段,将不同部分的内容联系起来,使文章更具连贯性。

(1)词汇的复现

词汇复现对语篇中的句子构成相互衔接。

以文章第一段为例。

"① Imagine mountains wrapped in silver water, shining in the spring sun. ② Summer sees the mountains turn bright green with growing rice. ③ During autumn, these same mountains are gold, and in winter they are covered in sheets of white frost. ④ These are the colours of the Longji Rice Terraces."

①②③中的 mountains 属于原词复现,①和③中有两对同义词或近义词,分别是 wrapped 和 covered、silver 和 white。前三句中的 silver, green, gold, white 跟最后一句中的 colors 构成了上下义复现。

第二段开头 These terraces 跟第一段中的 mountains 构成了概括词复现。

(2)词汇的同现

词汇的同现关系指的是词汇共同出现的倾向性。语篇中围绕主题构成的语义场,相关词汇出现的频率增大。

第一段围绕描绘四季中龙脊梯田的颜色变化展开,使用了一系列与颜色、季节、地点相关的词汇和短语,不仅增加了文本的表达力,也构建了生动的视觉画面,让读者能够更好地理解和感受龙脊梯田的美景。其中有不少词汇构成同现关系,如 spring,summer,autumn 和 winter 构成了同现关系;几个颜色词彼此间构成词汇同现;mountains,water,sun,growing rice,the Longji Rice Terraces 构成词汇同现。还有 spring 和 autumn、summer 和 winter 同时构成反义关系。

在语言实践中,同主题的语篇中常出现意义关联的词语,形成词汇链。词汇链中某个词的出现会引发对链中其他词的联想,它们不仅衔接句子,更有助于构建完整篇章。了解这一规律有助于读者快速预测语篇内容和上下文语义关系。在日常教学中,学生按话题整理词汇,实则构建主题语境下的词汇库,便于语义记忆。

关注文本连贯性有助于展现各要点逻辑,将零散内容串联,实现顺畅理解。然而,除了上文中提到的显性衔接,语篇中还有一些隐性衔接,就是在语篇中找不到明显的衔接手段,但是能使文本连贯可读地衔接。张德禄和刘汝山认为"隐性衔接是一种在句子级甚至更大单位上的省略现象……省略的部分无法在上下文中找到,只能由听话者或解释者根据情景语境和文化语境推测出来……语句的准确程度将决定语篇的连贯程度。"(张德禄、刘汝山,2003:28)隐性衔接主要从语篇的语境与语用层面来表达,借由非言语手段,比如沟通双方共知信息和相似文化背景、思维模式、上下文中的文化语境和情景语境。比如下面两个句子间的因果关系就需要根据上下文来判断:"Secondly, …, the mountains are steep and the soil is shallow. The flat terraces catch the rainwater and prevent the soil from being washed away."

(二)词语搭配

系统功能语法把搭配,即语义上具有联系的词汇同现,也作为语篇的衔接手段。词语搭配通常指各种形式的短语搭配,课程标准中,把短语作为句子成分,分为五类:"在语篇理解中借助五类句子成分(动词短语、名词短语、形容词短语、副词短语、介词短语)有选择地对长句和难句进行分析。"(中华人民共和国教育部,2020:24)

各种短语是英语表达中非常活跃的表现形式,加强短语记忆可以有效扩大词汇量。短语作为英语中的活跃形式,准确使用,体现了语言的地道,同时会极大地提升语言的流畅度。

(三)句子内部的语法结构

本节对于语法结构,主要按照课程标准中对于高考要求的语法分类和表述为主要依据。

课程标准对语法知识内容的要求,首先是要"意识到语言使用中的语法知识是'形式—意义—使用'的统一体,学习语法的最终目的是在语境中有效地运用语法知识来理解和表达意义"(中华人民共和国教育部,2020:24)

"英语语法知识包括词法知识和句法知识:词法关注词的形态变化,如名词的数、格,动词的时、态(体)等;句法关注句子结构,如句子的成分、语序、种类等。"(中华人民共和国教育部,2020:23)

由于中西方在文化和思维上的差异,体现在语法上,"英语常用'突显'语序;常用形合法、结构被动式和概括笼统的抽象性词语;注重显性衔接、语法关系和语义逻辑,注重形式接应,'前呼后应';喜欢词语和结构的主从分明、长短交错和替代变换;表达方式比较严谨、精确,模糊性较小,歧义现象较少,用词造句遵守严格的词法和句法,造句成章也服从某种逻辑规则,适合于科学思维和理性思维。"(连淑能,2010:6)

根据连淑能教授关于语法方面的陈述,英语属于综合语,其特征是运用形态来表达语法关系。"形态变化、语序和虚词是表达语法关系的三大手段,三者之间有密切的关系。"(连淑能,2010:25-48)

(1)"英语有形态变化。现代英语的形态变化主要是动词的变化和静词(名词、代词、形容词、副词)的变化,以及上述的词缀变化。这些变化有:性、数、格、时、体、语态、语气、形容词和副词的比较级和最高级、人称和词性等。有了这些变化,一个词(或词组)常可以同时表达几种语法意义。"

以 *Longji Rice Terraces* 语篇中的最后一句话为例:

"Today, the Longji Rice Terraces attract thousands of visitors who come to admire this great wonder created by people and nature working together."

Today 决定了句子的时态要用现在时;主句和从句中都有动词的主谓一致形式,attract 和 come 是第三人称复数的谓语;created 是过去分词做后置定语；working 是现在分词表示主动，做 people and nature 的补语。

（2）"英语的语序比较灵活。形态变化与语序有密切的关系。形态变化越多的语言，语序越灵活。一般而言，英语的排列顺序是：主—动—宾（表），但英语中的倒装形式很多，部分是由于语法的要求，部分是出于修辞的需要。

（3）英语中有大量的虚词。英语的虚词，也称结构词或功能词，包括冠词、介词、助动词、并列连词、从属连词等。它们在句中主要起辅助和连接作用。

西方的理性思维在英语语法中所体现的'法治'，重形合，重形式接应，结构要求齐整，句子以形寓意，以法摄神，句段严密规范，采用焦点句法，因而'语法是硬的，没有弹性'且富于强制性。"（连淑能，2010：13）

（四）句子的信息展开方式

在连贯的语篇中，所有句子的排列都受到制约，但都是根据语境考虑的。本节主要根据语言大家的理论介绍句内信息展开方式，主要涉及句子的主位和述位、句末中心和句末重心等几个方面。语篇或段落内的信息展开形式将在后面说明文章节中的七选五专题中进行介绍。

"英语句子有严谨的主谓结构。主语不可或缺，谓语动词是句子的中心，二者协调一致，提纲挈领，聚集各种关系网络。因此，英语句子主从分明，层次清楚，多层递进，前呼后拥，严密规范，句式呈'聚集型'。"（连淑能，2010：51）

"一般说来，句中若有叙事部分和表态部分，英语常常是表态部分（判断、结论等）在前，叙事部分（事实、描写等）在后，即先总提后分述，或先讲结果后追叙过去。"（连淑能，2010：35）

从理论上讲，同一意义可以用不同的词汇和语法结构来表达。但是，在实际语言使用中，不同的结构之间都存在着语义、语域、语篇、语境等方面的差异。我们在选用某一特定结构时，就必须考虑这些因素。

1. 句子的主位与述位

按照系统功能语言学理论，对语言的选择是根据意义来决定的。在进行语言分析时,要看意义是如何表达的。作为语义驱动的语法,系统功能语法坚持形式是意义的体现、形式为语义和意义服务的观点,明确句法、结构是手段,表达和创造意义才是目的。

系统功能语法把句子从交际功能的角度划分为两个语义组成部分:主位和述位。主位是交际起点,传达已知信息,帮助读者明白句子的焦点;述位则进一步描述和说明主位,传递新信息。语义相同的句子,如果它们的主位和述位不同,就会传递出作者的不同关注重点,以及交际双方对信息的不同掌握情况。

如果学生能充分理解这一点,就可以在高考解答七选五的过程中,根据主位和述位的信息推进方式,更清晰地理解段落间逻辑和句子间逻辑,清晰判断语篇和段落的信息推进模式,准确判断空格处应填的信息。

2. 句末中心

"英语句子呈现句首封闭、句尾开放的特征。修饰语、插入语可以后置,又有关系词与被修饰语连接,句子可以不断地向句尾扩展、延伸。"(连淑能,2010:94)

"英语语段甚至句子,通常突出关键词语或主题句,喜用主从结构,注重分析推理,直线性、有秩序、有层次地围绕主旨展开,信息安排往往采用'突显'语序:由近及远,开门见山,一语破的,头短尾长,可以向后延伸、扩展。"(连淑能,2010:97)

这种线性特点使语言在信息安排上遵循从已知到未知,从确定到不确定的原则。"一般说来,带有定冠词的短语是确定成分,往往表示已知信息;带不定冠词的短语往往是不确定成分,表示的常常是未知信息。

句末中心指把新信息安排在句子的后半部分,新信息中最重要的部分则安排在句子的末端。一段信息中的新的或最重要的内容应该置于接近句末的地方;在说话时,语调群的语调核心通常也在末尾。如果把要点安置于句末,那句子一般更为有力(特别是在书面语中)。"(黄国文,1988:66)

句末中心原则可以帮我们在特定的语境中选择合适的语言结构。例如,下面这对主动—被动句子:

The rain destroyed the crops.(可用来回答:What did the rain do?)

The crops were destroyed by the rain.（可用来回答：What happened to the crops?）

虽然两句话表达的意思相同,但其强调的中心内容不完全对等。

对读后续写而言,可以利用所给段首句的句末中心,准确接续,确保故事发展的逻辑和信息的推进。很多学生在故事的衔接方面有问题,就是没有抓住给定段首句的核心内容。

3. 句末重心

句末重心是从句子成分摆放位置的角度,把句末留给比较长一些、分量重一些的句子成分。关于句末重心,黄国文认为:"句末重心指的是在排列句子成分时,把'重'的成分置于接近句末的地方。句子中较'重'的部分应该置于接近句末的地方,不然句子听上去就不自然和不平衡。一个成分的'分量'可以从长度(如音节的多少)或语法结构的复杂程度(如修饰语的多少等)来确定。

据我们的理解,所谓'重'的成分,在不同的场合可能体现为不同的内容。例如,副词比名词'重',短语比单词'重',介词短语比名词短语'重';音节较多的一般也'重'于音节较少的成分;单词数较多的一般也'重'于单词数较少的成分;结构复杂的通常也比结构简单的成分'重'。"(黄国文,1988:69)

其实,所谓的句末重心原则,就是把长而复杂的句子成分放在句尾的原则。这一原则能够使句子在结构上保持平衡匀称。

"实现这一原则,英语中通常有几种方式:

把结构较长的状语放在句末。例如,He studied them that night with the kind of care his wife had suggested.

把结构复杂的直接宾语放在句末。例如,She visited that very day an elderly and much beloved friend.

把结构复杂的间接宾语放在句末。例如,I gave a book to each of the boys.

避免主语部分太重、太长,可通过分割、倒装、外置等语法手段来实现这一原则。例如:

Yet the fact is we know very little about gorillas. Not really satisfactory photograph has ever been taken of one in a wild state...

定语 of one in a wild state 与其中心词 photograph 被谓语 has ever been taken 分隔。

There stood in the way of this conspiracy one great obstacle-Paris. 本句用了倒装。

It's certain that we'll forget the address.

英语中的句子主语由 that 从句，-ing 短语或不定式短语充当，那通常要用先行词 it 作句子的形式主语，把真正的主语放在句末。"（赵振才，2005：416-417）

句末中心和句末重心通常并行不悖，但有时候这两个原则可能会产生冲突。在这种情况下，应该优先考虑语义中心原则，可以考虑改变句子的表达方式。

以外研版教材 Book 2 Unit 3 *A Game for the World* 的第二段段首主题句为例："That football is such a simple game to play is perhaps the basis of its popularity." 这个句子没有采用 it 作形式主语，看起来违背了句末重心原则，但照顾到了语义。That football is such a simple game to play 是已知信息，the basis of its popularity 是句子中心，传递未知新信息。

语篇是学生学习语言知识、发展语言技能的重要载体。教师只有全面、深入地掌握语篇分析的角度和方法，才能有针对性地设计与实施教学活动，更好地帮助学生培养综合语言运用能力。本章内容重点呈现了语篇分析的重要理论，为语篇分析提供了学理支撑和方法指导。

第三节　语篇分析的 What, Why 和 How

前面两节，主要介绍了功能语言学中与高中英语教学相关的部分研究：语篇及其语境，以及语篇的宏观和微观结构分析。本节从语篇的角度全方位分析展开。

一、课标对语篇分析的要求

新课标的基本理念之一就是实践英语学习活动观,要求所有的语言活动都要基于语篇进行。"基于语篇的英语教学,并非在传统教学模式上增加一个语篇层次的教学,而是应该以语篇为单位设计和实施教学。也就是说,语言教学应该围绕语篇来进行。……虽然每一类语篇有其共同的语篇结构和语言特征,但这些结构和特征也不是完全固定不变的。教师要在教学中注意引导学生观察和分析具体语篇的结构和语言特征,即关注语篇的各个组成部分以及语篇所用的语言是如何表达意义的,避免单纯地讲授语篇知识。"(中华人民共和国教育部,2020:29)

根据课程标准六要素整合的英语课程内容,如图 2-3 所示。

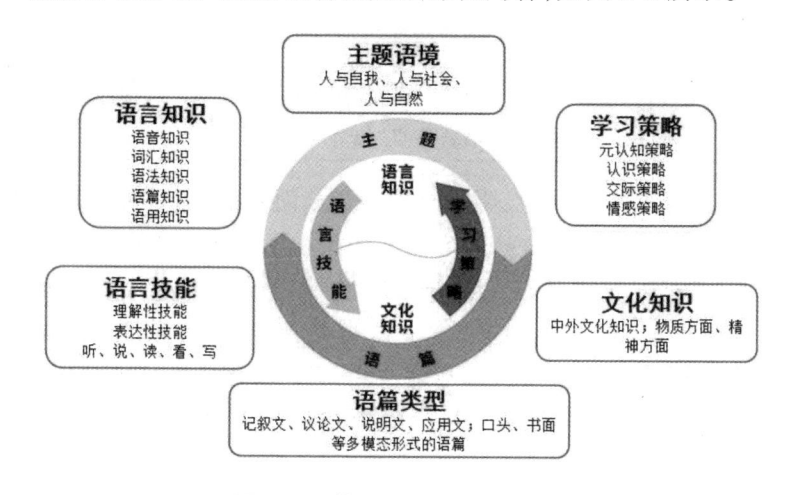

图 2-3 英语课程标准的六要素

英语教师要充分学习课标,深入研读语篇,从宏观和微观两个角度对语篇进行分析。课标认为"研读语篇就是对语篇的主题、内容、文体结构、语言特点、作者观点等进行深入的解读。建议教师首先尝试回答三个基本问题:第一,语篇的主题和内容是什么,即 What 的问题;第二,语篇的深层含义是什么?也就是作者或说话人的意图、情感态度或价值取向是什么,即 Why 的问题;第三,语篇具有什么样的文体特征、内容结构和语言特点?也就是作者为了恰当表达主题意义选择了什么样的文体形式、语篇结构和修辞手段,即 How 的问题。

对语篇的研读,教师还可以进一步关注语篇的选材出处和发表时间,分析作者或说话人的立场、观点和写作或表述风格,以及特定时期的语言特点和时代印记等。"(中华人民共和国教育部,2020:59)

"研读语篇可以帮助教师多层次、多角度分析语篇所传递的意义,依据语篇的主题意义、文体风格、语言特点和价值取向,设计合理的教学活动,同时利用作者视角、写作背景和时间等信息,帮助学生深刻理解语篇,把语言学习与意义探究融为一体,实现深度学习。"(中华人民共和国教育部,2020:59-60)

课程标准提出的语篇分析框架三要素(表2-4),为英语教师分析语篇、探究语篇主题意义提供了方向和抓手。

表2-4 语篇分析框架三要素

语篇分析 三要素	分析视角	语境
What	主题语境,内容信息	文化语境 情景语境(语场、语旨、语式) 上下文语境
Why	作者观点、写作意图、情感态度、价值取向	
How	文体特征、内容结构、语言特点、修辞手段	

同时,程晓堂教授认为,要对语篇进行全面分析,通常可以从以下八个方面来入手:"(1)语篇的内容与主题意义;(2)语篇隐含的意义与功能;(3)语篇对读者的思想和行为的影响,或者说语篇期望对读者的思想和行为产生的影响;(4)语篇产生的背景或语境,即该语篇是在什么情况下产生的;(5)语篇的类型与结构;(6)语篇的衔接性和连贯性;(7)语篇使用的语言和非语言手段;(8)语篇在内容和形式等方面的质量。"(程晓堂,2020)

如果说课标对于语篇研读的指导是提供了课堂语篇教学的分析框架,程教授对语篇的分析则更多是从教师备课的角度来考量,对文章的解读更细致。当然,我们的语篇分析实践,呈现给学生的不必这么全面细致,需要教师基于单元主题以及具体篇章进行取舍,抓大放小,有所侧重。师生可通过深入理解、分析语篇内容和结构,把握其主题意义,并挖掘文化价值。这有助于在解读过程中提升语言知识、技能和文化理解,促进多元思维发展,并培养正确的价值取向和学习策略。

二、语篇分析中的 What

语篇分析中的 what,首先要关注语篇的主题语境,判断话题,为随后的理解具体主题内容、探究主题意义奠定基础。课程标准在主题语境方面有很多陈述,可以帮助我们理解主题语境对语篇分析的重要性。

"所有的语言学习活动都应该在一定的主题语境下进行,即学生围绕某一具体的主题语境,基于不同类型的语篇,在解决问题的过程中,运用语言技能获取、梳理、整合语言知识和文化知识,深化对语言的理解,重视对语篇的赏析,比较和探究文化内涵,汲取文化精华。"(中华人民共和国教育部,2020:12–13)

"教材各单元提供主题语境和语言材料,构建学习活动场域,即以主题为引领,创设有意义的情境,依托多种题材和类型的语篇,使学生通过学习理解、应用实践、迁移创新等活动,学习语言知识和文化知识,发展语言技能,运用学习策略。"(中华人民共和国教育部,2020:109)

"教师要认真把握本课程标准对选择性必修课程所规定的各项内容要求,从深度和广度两个方面扩展三大主题语境的内容,同时补充更多的语篇类型,如:专题讨论,论说文、评论、散文等文体,以及小说、科幻故事等文学类文体。"(中华人民共和国教育部,2020:55)

课程标准中的三大主题语境,涉及了 10 个主题群下 32 个主题语境内容要求,涵盖高中教材和高考题目中所有的语篇。语篇题材多样、体裁丰富,语言地道鲜活,在主题内容的深度、广度和语言的难度方面逐步扩展和加深,符合学生的兴趣特点和语言能力的发展规律,提升学生的语篇意识,丰富他们的语言感知和学习体验。主题语境是引领教学目标制订与学习活动开展的关键,为语篇主题意义的分析和课堂活动教学设计确定基调,并给出了教学实践指导。

指导学生理解语篇内容信息,首先看课程标准对必修和选必修理解性技能中跟 what 有关的内容。所有这些技能都要在上下文语境中,运用阅读技巧和学生原有语言知识进行语篇表层及深层的内容理解技能,主要涉及学习理解类活动和应用实践类活动。在这个过程中,教师需要解决学生的理解问题,并提出开放性的问题,促进学生的思维在语言学习的过程中得到提升。

语言知识学习。在学习文本时,应注重词汇在不同语境中的积累和运用。对于关键的词汇,需要查阅词典深入理解其含义和用法,以及在上下文中的意义。深入解析长难句子结构,理解不同语法形式所表达的意义,培养正确的语感。

思维训练。在阅读文本前,根据标题、插图等信息预测文章的主题或内容,培养预判能力。阅读后,概括文章的主要观点和信息,并能基于语篇文本信息,进行多角度的思考和讨论,深入评价和分析,并能提出自己的观点和见解,批判思维的过程中培养创新思维能力。

三、语篇分析中的 Why

课标强调探究语篇主题意义为教学核心,阅读理解最终目的是理解作者的核心思想或深层含义。近年来,高考英语阅读试题日益注重主题意义的考查,涉及情感、态度和价值观,并围绕主题意义设计试题,以促进学生在语言能力、文化意识、思维品质和学习能力上的全面发展。

Why 因素下的语篇分析挑战性比较大,涉及探究和建构语篇主题意义。教师需要引导学生分析语篇的结构,理解段与段、段落与主题之间的关系,以及关键段落内的信息推进模式。同时,教师还需要引导学生关注、分析语篇中的关键词汇和语法结构,通过推断和归纳理解语篇中的隐含意义、作者的意图和写作目的,判断其情感态度和价值取向。这需要融语言学习与意义探究于一体,实现深度学习。通过对语篇的宏观和微观的分析,深入思考和严密推理,学生才能真正理解作者观点、写作意图、情感态度和价值取向。

四、语篇分析中的 How

课标倡导的英语学习活动观,主题语境作为其第一要素,为英语课程提供主题范围。学生对主题意义的探究是语言学习的核心内容。那么话题、主题、主题语境和主题意义等概念该如何界定?这里选用一些著名语言学家通俗易懂的定义来厘清这些概念:

"话题是文本内容(What is the text about?),通常可以在文本中直接获取。话题所包含的思想内容和精神实质是文章的主题。"(张金秀,2019)

"主题主要回答 what 的问题,即语篇主要传递了什么信息,包含什

么内容,是对语篇主要内容的总结。"(程晓堂、周宇轩,2023)

"主题语境包括'人与自我''人与社会'和'人与自然',每个主题语境由几个不同的主题群构成,每个主题群则包括多个更具体的子主题内容。"(程晓堂、周宇轩,2023)

"主题意义往往能够以陈述句的方式进行归纳和提炼,是学生在语篇学习以后的收获和体悟。"(葛炳芳,2022)"探究语篇的主题意义就是理解作者的写作意图、情感态度或价值取向,它强调读者对语篇内容的学习思考和价值判断。"(程晓堂、周宇轩,2023)

综上所述,主题是包含价值倾向的核心观念。如"气候变暖"作为话题,背后的主题是"保护环境"。针对主题,可以围绕"为何保护及如何实施"展开文本探究,自主构建并深化对主题意义的理解。

葛炳芳老师从读者视角(见表2-5)清晰直观地展示了这几个概念在不同维度上的区别(葛炳芳,2022)。

表2-5 话题等概念在不同维度上的区别

概念 维度	话题	主题意义	主题
意义特征	具体	介于二者之间	抽象
表达方式	直接	蕴含	拓展
核心意义	语篇讨论的中心	语篇的寓意	语篇寓意所属的范畴
本质特征	特定性	由语篇内容延长的普适性(去细节的)	普遍性

在明确相关概念后,语篇分析框架将更易理解。新课标强调的语篇分析框架注重整体性。其中,主题内容(What)是揭示深层含义(Why)的基础,而组织手段(How)是传递和实现主题意义的桥梁。语篇的最终目的在于实现交际功能,即影响听众或读者。因此,进行语篇分析时,应重视提炼主题与梳理信息,确保分析全面而完整。这一框架既关注表层内容,又挖掘深层主题,覆盖宏观与微观层面。教师运用此框架,能更清晰地规划教学目标,确保逻辑连贯,构建完整课程结构,避免片面解析。

语篇分析框架里三个步骤相比较而言,在理解难度上是逐渐递进的,这是因为:对于What(语篇内容的提取),可以以课文提供的各种信息为依据,指向一个相对比较客观的答案,但对"Why(语篇的深层含义)和how(语篇的组织特征)的问题,则通常没有唯一答案。因为对 Why 和 How 的解读更多地取决于每一位教师的教育背景、生活阅历、认知方式,以及教师在语篇互动的过程中所表现出来的分析能力和探究能力。"(中华人民共和国教育部,2020:59)同时还要了解语篇产生的背景知识,如文化语境和情景语境。

前面一节重点介绍了如何分析语篇的宏观和微观结构的角度和方法,这对应了语篇研读三要素中的 How 部分。因为教师在日常教学中已经对 What 层面的内容给予了大量的关注,而 Why(主题意义)层面的理解,有了 What 解读的铺垫,加上 How 层面的分析,将会更加水到渠成。

通过分析可以看出,教材中的语篇设问和高考真题中的阅读设问高度相似,阅读理解题目的设置都旨在考查语篇的关键因素,题目的设计以帮助学生进一步理解语篇为目的;而且题目以考查学生对语篇的基本信息理解为主,针对 What 的问题比较多,同时有意识地加大对学生高阶思维能力的考查,也就是 Why 和 How 层面的理解。对关键能力的考查并非都是难题,而是呈现出一定的合理布局。这对我们解读语篇,给出了提问以及思考方式和角度的提示。

五、语篇分析框架对课堂教学环节的指引

课标语篇分析强调文本深层价值与学生批判性思维的培养。学生需分析文体特征、结构和信息,整合、阐释并评判意义。在文化背景下感知文化差异,理解主题与文化价值。在语境中学习语言知识,理解意图,通过问题设计引导深入思考,培养批判性思维。

"从语篇分析的实践角度来看,对语篇的解析通常有以下五个步骤:观察、说明、描述、解释、评估"(黄国文,2002)。首先,教师需要判断语篇是否具备分析价值,并基于教学对象、目的和范围进行筛选。接着,教师需观察和分析语篇的语言层次和规律,并具备说明语篇的能力,包括解析其层次、意义、交际目的和引导效果。在分析过程中,教师应遵循科学步骤,在理论框架指导下梳理语篇层次,以确保分析的严密性和可重复性。分析的主要目的是解释语篇内容并揭示其表达意义的方法,而更高层次的目的则是对语篇进行基于语境的评估,以分析其传递意义的能力、表达目的的方式以及达成效果的程度。整个过程涵盖了从判断价值到深入分析再到评估的完整流程。

"要对语篇进行穷尽的功能分析,从理论上说是可以的,但实际上往往是不经济的,有时甚至是毫无意义或不可能的"(黄国文,2001)。教学实践中,不是每个语篇都需要细致地从所有角度去分析,分析的重点取决于语篇分析的目的,当然也受分析者的兴趣和水平的影响。教师需基于语篇的主题语境和语篇所处单元的总体目标,细化语篇分析角度,分解、制定符合 SMART 原则的课时教学目标和评价标准,设计教学活动。

黄国文认为,在对一个语篇进行功能分析时,如果采用自上而下的方式,可以遵循以下步骤:

"文化语境(语篇体裁:纲要式结构、体现样式)→情景语境(语域分析:语场、基调、语式)→语篇、语义{纯理功能:经验(及物性、作格、语态)、逻辑(相互依赖情况、逻辑—语义关系)、人际(语气、情态、评价)、语篇(主位结构、信息结构)、衔接(照应、省略、替代、连接、词汇连接)}→语言使用(词汇—语法、音系/字系)。值得注意的是,分析的步骤和括号中的各个部分在实际分析时都没有严格的先后之分。"(黄国文,2002)

朱晓燕老师把语篇分析三要素跟学科核心素养的培养进行了关联,认为语篇分析框架对阅读课堂教学有着明确的指导意义(见表2-6)。(朱晓燕,2023:66)教师通过三个层次的语篇分析和教学设计、三个阶段的教学过程的融合,努力落实英语学科核心素养的课程目标。

表 2-6　语篇分析框架对课堂教学环节的指引作用

英语学科核心素养的四要素	语篇初步理解阶段（What）Read for information /content	语篇内化提升阶段（Why）Read for ideas / values	语篇整体融合阶段（How）Read for structure /language
语言能力	理解标题、大意、生词	判断篇章主旨意义	理解语篇模式和特点
文化意识	物质层面	精神层面	两者综合
思维品质	低阶思维(记忆、分析)	高阶思维(推理、评价)	综合思维
学习能力	阅读初级技能	阅读高级技能	语篇知识和阅读技能

语篇教学目标的达成,需要在设定的具体的教学活动和环节中来进行。当下的阅读教学,教学活动基本遵循着读前、读中和读后三个大的

环节进行设计。表 2-7 来自王燕艳和崔林凤老师编著的《核心素养导向的 14 种英语课型设计框架及课例解读（中学英语教师版）》。（王燕艳，崔林凤，2023：20）经过严谨的评定，这些阅读教学步骤不仅具有较高的使用频率，更展现出科学性与专业性。它们易于参考且具有很高的可复制性，为提升阅读教学质量提供了有力支持。

表 2-7　阅读教学设计常用步骤

环节	步骤	学习者角色	学习者与文本的互动	学习者阅读行为
Pre-reading	lead-in（主题导入）	predictor（预测者）	——	Process: 分析
	predict（预测主题内容）			
While-reading	first reading: 文章大意	information-organizer（信息整理者）	extract（解读）：read between the lines	Process: 分析
	second reading: 文章结构			
	third reading: 逻辑化细节		decode（解码）：read the lines	Process: 分析 Product: 理解
Post-reading	复述总结	information-summarizer（信息归纳者）	——	Process: 分析
	深度阅读思考题	interpreter（思考者）	negotiate（沟通）：read beyond the lines	Social process: 评价
	读后应用活动	Problem-solver（问题解决者）		Practice: 应用

该阅读模式一个非常显著的特征就是真正体现了学为主体的理念。在阅读过程中，学生扮演的角色不断演变，他们与文本的互动逐渐深入。阅读活动的设计充分展现了从学习理解到应用实践，再到迁移创新的过程，这有助于提高学生的阅读素养和思维能力。

读前，通过主题导入和预测主题内容，调动学生原有认知，启动他们的阅读图式，为后续的新知学习作好准备。

读中，学生作为信息整理者，通过基于语篇、深入语篇的阅读，由整体掌握文章大意和文章结构，逐渐过渡到逻辑化细节的理解。逐渐培养学生的框架思维意识，对学生阅读能力的培养、语言学习的能力和思维品质的提升都有一定的帮助。

读后，学生有必要进一步巩固所学的语言知识和语言能力。作为信息归纳者，学生需系统组织所学的语言，加强记忆，以便更好地进行文本的复述和总结。通过教师设计的评估型问题，学生能够深入思考，并运用所学知识解决生活中的实际问题，从而超越语篇，实现真正的知识活用。

在教学中，教师应引导学生熟悉不同功能的语篇形式（如记叙文、说明文、议论文和应用文等),并教授他们关于这些语篇的类型、结构、特征以及语言特色。通过了解各种类型语篇的认知结构和体裁结构,学生不仅能够更深入地理解语篇意义,还能有效地运用这些语篇进行表达和交流,从而提升其语言能力和交际能力。特别是体裁分析法的应用有助于学生理解特定体裁语篇的社会功能、交际目的和认知模式,有助于他们创作出符合体裁惯例的语篇,并提升英语阅读和交际能力。高中英语教师应重视体裁教学法,并在阅读教学中积极尝试和应用。

第三章　记叙类文体

在教材和高考试题中,记叙文所占比重极高。本章主要围绕记叙文的特点、模式、鉴定方法以及拉波夫叙事分析等方面展开论述,探讨记叙文在课程标准中的篇章分析结构框架,并深入分析高考试题中常见且难度较大的完形填空和读后续写等题型。

第一节　记叙文的特点及判断要点

记叙文文体多以时间或空间为线索,按事件的发生、发展、结局展开。教师可引导学生围绕记叙文六要素,即时间、地点、人物、事件的起因、经过、结果对整个故事作全局性的解读,或者通过分析人物的语言、动作、心理描写来解读人物的性格特征,也可以按照拉波夫叙事原则进行解析。记叙文语篇的主题有时是隐性的,在语言形式上没有表现,即叙述的过程中没有主题句,这就需要读者从所提供的信息推测出语篇的主题。

一、记叙文简介

记叙文作为课程标准中的重要语篇类型,内容涵盖三大主题语境。通常以时间顺序叙述事件或故事,通过描述情节、人物、场景等元素来展现一个完整的故事情节。这种叙述方式不仅能够引起读者的兴趣,也能够传达信息和观点。

第三章 记叙类文体

记叙文作为其他语篇类型的基础，是课程标准要求的重点学习的语篇类型之一。它为其他类型的文章提供故事性、生动性和引人入胜的叙述方式，如说明文、议论文、描写文等，往往可以借鉴记叙文的叙述手法和结构。甚至可以在说明文中，通过嵌入一个小故事来更好地解释和说明某个概念或理论；在议论文中，可以使用一个具体的案例或故事来支持和证明自己的观点；在描写文中，可以运用记叙文的描写技巧来生动地刻画一个场景或形象。通过运用记叙文的特点和技巧，可以增强其他类型文章的表达力和吸引力，从而更好地传达作者的意图和观点。

记叙文因其主要用来讲述过去的故事，所以谓语动词通常用一般过去式形式，但谓语动词用一般现在时也不少见。叙事中用现在时态主要是为了创造紧迫感和紧张气氛，如下面选自外研版 Book 2 Unit 6 的 Sharks：Dangerous or endangered? 的第一段 "We see a woman swimming at night in a dark sea. Suddenly, she is pulled underwater. She surfaces, cries in fear, then disappears forever. This is the opening scene from the 1975 film *Jaws*, showing a shark attack. It tells the story of a great white shark that attacks and kills swimmers..."

现在时的叙事，短句的运用，引起了读者的兴趣，使描写格外生动，给读者带来更直接的情感冲击，使文章更具感染力。另外，记叙文用现在时，也同时能表达叙述者与其所叙述的事件有关系，或表明叙述者参与了叙述中的动作。例如，Book 2 Unit 1 中 A Child of Two Cuisines，整个文章以第一人称来写，主时态用的是现在时。作者以亲身经历，给读者讲述发生在自身的两种饮食文化产生的趣事，代入感很强。

记叙文的语言表达通常遵循时间、空间或逻辑顺序，将故事情节分为背景描绘、事件过程和结果呈现等几个要素。在叙述过程中，动作顺序与时间线索相互呼应，展现一种层层推进的叙事方式。故事情节的设定主要包括时间、地点、背景及人物角色等元素，因此其结构体现为描述式结构，依次呈现各种情节要素。

如 Book1 Unit 5 中 An Encounter with Nature 语篇中的第三段，就非常好地展示了人、熊的意外相遇、相处和分开的过程，动作链条完整。段落中，除了运用了大量的时间状语，如：Last spring..., When...finally..., While..., suddenly...Slowly..., A second later..., When..., now... 还运用很多动词，如：followed..., was concentrating on..., had a feeling..., was being watched..., turned..., froze..., stared back..., stood still..., started shaking..., forced..., turned and ran back..., recovered..., looked at...was captured... 表明动作推进的过程,同时也能从描写和动作中读出作者心情的变化,the view was breathtaking(thrilled)..., suddenly had a feeling (alert)..., turned...and froze(shocked), only meters away(frightened)..., time stood still(frightened)..., started shaking(frightened)..., recovered from shock(relieved)..., most frightening but magical experience was now captured forever...(excited and happy)。

"然而,语言交际不仅仅是客观实际地描述客观世界和内心世界的情况,而是总是为了一定的交际目的,完成一定的交际任务,实现一定的交际目标。所以,事件、概念和过程的叙述顺序要受到交际目的的制约。"(张德禄、刘汝山,2003:71)"客观外界的事件的发生顺序不是决定语篇连贯的主要因素。决定其连贯的主要因素是社会交际的需要。作者在关注客观事实发生的顺序的同时,考虑它们在整个语篇中的交际功能。"(张德禄、刘汝山,2003:74)

以人物传记类的记叙文语篇为例。语篇结构通常会以该人物最显著的成就来开篇,说明介绍该人物的必要和意义,然后会从该人物的出生开始倒叙。这是此类语篇的典型写作模式。

在选必二 U4 的 My 100 days with MSF 中,作者多次运用倒叙的手法。比如,日记的开头记叙了在利比里亚的无国界医生因为有一个月没有埃博拉病例而庆祝。接下来以倒叙的方式叙述了主人公自愿前往利比里亚并参与抗击埃博拉的故事,包括接受任务、认识新同事以及在疾病暴发现场工作的情况。第四段以下面一句话结尾"But, although the death rate is very high, we will never give up on a patient, and our efforts do sometimes end in miracle",第五段又倒叙到作者刚到利比里亚的时候,以实例证明他们的工作有时会真的出现奇迹。"Just after my arrival, a family of six were brought here in the back of a van. All of them were infected..., both boys were still alive. Pascal and Daniel have since made a full recovery. This small but unexpected success compensated for many other less fortunate cases."

这种倒叙手法完美呈现了语篇的语义连贯,为读者呈现了意外的希望和奇迹,激起强烈的情感共鸣。两种记叙方式的结合,使整个故事更加生动感人,展示了人与人之间的情感联系以及全球合作抗击疾病的伟大事业。

二、拉波夫叙事模式分析

"在写作谋篇的过程中,西方人偏重直线式思维,偏爱演绎推理,注重追溯因果;西方人习惯开门见山,一落笔就点明主题、交代要点,然后再逐层细叙、分析推理,较常按照从一般到细节、从概况到具体、从整体到个体的原则。"(连淑能,2010:39)。这个原则很好地解释了拉波夫的叙事模式分析中,为什么会有第一条的点题。

在记叙文的语篇分析中,美国语言学家拉波夫的叙事原则应用比较广泛(图3-1)。"他指出完整的叙述可以包括六个部分,分别是点题、指向、进展、评议、结果或结局以及回应。图3-1清晰地展示了这几个要素之间的关系。"(转引自黄国文,1988:147-153)

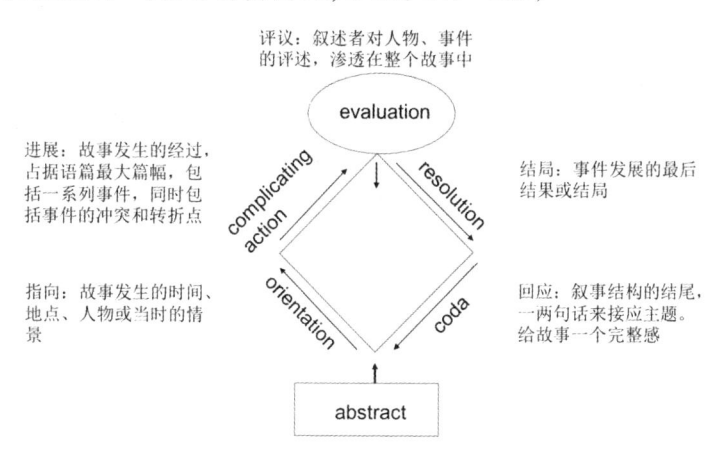

评议:叙述者对人物、事件的评述,渗透在整个故事中 — evaluation

进展:故事发生的经过,占据语篇最大篇幅,包括一系列事件,同时包括事件的冲突和转折点 — complicating action

结局:事件发展的最后结果或结局 — resolution

指向:故事发生的时间、地点、人物或当时的情景 — orientation

回应:叙事结构的结尾,一两句话来接应主题,给故事一个完整感 — coda

点题:通常出现在文章首段。有标题的文章,标题就是点题,对文章高度概括 — abstract

图3-1 拉波夫叙事原理示意图

```
                          So what?
                        ┌─────────┐
                        │evaluation│
                        └─────────┘
       Then what happened?   ↑    What finally happened?
              complicating      resolution
                action
       Who, when, what, where?        coda     通常不回答问题。
              orientation                      可以没有该部分。
                        ┌─────────┐
                        │ abstract │
                        └─────────┘
                    What was this story about?
```

图 3-2　拉波夫叙事原理各部分对应的潜在问题示意图

从图 3-2 可以看出，Coda 部分通常不直接回答问题，在有些语篇中可以省略。这为高考读后续写提供了理据：在文本结尾，当对故事情感和价值观把握不足时，考生可省略升华部分。留白可为读者提供解读空间。若能做到恰当升华更佳，但偏离主题会影响得分，需谨慎。

黄国文认为，并非所有的叙事结构都有这些组成部分，"有些部分在某一个叙事语篇中都必须出现，而有些部分则可以不出现……Labov 所说的六个部分哪些是可有可无的呢？我们认为，'进展'和'结局'部分是一定要出现的成分，因为这两个部分是叙事的主旨。……从我们掌握的语言实例看，有的句式并没有'评议'这一部分，所以我们把它与'点题''指向'和'回应'一起当作是可有可无成分。"（黄国文，2001：198-199）

一般而言，记叙文主要用于叙述人物的经历以及事物的发展和变化，其基本结构包含背景、过程和结局或评价这几个必要组成部分。除了基本结构，可酌情添加其他成分，但非必要不添加。教师应通过实例深入解析这一特点，并指导学生以此结构为模板，应用于口头和书面记叙文表达。

拉波夫叙事结构为叙事提供了基本框架，让我们明晰其整体组织结构和发展趋势。记叙文六要素——人物、时间、地点、事件、情感和目的，深入描绘了叙事文本的详细内容，帮助我们分析其人物塑造、时空背景、事件进展和情感表达。这两种工具在分析叙事时相辅相成，共同促进对叙事内容的深入理解。

三、记叙文语篇的判定

判断记叙文的要点在于,描述的对象通常是人物或事件,内容是对其进行叙述和想象创作,通常以第一人称或第三人称(也就是上帝视角)来进行叙述。如果以第一人称来叙写,叙述者只能描写自己的所见、所感,不能写其他人的心理活动;但如果是第三人称来叙述,以全能视角,叙述者可以写所有人的所见、所感及心理活动。在叙述文中,除了按正常顺序叙述外,还有倒叙、插叙等。

"事件和活动一定要有参与者,事件本身不能发生和发展。"(张德禄、刘汝山,2003:55)。也就是说,即便是以叙事为主的叙述文,也必然涉及人物角色。除了以事件的进展为明线推进故事,还有一条暗线,即人物的情感变化,来辅助故事的展开。作者通常会用字里行间的措辞去丰满人物个性,这是非常重要的记叙文的写作特点。教师通过让学生在阅读中思考人物性格,既可以让学生关注文本的词、句、篇,做到精读,感受语言的精妙;又可以让学生读出文本之意,锤炼阅读技巧和深度思考的能力。

"一般说来,句中若有叙事部分和表态部分,英语常常是表态部分(判断、结论等)在前,叙事部分(事实、描写等)在后,即先总体后分述,或先讲结果后追叙过去;句中若有连用数个前置定语,英语常常是越能说明人和事物本质的越靠近名词,或越能让人印象深刻的越靠近名词。"(连淑能,2010:35)

综上所述,记叙文的特点见表3-1。

表3-1 记叙文的特点

语篇目的	叙述人物的经历,描述事件的发展,想象创作
语篇形式	配图故事、叙事性日记、人物故事、寓言、幽默故事、童话、人物传记(介绍)、(简版、短篇)小说、科幻故事、剧本、文学名著等
语篇模式	叙事模式,拉波夫叙事:点题(abstract)叙事前对事件做出简要的概括、介绍;指向(orientation)事件发生的时间、地点、人物、活动和当时的情境;进展(complicating action):事件实际的发生、事态的进展;评议(evaluation):角色对故事发生的原因、故事的要点、人物、动作等方面的评论;结局(resolution):故事中发生的事件的结束情况,如后果、结果;回应(coda):角色对事件做出的行动、情感变化或认知转变

续表

语篇目的	叙述人物的经历,描述事件的发展,想象创作
语篇结构	通常是三部分:主要按时空顺序,遵循"背景—过程—结局或评价"的结构
叙事线索	主线:故事线/情节线;记叙人物、事件副线:情感线(表达主人公的情感及作者的评价),有时以暗线的形式出现,需要从字里行间分析
判断要点	描述的对象通常是人物或事件,内容是叙述(non-fictional)或想象(fictional)
叙述人称	第一人称:只能描写人物的所见、所感,不能写其他人的心理活动;第三人称(上帝视角):全能视角,可以写所有人的所见、所感及心理活动
语言特点	过去时为主,其他视具体情况而定(对话内容的时态按照说话时的情形决定)

图式理论指出,形式图式涉及读者对语篇体裁、修辞和写作手法的认知。掌握记叙文的整体特征有助于学生构建记叙文的形式图式,进而在阅读记叙文时更容易理解文章主旨、结构和段落间的逻辑关联。激活正确的图式让学生能在阅读记叙文的某个部分时,预测后续内容;在运用记叙文形式表达时,他们脑海中将浮现清晰的记叙文结构模板,这有助于提升阅读效率,深化对材料的理解。

第二节 记叙文的语篇结构及分析

本节会重点介绍常见的记叙文类型及结构,根据教材语篇设题看记叙文的教学重点,并根据课标要求的语篇分析框架 What, Why 和 How 的角度进行语篇分析示例。

一、记叙文的常见结构

在阅读教学中,语篇解读不仅能塑造学生的思维品质,还能增强其学习能力和文化修养。记叙文以其叙述性和描写性为特点,其中时间、地点和人物构成其核心骨架。叙事文的开篇往往聚焦于这三者,确保读者能迅速把握事件发生的时空背景与人物角色,从而深入理解故事走向。

常见结构有以下几种。

(1)时序展开式。叙事类记叙文常以时序展开,通过时间线推进中心事件,强调事件间的时间顺序关联,核心在于清晰叙述特定事件与主体人物的经历。

(2)平列展开式。引出主题后,依次从不同侧面围绕主题进行叙述,是人物类记叙文最常见的写作模式。

(3)穿插回顾式。以倒叙的形式以最令人印象深刻的场景或事件吸引读者的注意,开展后续的故事,过程中需要特别关注人物的心理和情绪的变化,如 My 100 days with MSF,以及下一节中将要分析的 2010 年全国高考 E 篇阅读。

(4)对比映照式。引出话题后,对照不同的人、事,凸显主题,最后进行评价、抒情,如 Life behind the lens。

在阅读教学时,教师可根据语篇类型及结构开展教学活动,训练学生的阅读策略,使学生迅速理解语篇结构与内容。在教学中,教师先创设情境激活学生知识,引导他们分析文章主题、结构和语言特点,并教授体裁分析技巧。同时,注重故事发展,指导学生识别描写手法,如动作、心理和语言的描写,从而增强对实词的敏感度。文中重复句型和关键动词是理解主题与文本分析的重要语言目标。

二、教材中的记叙类文体

记叙文是教材中的重点文体,在外研版高中教材必修和选择性必修的 42 个单元中的 84 篇主文章中,叙事类文体占了 33 篇,涵盖人与自我、人与社会和人与自然三大主题语境。大量的记叙类文章给学生提供了丰富的话题,内容涉及校园学习、人际交往、人物介绍、生活态度、社会历史和自然环境等。笔者基于自己的理解,把这 33 篇文章粗略分成了七个类别,分别是日记、个人故事、叙事故事、游记、小说戏剧、人物介绍和新闻特写(如表 3-2 所示)。

这些类别的划分主要根据语篇形式,但彼此交叉,都体现记叙文的特征。无论是真实的还是虚构的,文章结构严谨、情节连贯、语言生动,并通过时间顺序或空间关系进行故事情节的展开,将读者带入一个有情节发展和人物情感的世界，使读者沉浸其中、产生共鸣，并在阅读中感受到故事背后所蕴含的情感、价值观念和思想。

表 3-2　外研版高中教材必修和选择性必修中记叙文的类别

教材	单元	语篇	类别
1	Unit 1 A new start	My first day at senior high	日记
选必 2	Unit 4 Breaking boundaries	My 100 days with MSF	
2	Unit 1 Food for thought	A child of two cuisines	个人故事
2	Unit 4 Stage and screen	When Hamlet meets Peking Opera	
3	Unit 6 Disaster and hope	Hot! Hot! Hot!	
3	Unit 6 Disaster and hope	Stars after the storm	
选必 1	Unit 4 Meeting the muse	What inspires you？	
1	Unit 5 Into the wild	An encounter with nature	叙事故事
选必 1	Unit 1 Laugh out loud!	The best medicine	
选必 1	Unit 5 Revealing nature	A journey of discovery	
选必 2	Unit 3 Times change!	A new chapter	
选必 3	Unit 3 War and peace	The D-day landings	
选必 3	Unit 3 War and peace	Lianda: a place of passion, belief and commitment	
2	Unit 5 On the road	Coast to coast	游记
3	Unit 4 Amazing art	Live from the Louvre	
选必 1	Unit 6 Nurturing nature	The sky railway	
选必 4	Unit 3 The world meets China	Welcome to Dunhuang	
1	Unit 3 Family matters	Like father, like son	小说戏剧
1	Unit 4 Friends forever	After twenty years	
3	Unit 5 What an adventure!	Twenty thousand leagues under the sea	
选必 2	Unit 1 Growing up	The little prince	
选必 3	Unit 1 Face values	The Hunchback of Notre-Dame	
选必 3	Unit 4 A glimpse of the future	A boy's best friend	
选必 4	Unit 2 Lessons in life	The blue bird	

续表

教材	单元	语篇	类别
3	Unit 2 Making a difference	The well that changed the world	人物介绍
3	Unit 2 Making a difference	The power of good	
3	Unit 4 Amazing art	Han Gan and his horses	
选必3	Unit 2 A life's work	Masters of time	
1	Unit 3 Family matters	Just a brother	新闻特写(人物)
选必1	Unit 3 Faster, higher, stronger	The road to success	
选必1	Unit 3 Faster, higher, stronger	The return of the champions	
选必3	Unit 2 A life's work	Life behind the lens	
选必4	Unit 4 Everyday economics	Business blossoms	

高考真题阅读理解中的记叙文主要在 B 篇,虽然出现频率高,但是考查文章的主旨大意的题目较少,以事实细节和细节推理题为常考点。记叙文主旨类题目的正确选项以故事寓意类为主,阐明故事背后的寓意和道理,或者作者的观点态度。选项表述形式统一,要么是事件概括,要么是故事寓意,一般不会进行二者的混杂。本节所采用的说明材料都是来自 2023 年全国高考题中关于记叙文的设题。

因为记叙文通常会通过丰富的细节描写来展现故事情节和人物性格,因此阅读理解题目往往会涉及细节理解。找到这些信息不仅能够锻炼学生阅读细节、查找信息的能力,还能通过对信息的加工处理,深化对文本的理解。

What is the basis for John's invention?(全国新高考Ⅰ卷)

Why did Terri's grandfather give her £5 a day?(全国甲卷)

How does the author deal with the challenge as a landscape photographer in the Midwest?(全国乙卷)

What is the key to successful landscape photography according to the author?(全国乙卷)

记叙文往往融入了作者的情感、态度和价值观,题目可能会要求考生理解作者的情感表达、观点立场,从而推断出作者的态度和意图。

What can we learn about John from the first two paragraphs?(全国新高考Ⅰ卷)

What is the author's purpose in mentioning Fuzhou?（全国新高考Ⅰ卷）

What trend in DIY does the research show?（全国甲卷）

How does the author find his photos taken at Devil's Lake?（全国乙卷）

记叙文中的事件发展常常有一定的逻辑顺序和因果关系,题目可能需要考生根据文中线索推断事件的发展或人物之间的关系。

Why did John put the sludge into the tanks？（全国新高考Ⅰ卷）

How did Terri avoid losing the deposit on the house she rented?（全国甲卷）

What can we infer from the author's trip with friends to Devil's Lake?（全国乙卷）

这些题型,在教材记叙文语篇的配套练习中都能找到影子。

叙事类语篇形式各异,特点与功能有所区别,但记叙文阅读理解题主要评估考生对文章的整体把握,以及对细节、情感和逻辑的深入理解与分析能力。教材的配套练习为一线教师提供了明确的教学方向和指导。在此基础上,我们将依据这些练习,探讨各类叙事语篇的教学重点。

（一）日记类记叙文

日记类记叙文独具格式,要求标注星期、日期,并可记录天气。其特点在于真实性和个性化,作者借此形式记录生活点滴、情感波动与思想变化,展现内心的成长与蜕变。写日记不仅是记录生活琐事,更是一次自我探索与审视的旅程,有助于作者理解自我、规划未来。通过日记,作者可抒发对生活的热爱,表达对人生的深邃思考,以及对特定事件的独特见解。这使日记类记叙文充满了个人风格和深情投入,能够触动读者内心,让其感受到作者的真挚感悟与深刻思考。

读日记类的记叙文,我们首先要整体把握文章的内容,了解发生的事情、呈现的问题、解决问题的方式以及作者要表达的情感。日记不限于记录一天内发生的事情,可以根据个人习惯和需求来安排日记的内容和时间跨度。教材中的两个日记语篇,第一篇就是按照时间顺序,详细记录了初入高中的 Meng Hao 这一天的所做、所见和所思；另一个语篇对 100 天内发生的重要的事情进行记录和思考,运用了顺叙和倒叙的方式,所以在捋事件顺序的时候,就需要利用好语篇中的时间线索。

对 My first day at senior high 这个语篇,教材配套了三个练习,分别要求:(1)Read the passage and find out what the author wrote in his diary about the first day at senior high. (2)Choose the best description of Meng Hao's first day at senior high. (3)Complete Meng Hao's experiences with expressions from the passage.

对 My 100 days with MSF 这个语篇,教材同样配套了三个练习,分别要求:(1)Read the journal of an MSF doctor and find out what problem he was involved in tackling. (2)Choose the ideas conveyed in the passage and find evidence to support your choice. (3)Organize information from the passage and complete the table.

教材中两篇日记文体,一篇作为高中教材第一个语篇,另一个出现在高二。从配套练习中可以看出,教材对学生理解深度的要求、对语言的要求逐步提升,但教材给出的处理方式非常相似,分别给出了图表提示读者可以从作者的经历中体会作者的情感历程。

两个语篇最后都有一个对文本句子的深度理解:What is your understanding of the saying "Well begun, half done" 和基于对习近平总书记倡导的 a community with a shared future for mankind 的理解,进一步理解文本句子 "To be caught up in such a crisis creates powerful bonds between people, not only between careers and patients, but also between all those who have come from different parts of the world and joined together in a common cause." 通过结合自身经历,读者可以更深刻地感受到日记作者的情感、思想以及背景。这种分析能够帮助读者更全面地把握日记的内涵与意义,也有助于读者提升阅读体验和对文本深度理解。

(二)个人故事类记叙文

个人故事类的记叙文是以作者个人经历、遭遇或成长为主线,通过叙述具体事件或情节来展示作者的内心变化、思考和成长过程。这种记叙文通常以第一人称进行叙述,让读者更容易与作者产生共鸣和情感联系。个人故事类的记叙文可以包括作者的童年回忆、重要生活转折点、挫折与成长、梦想与追求等内容,通过真实的个人经历展现出作者独特的人生感悟和情感体验,能够打动读者的心灵,让读者在阅读中感受到情感共鸣和启发。

教材中这五篇个人故事类的记叙文,设题涵盖了理解题、主旨大意题、细节理解题、写作目的题、文章出处题等。记叙文语篇的主题常常需要读者从所提供的信息推断。What inspires you 这个语篇以并列微语篇的形式,呈现了三位艺术家的作品及其灵感来源,以表格的形式呈现语篇的结构。另外,好几个语篇都以表格形式考查了学生对作者情感态度的理解并要求提供支持观点的细节。

阅读个人故事类记叙文,重点是要透过文字表达的情绪、细节描写等,感受作者想要传达的情感,并试着站在人物的角度去感受、理解他们的内心和处境,体会他们的痛苦、喜悦、忧虑等。思考人物的行为背后的动机和原因,挖掘他们的内心世界,理解他们的选择和冲突,联系自身经历,达到与作者共情。

(三) 叙事故事类记叙文、戏剧小说

叙事故事类的记叙文可以是虚构的小说,也可以是基于真实事件改编的故事,无论是哪种形式,都需要通过生动的语言和丰富的细节描写来吸引读者的注意力,让读者与故事中的人物产生共鸣。教材中的记叙文篇幅虽然不是很长,但故事情节都很完整,通过描述人物、事件的发展和变化来展现故事的起承转合,最终达到传达主题或启示读者的目的。通过情节的设置、人物的塑造、环境的描写等手法来引导读者进入故事情节。

小说和戏剧在叙事上有各自的特点和表现方式,但都可以通过生动的描写和叙述带领读者进入故事的世界,感受其中的情感与冲突。

小说通常通过第一人称或第三人称的视角来叙述故事,包括对场景、人物内心世界、事件发展等方面的描写。作者可以通过详细的描写和铺陈,深入展现人物的性格、情感和命运,使读者能够身临其境地感受故事的发展和情节的转折。戏剧则是一种适合舞台表演的文学形式,强调对话、动作和舞台设置等因素。在戏剧中,记叙文更多地体现在台词和舞台指示中。剧本中的对话和舞台布景通过记叙来表达剧情和人物关系。

高考读后续写类的记叙文,与以上两种类型的记叙文类似,其基本特征是双线结构。需要学生基于已给的故事情节和线索续写故事中问题的解决及人物的成长变化。显性主线是以时间或空间顺序发展的具体事件,最关键的感情线索却是不易察觉的隐形支线,很多学生在续写时最大的问题是难以深度把握时序式记叙文的深层内涵与现实意义。

阅读时,需关注背景、进展和高潮,特别是冲突的解决;理解角色发展、故事起承转合;注意主要人物的性格、言谈举止、成长变化及与其他人物之间的关系;让自己代入情感,感受故事情绪;留意作者对场景、环境和细节的描写;注意故事结构、时间顺序和组织方式的逻辑性,包括时间顺序、回忆、倒叙等;理解作者语言风格,把握故事主题和价值观。阅读中通过关注以上的几个方面,引导学生体会和模仿语篇结构、语篇的衔接和连贯、语言的运用,从拉波夫叙事的角度建构故事情节,更深入地体验和领悟故事所蕴含的意义,提高他们的表达能力。

教材中的叙事类记叙文设题,除了排列故事中事件发生的顺序、细节理解、段落主旨等,还运用维恩图设置了信息对比题目。例如,The best medicine 中,对比小丑医生跟传统医生的异同;A new chapter 语篇中,对比新旧书店的异同。信息对比题目的设置,目的是培养学生的批判性思维、分析问题的能力和归纳总结的能力。阅读时,学生需对比不同事物、观点、数据,以深入理解文本。在整合对比信息中,形成独到见解,深化对问题的理解,同时培养客观分析、批判思维、逻辑思考及问题解决能力,亦提升语言表达水平。

(四)游记类记叙文

游记通常记录作者在旅行或游览过程中的见闻、感受、体验以及对所到之地的描述和评价。在结构上通常包括游记的动机或目的、旅行的路线和计划、所到之地的景观、文化特色等内容,记录旅行中的趣事,同时也会插入作者的个人感受、思考和评价。通过清晰、生动、具体的文字表达,使读者能够身临其境地感受到作者的旅行经历。游记类记叙文不仅可以展示作者的旅行体验,还可以让读者从中获取知识、启发思考,激发他们对旅行的向往和探索欲望。读者可以从此类文章中学到对环境的描写。

（五）人物传记类记叙文

人物传记类的记叙文以第三人称视角叙述某个特定人物一生的经历和成就。一般分为两类,名人传记和励志型小人物记。此类故事以简介人物生平为核心,重在展现人物的杰出成就与非凡品质,意在引导学生领悟并学习这些品质。试题的考查焦点在学生对人物事迹的深刻理解和对其品质的领悟上。一旦学生掌握了该文体的图式,便能迅速把握文章脉络,精准抓住要点,进而提升对文章内容的理解准确度。

人物传记篇章常遵循的结构为:人物、时间、事件、成就和评价。起始于该人物的标志性成就,再追溯其生平,如出身、家庭背景、成长环境及教育经历,以呈现人物起点。随后详述其生涯中的重要事件和成就,包括遇到的困难、挑战及克服过程,凸显其性格、智慧和毅力。最后,评价其影响力,包括在特定领域的贡献及对后世的启示。教学活动应围绕这一结构,训练学生的阅读策略,以迅速理解篇章结构与内容。

教材中的几篇人物传记类文章结构相似。Han Gan and his horses 就是非常典型的人物叙写。开篇第一段先从对韩干的代表作《照夜白图》的介绍开始 "What a magnificent horse! Even after more than a thousand years have passed, we can still feel the power within its burning eyes, bared teeth and kicking hooves. Night-Shining White, ..., is regarded as one of the most significant horse paintings in the history of Chinese art. Its artist, Han Gan, is known for his skill in capturing not only the physical features of the animal, but also its inner spirit and strength." 文章的第二段以 Born into a poor family in the early Tang Dynasty 开始讲述韩干的人生,第三段和第四段介绍韩干的工作及他如何精进画技,最后一段 Those who saw Han Gan's horse paintings all sang high praise for his unique skill, saying that his horses "could gallop off the paper" 高度评价韩干的画技,甚至还以苏轼对韩干的评价来佐证他技艺的高超。

教材语篇的结构可以迁移应用到高考真题中。人物类介绍一直都是高考应用文中的热点考点。近几年高考题中关于人物的应用文如表3-3所示。

表 3-3　近几年高考题中关于人物的应用文

试卷年份	试卷名称	考查体裁	题材内容
2023 年 6 月	全国甲卷	短文投稿	写一位历史人物
2020 年 6 月	全国新高考 I 卷	记叙文	身边值得尊敬和爱戴的人
2020 年 6 月	北京卷	推荐信	推荐一名外籍指导教师
2019 年 6 月	全国卷 I 卷	申请信	申请中国画展志愿者

在语篇学习过程中，学生不仅深入理解了人物类文章的基本结构，还通过教材语篇的学习，积累了与主题语境紧密相关的语言知识。结合这些积累与体裁格式的要求，再参照高考应用文的评价标准，学生便能够流畅地撰写出一篇结构清晰、内容充实的人物类应用文。

（六）新闻特写类记叙文

新闻特写类的记叙文不仅仅是简单的事实报道，更是在新闻报道的基础上，通过对人物、事件、背景等方面的深入挖掘和呈现，展现出丰富的细节和情感，使读者更加深入地了解事件背后的故事和意义。这类记叙文通常会通过丰富的描写和翔实的描述，去呈现出一个特定事件或主题的全貌，让读者能够更加生动地感受到其中的情感与故事，更注重于情感共鸣和读者的思考，帮助人们从不同角度去理解和思考所报道的事件。

这类记叙文常以一个抓人眼球的特写镜头作为开篇，瞬间吸引读者的注意与好奇。例如，教材中的五个新闻特写，皆以此手法引人入胜。其中，Just a Brother 以 Alistair 兄弟在铁人三项中的争议行为开篇，直戳人心，引发读者对兄弟情谊与竞技精神的深思。The Road to Success 则以 Steven Curry 童年的篮球起点为镜头，描绘了简陋的乡间小道与爷爷亲手搭建的篮球框，彰显了他日后辉煌之路的艰辛与不易，更加突出了 Curry 坚定的信念与勤奋精神。The Return of the Champions 则以中国女排在里约奥运夺冠的震撼瞬间开篇，让读者置身现场，探寻女排胜利的秘诀。Life behind the Lens 以知名摄影师 Bill Cunningham 的摄影作品描述开篇，巧妙地描绘了他的形象特征，勾起了读者对他人生故事的浓厚兴趣。Business Blossoms 则以主人公紧张的投资面试场景开篇，吊足读者胃口，让人迫不及待想要知道她的创业故事与现状。

教材中对这类语篇的设题主要有几种,包括写作目的、要传递的信息、题目题等,频率最高的题目是探求这些人物的品质和成功的原因,激发读者学习这些榜样人物。在阅读该类语篇时,首先我们要引导学生关注和分析新闻事件本身,了解历史背景、影响以及可能的深层含义;聚焦文本内容,进行深度阅读,探究事件、人物背后的关键因素,把握作者的写作目的及要传递的价值观。

三、记叙文语篇分析

在语篇分析备课中,教师需要深入理解语境,涉及文化和情景语境,特别是时间、地点、社会背景等关键要素。同时,教师应全面把握语篇的整体结构,包括段落间的逻辑联系、话题的演变以及信息的布局。此外,还需研究交际参与者的意图和选择特定表达形式的原因。

以必修二 Unit 1 A child of two cuisines 为例,从课标中的语篇分析三要素角度对该语篇进行分析。

(一)首先是语篇的主题和内容(what)

主题:跨中英文化背景下的饮食文化。

语篇共配四幅图:一个红油火锅图,一份英式早餐图,一份西式点心图和一杯茶。从配图可以大胆预测题目中的 two cuisines 指的是中英两国的饮食。题目中的 a child of two cuisines 提示作者的身份是中英混血。从语篇第一段可以证实这个猜测。

内容信息:主人公具有中英两国血统。通过描述一家人在烹饪和饮食上的不同文化体验,他在中英两种食物之间找到了自己的喜好,也感受到了两种文化之间的碰撞和融合。

(二)语篇的主题意义(why)

通过食物和家庭文化的描述,展现了主人公在跨文化环境下成长的心路历程和对多元文化的包容态度,强调了文化间的相互尊重和理解,以及对于不同文化食物的接受和尝试的重要性。语篇最后一段"...but I feel at home with food from both my cultures. To me, there's nothing better than a cross-cultural afternoon tea of English biscuits and a cup of Chinese oolong tea in a fine china cup." 展现了作者对于两种饮食文化的接纳和享受。

(三) 语篇的组织特征(how)

(1) 语篇体裁：记叙文

篇章结构：采用平列展开式结构。首先介绍了主人公的家庭背景，然后详细描述了作者及其父母对中国和英国饮食中不同食物的见闻和感受，最后总结了对于跨文化食物的态度和看法。

(2) 衔接手段

语篇中有时间上的衔接，也有地点上的变换，但最主要的是针对不同食物的体验和好恶来展开语篇，最后仍然归结于文化的融合和接纳。

(3) 段与段之间的衔接

第一段作为背景介绍，最后一句 "I've enjoyed food from both countries ever since I was able to hold a knife and fork—and chopsticks." 可以作为全篇的总起，下面要分说中英两国饮食。

第二段和第三段间以 but 构成了转折，作者表明了自己可以接受爸爸不喜欢的鸡爪子和猪蹄等动物身体部位。

第二、三段主要说了中国的两种饮食 hot pot 和 animal parts，接下来的第四段跟第二段形成了对比，开始讨论一家人对英式餐点 full English breakfast 和 Sunday Roast 的情感。

第五段通过空间的转换，又回到中国饮食。通过在中国勇敢试吃臭豆腐的经历，发现也有自己暂时不太喜欢的中国饮食。

最后一段，通过对比表达了对中英两种饮食的接纳和喜爱。

语篇中使用了大量的显性衔接手段。

(4) 语法衔接手段

①照应。照应中的人称指代，除了指代父母的 he, she, her 等，还有第五段中的 You don't need to try it if you don't want to 中的 it, I was amazed to find it wasn't so bad 中的 it 以及 It reminded me of blue cheese 中的 It 都指代前文的 stinky tofu。

指示代词如：第二段中的 Thanks to this 中的 this 回指(mom) often cooks spicy dishes；第三段开头的 But I enjoy that sort of food myself 中

的 that 也是回指,指代上一段中最后一句话中的 things like chicken feet;第三段中,屠夫说的"just these ordinary ones"里用到了 these 回指 ears,还用到了 ones 替代前文的 ears。

比较词语如:第二段中的 even shocked;第五段中的 try different kinds of food 中的 different;smelt like a burnt sports shoe 中的 like;a similarly strong smelling type of food 中的 similarly;最后一段中的 there's nothing better than ... 中的 nothing better than 都构成了比较的关系。

②替代。除了上面提到的 ones 替代 ears,第四段中"He also does a typical Sunday roast"中的 does 替代前文的 cook;第五段中的 and I did 中的 did 替代上一句中的 try different kinds of food 这件事。

(5)词汇手段

词汇衔接手段运用了词汇复现和词汇同现两种手段。

词汇复现,用到了同词复现,如 ears, stinky tofu, love 等;同义词近义词用到了很多,特别是表示喜好的,如 love, take to, enjoy, feel at home 等,还有 surprised 和 shocked 等;上下义词有 food from her hometown 和 spicy food, hot pot,以及 every part of an animal 和 chicken feet 等。

整个语篇作为关于中英饮食的一个语义场,很多关于饮食的词汇,甚至包括文化差异的餐具 knife and fork, chopsticks 等都构成了同现关系,另外还有反义词 love, hate 等。

使用的连接手段主要通过连词 and, but, even, still, or 等,使整个语篇结构更加流畅自然。

在语篇分析中,读者能够深入了解作者的身世背景、成长经历以及跨文化交融下的美食和家庭文化,感受到其中蕴含的趣味和情感连接。

当然,在教学实践中,我们需要在遵循课程标准的前提下,根据学情和需求进行灵活调整。同时,要避免在每堂课中面面俱到,要有所侧重,合理取舍教学内容,确保学生能够高效、有效地掌握关键点。因此,在教学设计和实施中,应当关注个体差异,实施同课异构的教学策略,以最大限度地满足学生的学习需求,并提升教学效果。

第三节 记叙文语篇中的语言学习

在文本解读中,除了分析文章的体裁和主题,还需理解故事情节、事件进展和人物性格的描绘,以了解文章结构。特别值得注意的是,对文章语言进行深入剖析对提升整体英语能力至关重要。这包括对词汇、短语、句型结构和写作技巧的综合考量,尤其是对高频词汇、固定搭配及复杂句型的详细解读。此外,当面对记叙文特有的双线结构时,情感线索的展开和表达方式同样不容忽视,教材中的范例为学生提供了宝贵的写作借鉴。

除了语音语调可以表情达意(不在本书的研究范围),教材中还有很多其他的方式可以表达各种情感,特别是形容词、副词、名词、动词、情态动词、标点符号和修辞等。下面利用外研版高中教材中的片段举例说明。

一、表情达意的形容词和副词

形容词可以用来描述物体或人的特征,常用来修饰名词以表达情感。副词通常用来修饰动词、形容词或其他副词,可用来修饰情感的程度或方式。它们在表达情感方面最直接。例如:

Mum has **sweet** memories of the food from her hometown in Sichuan, ...

Seeing the main characters come on the stage, I was **surprised**! The costumes and masks were **amazing**.

Moreover, what made Cunningham **great** was his devotion to photography, and the hours and hours of **sheer** hard work he put into his work.

副词的叠加运用,不仅能够更加深刻地诠释情感,还能使句子更具感染力。

It was August, so it was **really, really** hot and it smelled so bad everywhere!

形容词、副词如果结合标点符号,表达的情感会更强烈。如:

That was **simply incredible**! It was so **dazzling** and **energetic** that I wasn't sure if the characters were performers or athletes!

人教版教材第二册中的 A day in the clouds 语篇中有这样一句话:They (antelopes) were hunted, **illegally**, for their valuable fur. 作者使用逗号将副词 illegally 单独隔开,体现了其对非法狩猎藏羚羊的谴责、愤怒和强烈反对的心情。

写作中,如果能利用不同的形容词和副词构成对比,也会产生格外的效果。例如:

What made Cunningham so great? It certainly wasn't the use of **expensive, technologically-advanced** equipment. Cunningham always used **simple, relatively cheap** cameras and took all his pictures on the streets of New York, not in a studio. Nor was it a wide range of contacts and connections...He found inspiration where others could not in **simple, everyday** scenes...

语段中除了地点的对比、隐藏的人脉对比,还通过形容词的对比,表达了对 Cunningham 的钦佩、尊敬和欣赏,因为他能够在简单、日常的场景中发现灵感,不依赖昂贵的设备或广泛的人脉,展示出了他的独特才华和创造力。

It is August 1939, and a group of **frightened** children are boarding a train at Prague's Wilson Station. Their **heartbroken** parents do not join them.

受惊吓的孩子和心碎的父母形成了强烈的对比,而且语段中运用了一般现在时,营造了紧迫感和紧张气氛,让人忍不住要考虑这背后的原因,为什么家长不能带着孩子一起乘车?

Even after more than a thousand years have passed, we can still feel the power within its **burning** eyes, **bared** teeth and **kicking** hooves...Its artist, Han Gan, is known for his skill in capturing not only the **physical** features of the animal, but also its **inner** spirit and strength.

在这个语段中,韩干高超的绘画技巧,通过形容词 burning, bared 和 kicking 有针对性地描述了马的外在特征,同时捕捉到马的内在精神和力量,表达作者对韩干及其画作的赞叹。

情感的发展有进阶,可以用形容词和副词的比较级来表达。

But I know Jimmy will meet me here if he's alive, for he always was the **truest, staunchest** old chap in the world.

句中的两个最高级形容词表达了说话人对 Jimmy 在真诚和忠诚方面的极高评价和赞美,传达了说话者对 Jimmy 深厚的感情和信任。

To me, there's **nothing better than** a cross-cultural afternoon tea of...

句中的 nothing better than 强烈表达了对英式饼干配中国乌龙茶的喜爱,视其为无可替代的最佳组合,流露出对这一文化交融的积极感受。

It's just typical that my journey is on one of the **oldest** lines, as well as one of the **deepest**. It's the **hottest** on the whole Tube system.

句中连用三个形容词最高级形式表达了作者对于地铁环境闷热的不满和不适。

直接用表达不同层级情感的形容词和副词。

He once told me he was **surprised** by what he saw on the table ... He was **even shocked** at their wedding...

句中 surprised 指对中国饮食超出预期的轻微惊讶,而 shocked 则表达了对所见所闻的强烈震惊和困惑。

形容词、副词表达情感,虽然直接,但是学生习作中如果全用它们表达情感,就显得单调乏味,还需要考虑其他表达情感的方式。

二、运用名词表达心情

名词通常用来表示特定的情感或状态,特别是介词搭配,可以直接描述某种情感。例如:

I woke up early and rushed out of the door **in my eagerness** to get to know my new school.

句中的 in my eagerness 表达了作者渴望去了解新学校而表现出急切的行动和心态,强调了对新环境的兴奋和期待。

With butterflies in my stomach, I breathed deeply...I looked at them **in panic**.

从 with butterflies in my stomach 表示主语感到紧张到 in panic 强调了恐慌的情绪,描绘了主语在紧张不安的心情下作出的反应。

This **insight** grew from the **determined attitude** of a six-year-old boy who had the **courage and perseverance** to make his dream a reality.

作者赞美和肯定 Ryan 六岁时就展现出的坚定态度、勇气和毅力。

Due to Han Gan's **natrual talent** and **years of hard work**, he was eventually chosen to serve Emperor Xuanzong in the royal palace.

句子中的 natural talent 和 years of hard work 是作者对韩干的卓越才华和不懈奋斗的品质赞赏和钦佩。

Through **self-belief**, **hard work**, **perseverance** and some help from an old hoop, he has shown that anything is possible.

作者对 Stephen 的欣赏和赞叹通过 self-belief、hard work 和 perseverance 得到体现,对未来充满信心和希望。

三、运用动词表达心情

在语言表达中,运用恰到好处的动词和时态可以有效地传达思想和感情。尤其是搭配副词或短语使用动词,不仅可以提升句子的情感表现力,还能够丰富句子的内涵和意义。

首先,根据情节和背景选择最合适的动词,形象生动地展开想象情节和场景以准确、生动地描述人物的行为和内心感受。

"...a friend asked Winton to come to Prague to **aid** people who **were escaping** from the Nazis. In Prague, Winton **saw** people living in terrible conditions...He **decided to help transport** children to safety in Britain. He **established** an office to **keep records of** the children, and then **returned to** Britain to **find** temporary homes for them. He **used** donated funds and his own money to **pay** the 50 pounds per child...By August 1939, Winton **had saved** 669 children."

该语段的前半部分以过去进行时态以及 Winton 的所见所闻,创造了充满紧迫感的氛围,描绘了试图逃离纳粹迫害的犹太人的悲惨生活。后半部分通过一系列动作描写,详细描述了 Winton 如何拯救这

669 名儿童的全过程，充分表达了作者对 Winton 的敬佩和感激之情，向 Winton 的无私、勇敢表达了敬意。

It looks like she **has just flown down** out of the sky and **is standing** on a ship... but you **can imagine** her **holding her arms up high**, **celebrating** the result of an ancient battle. And just look at how her dress **is being folded** by the wind!

作者使用了多种时态，如 has just flown down, is standing, is being folded 以及祈使句 just look... 和非谓语动词 celebrating 等详细描绘了雕塑的细节和状态，表达出作者对栩栩如生的雕像的惊叹、对雕塑家高超技艺的赞赏和钦佩。

使用多样化的动词，以避免重复使用相同的动词，可以丰富文采，使叙述更加生动有趣。

在 A child of two cuisines 语篇中，除了形容词、名词等方式，作者运用了不同的动词表达对饮食的喜爱。如：

...I'**ve enjoyed** food from both countries ever since I was able to hold a knife and fork——and chopsticks!

Thanks to this, Dad has **come to love** hot pot!

Even today, he still does not easily **take to** eating things like chicken feet.

...Mum and I just have to **find a way to get him into** the kitchen!

We **all love** roast beef and vegetables, ...

Maybe I'll **fall in love with** stinky tofu——someday.

...but I **feel at home with** food from both my cultures.

动词的时态语态也可以在恰当的场景下，表达人物的心情。

He also saw hundreds of delighted students who had turned out to welcome him. They sang and danced happily. Some even offered him food and gifts.

在这个句子中，过去完成时凸显了学生们在 Ryan 到达之前便已在等待，他们对 Ryan 的感激与迫切相见的心情跃然纸上。

四、运用情态动词以及虚拟语气表达心情

情态动词是用来表达对某个动作或状态的看法、推测、建议、能力等情感的助动词。情态动词与动词搭配使用,能够用来表达各种不同的情态和语气。

课程标准对虚拟语气的具体要求是"选修(提高类),在语篇中恰当地理解和使用虚拟语气"(中华人民共和国教育部,2020:25)。也就是说,虚拟语气高考考察要求不高。但虚拟语气在多种体裁的语篇中广泛运用,尤其在记叙文中,它能够精准地表达主人公的情感变化,以及情感和意图的微妙转变。

情态动词还可以用来表达说话人对所说内容的怀疑、愿望、建议等,帮助我们更准确地传达自己的情感。情态动词会在第七章里详细介绍。

五、运用标点符号表情达意

英语写作中,标点符号的使用也可以帮助我们更好地表达情感。比如,感叹号可以表示强烈的情感、惊讶或兴奋;问号可以表示疑问、追问或不确定;省略号能表示语气的拖沓、停顿或悬念,增加神秘感。例如,Erm...Dad, can we talk? 通过巧妙运用这些标点符号,作者可以更好地传达文字背后的情感,使文本更加生动、情绪化并引人入胜。

感叹号本身就表示比较强烈的情感。感叹号和问号并用时,能表达强烈的复杂情感,融合疑惑、困惑与惊讶、震撼,有效增强语句的表现力,使对话更为生动有趣。

You can't be serious! What about your future career as a lawyer?!

前句感叹号流露父亲对儿子选择的不满与难以置信,后句问号与感叹号连用,彰显出强烈不满与质疑。

"You're Jimmy's son?!" Bob shouted in surprise.

以介词短语 in surprise,Bob 连用问号和感叹号,强烈表达了对 Jimmy 儿子接他出狱的惊讶、激动,以及对先前疑虑的确认。

Having seen quite a few productions of Hamlet and read the play many times, **I was full of confidence**—until the Peking Opera came to town!

现在分词完成形式揭示作者观看、阅读《哈姆雷特》的丰富经历,是作者信心的来源。破折号、感叹号交织,展露了作者在京剧前的意外震撼及对新体验的喜悦兴奋。

教材中标点符号的使用非常多样,第七章有专门的介绍。这里仅以现行高中英语外研版教材中带有标点符号的题目为例,说明我们如何可以通过题目,加上标点符号,就可以初步判断把握作者的态度和写作意图。

三篇带有感叹号的文章,都比较强烈地表达了文章中人物的情绪。

从题目 Absolute agony! 中就能非常清晰地看到文中人物的愤怒和痛苦的情绪。文章含两封书信:一封求助信反映同学相处难题;另一封回信则给出解决方案。

正可谓重要的事情说三遍,Hot! Hot! Hot! 不仅三遍,还连续三个感叹号,作者热不可耐的心情跃然纸上,画面感很强!作者以乘坐伦敦地铁的经历生动描写伦敦的酷热,并由报纸上关于飓风的灾害,引发对环境问题的思考。

It's all about me! 用感叹号旗帜鲜明地表明了三位年轻人对自我形象的认知和对内美与外在美的不同看法。

十二篇以疑问形式作题目的文章,根据各种疑问句本身的特点和用法,功能和表达的内容各不相同。

特殊疑问句作为题目,旨在激起读者好奇心,促使他们对特定问题进行深入思考与探索,其明确具体的答案常用于营造悬念或激发争议。

What's really green? 以特殊疑问的形式设置悬念,介绍生活中常见的关于环保的误区,并针对问题进行解答:如何做才是真正环保的。

What inspires you? 引起读者兴趣,关注三位著名艺术家对艺术灵感的解读和他们的作品,答案明确直接。

Franklin's experiment:how much is true? 质疑大家相信了多年的富兰克林的风筝实验,问题代表了对这个风筝实验的怀疑,以及由此带来的求证,客观说明实验情况,同时提出作者自己的观点。

Why Shennongjia? 以省略的特殊疑问形式作演讲的题目,唤起听众的好奇心,进而引导听众了解神农架的神秘独特之处。

选择疑问句作题目,通常用来给出两个或多个选项,让读者在文章中作出选择或判断。选择疑问句的答案通常简单明了,因此也常用于引导读者进行思考或权衡利弊。例如,Sharks:dangerous or endangered? 以选择性疑问形式引发读者对于鲨鱼的思考。文本解释了人们对于鲨鱼的误解的变化,得出了鲨鱼目前是 endangered 的结论,提升人们保护鲨鱼的意识。

一般疑问句作题目,通常用来提出一个普遍存在的问题或观点,激发读者的思考和讨论。这类问题的答案通常取决于个体的观点和经历。教材中的七篇以(省略的)一般疑问形式作题目的文章都属于这种情况,但表达观点的主体和文体略有不同：

Click for a friend? 和 Good book, bad movie? 都是论说文，引发读者对于题目表达的内容的思考和讨论，最终都给出了作者自己对于题目的态度。前者的结论是：网上可以交友，但必须谨慎。所以，如果文章继续写，就需要提出具体的做法。后者讨论了文学作品改编的电影常不尽如人意的原因，最后提出要在各种作品的类别内进行判断，交叉评判没有意义。

Emojis: a new language? 是说明文，但是题目激发了读者的兴趣，随后作者引领读者逐步了解 emoji 的发展，表明自己的观点。

剩下的四篇 Time for a change? Climbing Qomolangma: worth the risks? Plan B: life on Mars? Artificial intelligence: a real threat? 基本属于专栏文章或杂志文章，通常发起问题的人不展示自己的观点，给予读者以充分的自由，思考问题，表达观点。对问题的答案，往往出现对立的现象，孰优孰劣，由读者自行评判。

总之，英语文章题目中的多种疑问句类型，各自承载着不同的含义和用法。作者依据文章的主题、内容和目的精心选择疑问句类型，以吸引读者并激发其深入思考。

六、运用修辞表达人物心情

英语中修辞手段有很多，包括语义上的修辞、结构上的修辞以及音韵上的修辞等。但高中生不必太细究修辞，更多体现在语义理解即可，并能尝试使用比喻、拟人、夸张、对比、排比等手段表达情感。下面将从教材中选取部分例句进行介绍。

（一）比喻

比喻是语言中极富表现力的修辞方式，主要包括明喻、暗喻和提喻等形式。通过具体形象描绘抽象概念或情感，以传达情感、情绪和思想，引发读者在视觉和感知上的联想，使文辞更加丰富多彩，加深读者的理解和感受。高中学生了解一些常见的比喻方式即可，如明喻的表达方式主要用 like/as, as if/as though, as...as, A is to B what C is to D 等。比喻的修辞手段，在教材中随处可见。

Just as I thought I could deal with all Chinese food, I came across stinky tofu, a horrible grey thing that looked and smelt like a burnt sports shoe.

句中使用了比喻修辞手段,将臭豆腐比作烧焦的运动鞋,强调了其外观和气味之恶劣。通过生动的比喻让读者更直观地理解作者的不快与反感情绪。

Sure enough, going down the stairs and onto the platform is like jumping into a volcano that's erupting.

句中的比喻 like jumping into a volcano that's erupting 表达了一种极为强烈的情感,一方面展示地铁站台里面的温度特别高,另外也体现了作者的焦虑和不适的感觉。

Living in the open air, we became **breakfast, lunch and dinner** for the mosquitoes.

通过将被蚊子叮咬的痛苦形象地比喻为蚊子每天的三餐,表达作者被蚊子困扰的程度和频率。将抽象的感受具体化,增强了表达的生动性和情感共鸣,使读者更容易理解和感同身受。

Although it was only a few days before we were rescued, it felt like months.

比喻的运用,体现了作者在等待被救援时的度日如年的心情。

(二)夸张

夸张是表达上的需要,故意言过其实,对客观的人、事物尽力作扩大或缩小的描述。深刻、生动地揭示事物的本质,增强语言的感染力,给人以深刻的印象。

I'm sure the passenger next to me and **I are melting and becoming one**! I had bacon and eggs for breakfast, and now I'm feeling a bit sick—I hope I can make it to Bank station...

通过夸张描述自己与身边的人融化后合二为一的场景,以及由于吃了早餐后感到有些恶心而表现出近乎无法承受的感觉,强调了作者内心的焦虑和不适,从而增强了句子的表现力和吸引力。

（三）讽刺

讽刺常用较为温和、委婉的词语来论述、评价事物或人物，或采用转弯抹角、旁敲侧击、含沙射影的方式去暗示某人，以免引起讽刺对象的心理不适。适当地使用讽刺手法可以获得生动活泼、幽默风趣以及强调的语言效果。

教材中节选的《小王子》片段中，两处运用了讽刺的手法：

In the course of this life, I have had a great many encounters with a great many **people who have been concerned with matters of consequence**.

许多人过分追求表面事务的重要性，忽略了真正的价值，定语从句讽刺成年世界常被物质利益和功利心左右，忽视内在纯真与真诚。

I would bring myself down to his level. I would talk to him about bridge, and golf, and politics, and neckties. And the grown-ups would be greatly pleased to have met **such a sensible man**.

本句揭示了主人公为迎合成人世界放弃真我，迎合其品位与话题，讽刺了成人对表面功利的热衷与对真诚精神交流的漠视。

（四）排比

排比通过结构相似、语义重复且语气一致的词语、短语或句子，形成整齐、明快、简练且语义突出的整体，旨在强烈表达情感，凸显关键内容，增强语言力量。

高中教材中有大量的排比的例子，例如，Three days to see 中的最后一段："**Use** your eyes **as if** tomorrow you would be stricken blind...**Hear** the music of voices, …, **as if** you would be stricken deaf tomorrow. **Touch** each object...**as if** tomorrow your tactile sense would fail. **Smell** the perfume of flowers, **taste** with relish each morsel, **as if** tomorrow you could..."

作者用"感官动词+as if"的形式进行了多重排比，通过强调要像明天就会失去某种感官一样去珍惜和充分利用它们，表达了对生命中每一个细微之处的重视和感恩。

在《葛底斯堡演说》的最后一段，林肯运用了多重排比，包括两个 It is for us to... 句型，四个 that 引导的同位语从句，加上最后一句的三个作定语的介词短语排比，表达了对死去士兵的悼念、保卫国家完整的决心和希望，很大程度上坚定了人们的信心，推动了内战的走向。

It is for us, the living, ...**It is rather for us** to be here dedicated to the great task remaining before us—**that** from these honored dead ...—**that** we here highly resolve that...; **that** this nation shall...; **and that** this government **of the people**, **by the people**, **for the people**, shall not perish from the earth.

教材中包含了许多修辞，老师们在讲解语篇时，可以根据需要选择讲解的内容。

七、其他可以表达情感的形式

（一）祈使句

祈使句常用于表示命令、请求、建议、劝告等意图。通常情况下，祈使句的语气带有命令或者建议的意味，表现出权威性和明确性。例如：

Stop daydreaming! Playing in a band is not a job.

（二）内心独白

人物的内心独白常常被用来表达人物的情感、想法、挣扎和矛盾等内在世界。莎士比亚的戏剧 Hamlet 中的 To be or not to be 就是最好的例证。通过人物的内心独白，读者可以更深入地了解人物的性格特点、心理活动以及故事情节的发展，从而增强作品的情感表达和阅读体验。

"What?!" I tried to turn on my brain but the engine just wouldn't start. "I should say my name, of course. But what else? What could I say to make a good first impression? Something about my insect collection, perhaps."

这段独白描绘了主人公内心的紧张与焦虑，他努力激活思维却觉困难重重，并在构思自我介绍时犹豫不决，竭力营造最佳初印象，尽显不安与压力。

Ryan asked himself, "Why do some African children have to walk...? And why is the water so dirty that it makes them sick?" ... "Life is easy for me, but hard for those people. Why don't I help?"

Ryan对非洲孩子长途取水及水质污染致病的困境深感不解与忧虑，对比自身生活，萌生助人之心，彰显其善良、感恩与乐于助人的品质。

除了以上介绍的几种表达心情的方式，还可以通过氛围的渲染、人物的对话等很多其他方式表达。我们要做有心人，充分挖掘和利用教材语篇和其他学习资源，为语言表达积累各种地道语言素材。

八、片段及语篇解读

（一）片段解读

作者在体现人物心情时，通常会运用多种手段从多角度进行描写，以期达到最佳效果。例如，Book 1 Unit 1 My first day in Senior High 第一段中，过去完成时加上 pictured over and over again，强调上学之前就已经在反复想象、描绘高中的样子，woke up early, rushed out of 和 get to know 以动作链的形式展现作者的迫切心情；另外，the big day, finally，冒号和感叹号以及 in my eagerness 也无一不在体现着作者的重视和期待。仅用两句话，作者就把自己迫不及待地开启高中生活的心情描绘得淋漓尽致！

Cunningham **would** go out...each and every day, regardless of the weather. He **would** even stay outside in a storm, ...He **hardly** ever took a day off...This **devotion and hard work** is what we see reflected within his photos. This is what makes them so **special**.

这个语段中连续用了两个 would 述说 Cunningham 的工作习惯，each and every day, regardless of the weather, even, hardly, not once 都说明 Cunningham 对工作的热爱和投入。加上 devotion, hard work 和 special，作者表达了对 Cunningham 的钦佩。

And my magic medicine does indeed seem to do the trick...Although she is clearly **still in some pain**, her **scared and anxious look** has been **replaced**—first by **a small smile**, and then by **loud laughter** as I "**magically**" **produce** her sock...Seeing their daughter so **much happier** has in turn made Lara's parents **more relaxed**.

段落第一句话以 does indeed seem to do the trick 的动词强调形式，展示了作者作为小丑医生能够缓解就医孩子的痛苦的骄傲心情。Still insome pain, scared and anxious look, a small smile, loud laughter, much happier 这一系列的心情和表情的变化，以及孩子父母 more relaxed 的心情都进一步证明作者工作的价值，也隐含着作者自身的喜悦心情。

(二) 语篇解读

很多记叙文语篇中有非常值得学习的情感表达方式。2010 年全国高考题 E 篇阅读，在情感表达方面给我们提供了范本。

"There were smiling children all the way. Clearly they knew at what time the train passed their homes and they made it their business to stand along the railway, wave to complete strangers and cheer them up as they rushed towards Penang. Often whole families stood outside their homes and waved and smiled as if those on the trains were their favorite relatives. This is the simple village people of Malaysia. I was moved.

I had always traveled to Malaysia by plane or car, so this was the first time I was on a train. I did not particularly relish the long train journey and had brought along a dozen magazines to read and reread. I looked about the train. There was not one familiar face. I sighed and sat down to read my Economics.

It was not long before the train was across the Causeway and in Malaysia. Johore Baru was just another city like Singapore, so I was tired of looking at the crowds of people as they hurried past. As we went beyond the city, I watched the straight rows of rubber trees and miles and miles of green. Then the first village came into sight. Immediately I came alive; I decided to wave back.

From then on my journey became interesting. I threw my magazines into the waste basket and decided to join in Malaysian life.

Then everything came alive. The mountains seemed to speak to me. Even the trees were smiling. I stared at everything as if I was looking at it for the first time.

The day passed fast and I even forgot to have my lunch until I felt hungry. I looked at my watch and was surprised that it was 3:00 pm. Soon the train pulled up at Butterworth. I looked at the people all around me. They all looked beautiful. When my uncle arrived with a smile, I threw my arms around him to give him a warm hug. I had never done this before. He seemed surprised and then his weather-beaten face warmed up with a huge smile. We walked arm in arm to his car.

I looked forward to the return journey."

本文开篇运用倒叙手法,选取旅行中作者情感变化的关键内容作为引子,吸引读者兴趣。在调整游记类记叙文的叙述顺序时,需按照时间线重新排列,确保与旅行过程相符。此外,文章采用了双线结构,既包含地点和环境的变化,又隐含了人物情感的起伏,丰富了情节,深化了情感表达。如图 3-3 所示。

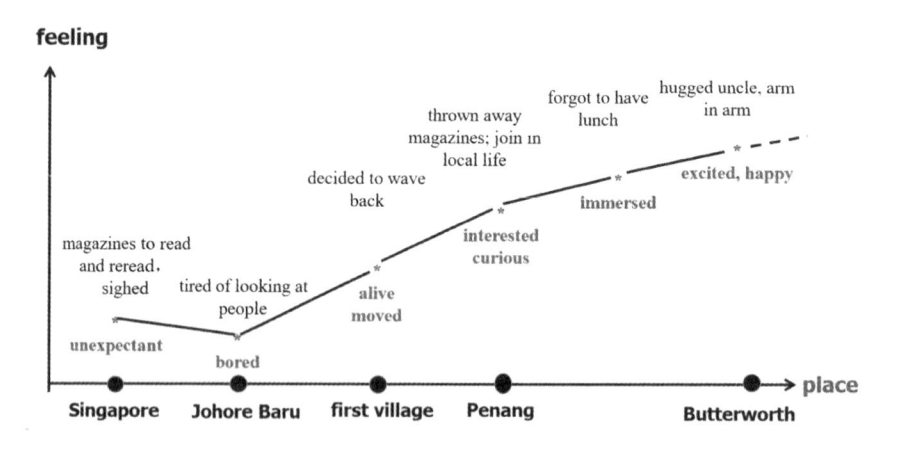

图 3-3 情感经历暗线

在本文中,情感经历作为暗线贯穿全文,作者借助形容词、副词、动词、名词以及环境描写等多种手法,巧妙呈现心境的微妙变化。图示中的曲线起伏反映了作者心境的波动,融合了具象时空与抽象情绪。

从 Singapore 离开之时,作者对旅行没有多大期待, not particularly relish。带着一打杂志,且认为需要在 to read and reread 中来度过旅途!

周边没有熟悉的人，所以作者只能 sighed，开始读杂志。

Johore Baru 跟新加坡相似，作者厌倦了看城市人群。到达第一个村庄，看到笔直的树和满眼的绿，作者 immediately came alive。特别是看到无论大人还是孩子跟陌生人挥手 to cheer them up，作者 was moved。

后面的旅途中，作者的心情开始高涨。第四段首先以 interesting 界定了旅途；随后运用了动作描写 "threw my magazines into the waste basket, decided to join in Malaysian life"；环境描写运用了拟人的手法 "mountains seemed to speak, trees were smiling"。作者第一次以极大的兴致看着周围的一切。

美好的时光总是过得飞快！第五段开头的 fast 和 forgot to have my lunch 都能看出作者对旅途的专注和投入。火车到站时，再看周围的人，all looked beautiful。人还是那些人，不同的是作者的心境发生了变化。作者的美好心情还体现在对叔叔的态度上，动作链 "threw my arms around him to give him a warm hug, walked arm in arm" 呈现的亲密举动是之前从未有过的，且带来了叔叔的变化，a smile, warmed up, a huge smile，非常具有感染力。

最后的结论是 looked forward to 回程。

整个语篇传达了作者通过火车旅行重新发现生活中温暖和美好的感悟，以及美好心情所带来的感染力，其中表达心情的各种方式值得在实践中学习和运用。

第四节　高考记叙文的考查形式及重点

记叙文是高考中的常见语篇形式，它主要围绕人与自我、人与社会、人与自然三大主题展开。高考中，记叙文常以完形填空和续写的方式出现。下面将深入剖析这两种形式的记叙文及其考查方式，并运用拉波夫叙事原理和语篇分析框架指导学生分析高考记叙文，旨在提供解题的思路和技巧。

一、完形填空的考查重点及解题技巧

完形填空源自格式塔心理学,即完形心理学,它研究大脑如何以整体方式感知事物。此理论提出,由于个人经验的影响,人们在无意识中会用已知图式去填补图像或信息中的空白。类似地,面对不完整的语言现象,如句子、段落或篇章的缺失,人们会根据已有信息、整体语言现象的把握及个人经验来补全内容。大脑中的已知图式越丰富,补全过程就越简单;反之,如果心理表征不够完善,补全就会变得困难。

完形填空实际上是一种深入的阅读理解活动,不仅要求考生梳理文本信息、准确把握主旨,还需要理顺文本内部的逻辑结构,并通过已知的信息去推断未知的内容,从而深入体会作者的写作意图。这类题材具有多样化的特点,涵盖了丰富的内容和地道的语言,故事情节完整且发展脉络逻辑性强。

完形填空考查阅读技能时,既测试考生对句子层面的低阶处理能力,也突出了对语篇层面的高阶处理能力。考生需结合句子的语法信息和语篇信息作答。全国卷完形填空以名词和动词为主要考查点,辅以形容词和副词。近年来,更多强调段落和语篇层面的考查,命题人优先考查考生对语篇整体的感知能力,因此即便有空白也不会影响对整篇的理解。

"完形填空结合文义重点考查对词语用法的掌握,降低了对单词本身词义的考查要求,将考查的重点放在理解全文、通篇考虑、掌握大意、注重关联方面。文中一般没有生僻词,语言简单,长句不多;对熟词生义、一词多义进行适度考查;从词义辨析的角度,大部分题目都可以利用较小的语境和词汇的辨析来解决;从词汇难度来看,初中所学词汇占据大半,即便是高中阶段所学的词汇,也基本在必修范围之内。聚焦完形填空核心考点——逻辑推理,对综合判断和分析概况等进行考查。"(中国高考报告学术委员会,2021:90)

在完形填空中,重要的是要理解意义。"完形的'形'特别重要,这个'形'其实就是意义,更准确地说是一个完整的意义。因此,理解意义是完形填空的前提。"(陈新忠,2020)在高考英语全国卷中,完形填空考查的是对词汇在特定语境下的准确理解和运用,以及对整体篇章结构的把握。考生需结合上下文,深入理解词汇意义,避免在相似选项间徘徊。为提升这一能力,学生应注重词汇的英语释义和例句学习,这不仅能避免内容重复,还能提高语言水平和应试能力。

另外,完形填空语篇来源广泛,其文化语境对学生的意义理解,特别是语篇中的人物情感变化的理解产生影响。各国因其独特的语言、文化、历史和生活常识,形成了不同的思维和行为习惯。考生若掌握更多文化语境知识,将有助于他们更准确地理解和处理完形填空。

二、完形填空教学建议

在完形填空教学中,教师可以从以下几个方面来改善教学,提升学生的综合语用能力。

(1)学生需掌握辨识不同语篇类型及其组织形式的能力。记叙文以其清晰的行文脉络和明确的故事发展情节为特点,通常符合拉波夫叙事模式。在阅读教学中,教师可指导学生应用拉波夫叙事原理,分析语篇各部分,深化对文意的理解,并明晰故事线索与情感脉络。此方法有助于揭示语篇内部的逻辑关联,协助学生在文本中寻找连接点,从而高效获取信息。

(2)在阅读中,重视衔接与连贯是关键。捕捉语义关系,挖掘文字深层含义,有助于把握主题和提高阅读效率。完形阅读时,结合句子结构与整体语境,结合个人知识和作者意图,主动思考并适时调整判断,以完善理解。

(3)在日常教学中,单元词汇的整体教学至关重要。特别是在完形填空解题时,学生需整体把握语篇大意,但从意义连贯角度思考会受到生词过多的阻碍。若生词过多,学生难以通过构词法、语法知识或上下文推断其含义,导致阅读速度下降,注意力过度集中在片段信息上,从而失去对整体文意的把握。很多时候,学生的理解困惑正是源于词汇量的不足。

因此,在语篇教学中,词汇学习应紧密融入具体主题,让学生在语境中理解词汇。通过引导学生运用构词法技巧,结合丰富的上下文,深入理解词汇的意义。同时,鼓励学生积极利用词典等辅助工具,挖掘词汇的多样化用法。通过设计词义猜测和逻辑推理练习,学生能够准确把握词语在特定语境中的功能、深层含义及使用者的情感态度。

为了加强学生对词块的敏感度,教师可以在主题语境下引导学生反复运用词汇,并利用思维导图系统整理词汇。基于词性、常见搭配及主题内容,构建多元化的词汇语义网络。特别关注词块的呈现,如动词、介词、名词、形容词和副词短语等常见搭配和表达方式,使学生在不断的语言实践中积累知识,提升语感,最终实现知识的内化和灵活运用。

做好完形填空题的关键在于准确理解语篇、掌握充足的语言知识、文化背景知识、出色的分析、推理与判断能力、有效地预测语境和适当的语场图式,还需要拥有感知和把握作者言辞中所蕴含的语气和情感。最关键的是,注意整体理解语篇,不要过度拘泥于局部细节,严格遵循"整体优化、局部正确"的答题原则,这样能够更好地完成完形填空题。

在解答完形填空题时,成功的关键在于对语篇的深入理解和全面把握。这要求考生不仅要有扎实的语言知识和文化背景,还需具备敏锐的分析、推理和判断能力,以及预测语境和语场图式的能力。尤为重要的是,考生需要能够敏锐地感知并准确把握作者在言辞中所传达的语气和情感。同时,应避免过度关注局部细节,而应当坚持"全局优先、细节精准"的答题策略,从而更全面地完成完形填空题目。

三、高考完形填空语篇分析

高考中的完形填空多数是记叙文。根据前面提到的拉波夫叙事原理和语篇分析的宏观和微观结构,以 2023 全国新高考Ⅰ卷的完形填空为例,进行语篇分析。

文章首段以时间开头,介绍 Melanie Bailey 在越野跑中帮助对手完成比赛,因而耽误自己的比赛成绩。这是典型的记叙文特征,语篇体裁是记叙文。该记叙文的各个部分非常清晰地契合拉波夫叙事分析理论的结构:

点题。对整个事件作简要介绍。

指向。说明时间、地点、人物以及事情发生时的情境。

进展。说明事件发生的过程。

评议。对事件的过程进行评价,具体体现在 "She would have struggled with extreme pain to make it to that aid checkpoint without Bailey's help."

回应。主人公 Bailey 对突如其来的报道作出的反应。跟 Book 1 Unit 3 中的语篇 Just a brother 的主人公 Alistair 反应相似,都觉得自己只是做了该做的事情。

第六段,结局。虽然两个之前陌生的选手,都没有赢得比赛,但彼此成为朋友,文章的主题意义 the display of human kindness won the day 得以呈现。

故事进展的过程中,特别是后三段,能看到人物的情感变化。

与七选五题型不同,完形填空和语法填空侧重于语篇的微观分析,特别是上下文语境。在分析时,应着重关注语法衔接、词汇衔接和连接词衔接三个要点。

(一)语法衔接

该篇文章,语法衔接方面,主要涉及人称代词和不定代词的照应、定冠词 the 的回指照应、指示代词和地点副词的替代。

贯穿语篇始终的是 Bailey 和 Lenoue 及她们的人称照应 she, her。

第一段的 the course 和第二段中的 the way 中 the 都是照应,两个短语都回指第一段中的 a cross-country race。最后一段填空 display 前有 the 回指 Bailey 在比赛中展示出来的人性善的一面。

第二段中的地点副词 where 和第三段开头的指示代词 there 都照应下面的 checkpoint。

最后一段中的 the two young women 与段内的人称代词 they 和不定代词 neither 形成照应。

(二)词汇衔接

该语篇的词汇衔接,主要考查了词汇复现,包括同(义)词复现、上下义词复现,以及语义场内的词汇链,语篇中的句子通过这种复现关系达到相互衔接。

1. 同(义)词复现

Runner: Para. 1...hundreds of runners...; Para. 2...help her fellow runner...

Race: Para. 1...in a cross-country race in...the course earlier...; Para. 5 Neither won the race...

Finish: Para. 1...should have finished the course...across the finish line...; Para. 2...carried her all the way to the finish line.

Help: Para. 2...stopped to help her...if she could walk forward with aid; Para. 3...without Bailey's help

2. 上下义词复现

Runners and competitor: Para.1 hundreds of runners, ...a competitor...

3. 主题信息词汇链

这篇文章的主题语义场中的关键词,除了上文的 runner, race, help, 还有跟受伤需要帮助的一系列词, 如:

Pain: Para.2...crying in pain...get medical attention.
Para.3...assessed...a hospital...serious injuries..., struggled with extreme pain.

学生以这些主题信息词为语义场的核心,将其他的信息和段落进行梳理、重组和整合,形成与相关话题相连的词汇知识和语法结构的语篇主题网络。

完形填空的设空通常位于故事情节主线,多与语义场核心词汇相关,包括主题词、情节词、逻辑词和情感词。在记叙文教学中,应重视实词在语境中的实际运用。

(三)连接词衔接

语言学家韩礼德和哈桑把逻辑连接词分为四类:分别是增补、转折、因果和时间。本篇中运用的连接词衔接也很多,如第一段中的 because 表因果;第二段中的 as 表示增补, when 和 then 表示时间, and 和 then 表示增补;第三段中的 once 和 later 都表示时间;第五段中的 although 和 but 表示转折, before 和 since 表示时间。

分析文本时,宏观上把握整体架构,微观上洞察词语深层联系。注意词汇重现形式与构建文章意义的词汇链,利用显性衔接手段理解文本逻辑与连贯性,形成系统解析方式,应对完形填空题型。

四、高考真题中的记叙文续写

根据图式理论,写作过程是一种构建语篇图式的活动,涉及图式或背景知识与输入的语言和语篇信息之间的相互作用和匹配。整个过程中需要用到三种图式:形式图式、内容图式和语言图式。

课程标准强调撰写短文须语义连贯、语句通顺、结构完整。在高考读后续写中,考生须根据文本理解,完成故事接续,展现英语语言知识与语用能力,包括语言的恰当运用、句子间的逻辑严密、内容结构的合理创新。高考读后续写选材广泛,贴近学生生活,情节曲折、逻辑性强,强调立德树人,充满正能量,与考生生活认知水平紧密相关。

在真实的问题情境中,考生需准确运用英语词汇和语法,展现阅读理解、分析能力和创作能力。读后续写测试学生的理解思维和书面表达能力,更凸显基础性、综合性和应用性的考核标准,倡导社会主义核心价值观,同时评估考生的三观和心理健康。考生须在限定时间内完成一篇逻辑清晰、情节完整、结构合理且富有正能量的短文。

在《高考试题分析(英语)》中,教育部教育考试院对读后续写的评价标准有明确说明。"评价读后续写的质量主要从内容、语言表达和篇章结构三个方面考查,具体为:

(1)创造内容的质量、续写的完整性以及与原文情境的融洽度。

(2)所使用词汇和语法结构的准确性、恰当性和多样性。

(3)上下文的衔接和全文的连贯性。"(中华人民共和国教育部教育考试院,2023:172)

也就是说,写作的内容要逻辑合理、故事完整,语言要保证正确、语用得体且与语篇给定部分风格一致,语篇要衔接连贯,符合记叙文语篇的语体风格。

要完成一篇质量上乘的续写,读懂、读透给定部分是关键。考生应该重点读懂、读透以下几个方面。

(1)读主题语境,把握故事主题,将所给文章段落与拉波夫叙事的几个环节对应,确定故事的走向。

(2)读文章主题。主题立意积极向上,弘扬正能量。

(3)两条线:情节线+情感线,抓住冲突点;快速阅读时,教师应指导学生识别主要人物,分析角色关系,以加深故事理解;同时,注重情感处理,领悟故事深意。

（4）语言风格：阅卷过程中,语言风格不易界定,但须确保故事主线清晰合理。避免过多对话,以防情节冗长。可通过环境、动作及心理描写,展现人物性格与情感变化。

在记叙文创作中,第一步是构思情节,确保故事发展。为塑造人物,作者常运用语言、行为和心理描写。创作意图隐于情节、环境和动作中,引导读者自然领悟。根据拉波夫叙事原则,重点从以下几个方面进行考虑。

（1）Para.1 指向矛盾和解决方法,也就是故事的发展；Para.2 指向解决方法的结果,也就是叙事的结局。

（2）故事的人物、时间及故事发生的情境在指向部分已经确定。在续写中,除非已有人物无法解决难题需外部协助,否则不引入新人物,并保持故事时空紧凑。

（3）思考所给的两个首句,关注衔接：宏观上,段落间衔接构成语篇逻辑；微观上,段落首句与内容衔接反映内部逻辑,这与英语句子成分的位置和排列,特别是句末重点信息紧密相关。

（4）创造性的故事情节,首先要保证情节的合情合理,再考虑写得新颖。

（5）叙事结构未必有回应（coda）环节,续写结尾无需强求升华,尤其当升华点难以把握时,留白给予读者想象空间更为妥当。否则,升华不合理,就会被判定没有读懂原文,成为扣分点。

在正式写作过程中,首先要考虑人物活动的时间顺序、人物的主次和典型特征、事件发生顺序和空间变化,同时需要结合具体情况具体分析,以确保内容有条理、连贯。

（1）先列提纲。关注语言的衔接手段：词汇衔接、语法衔接和连接词等。

（2）记叙描写交替,表达要丰富。重点关注人物和环境描写,心理描写,语言(不要太多),动作描写(动作链)等。以时间顺序为主,兼顾情感发展线,铺排故事。

语言要多样,特别要关注所给部分的语言特点和运用。根据语言表达需要选用并列结构、复合句、非谓语动词、with 复合结构、倒装、无灵主语、虚拟语气等,特别是上文中出现过的语言表达形式,可以适当在接续中复现,并适当运用修辞手段。个人认为逻辑自洽和呈现符合语体要求的内容比所谓的高级句型或词汇更重要,不要刻意堆积所谓的高级句型和表达,否则给人的印象是刻板生硬,不自然,不地道,这样的作文难得高分。

(3)内容连贯和呼应。情节要符合原文逻辑,想象合理,围绕主题,三观要正。

(4)书写要认真工整,标点要准确达意。

下面分别以 2023 年和 2022 年高考续写语篇为例,分析语篇的走向及续写的切入点。

例 1:2023 年全国新课标 I & II 卷续写。

首先,根据拉波夫叙事原理,对已给部分的语篇进行分析:

段落 1 点题:作者在初中时被社会科学老师邀请参加写作比赛,但他拒绝了,理由是自己不喜欢写作。

段落 2 指向:作者回忆社会学教师的参赛邀请,描述了教师的赞赏与鼓励,这成为他尝试写作的契机。

段落 3 到 5 进展:作者选 Paul Revere,一匹马为题,写作过程中克服困难,不断修改,注重写作的乐趣而非成绩。

段落 4 评价:老师对作者的作文反应积极,鼓励其重写,显示文章趣味横生。作者享受写作,不再执着于竞赛胜负。

段落 6 结局 + 回应:作者因在比赛中获奖而深感欣喜和骄傲,这一成就是对他持续努力、不懈追求和得益于老师指导的回报,赋予了他新的信心和成就感。

段落 7 回应颁奖后,向老师表达感激之情;同时,老师也会对作者的成就感到骄傲,回应第二段中老师对作者的鼓励。

第二步,回看所给的两个段首句。

Para 1: A few weeks later, when I almost forgot the contest, there came the news.

Para 2: I went to my teacher's office after the award presentation.

无论从衔接角度还是从连贯角度看,句子内各成分的排列和句子之间的排列都是受到制约的,符合某种信息推进模式。"一般说来,在语言结构的安排上,要遵循从已知到未知;从确定到不确定的原则。同时,还要考虑句末中心和句末重心原则。"(黄国文,1988:64)

第一段给的信息中,明显看出,contest 是已知确定信息,news 是未知的不确定信息,从衔接和连贯的角度。紧接其后的句子一定是从

news 开始铺展。

第二段给的信息,after the award presentation 成为引发新信息的触发点。本段落的写作也必定是借由 the award presentation,作者去老师办公室感谢老师,老师作出正向回应。作者从这次经历中也看到自己的潜能和成长。整个文章由此完整展现了作者在老师的鼓励和帮助下,达到了个人成长的过程。

下面的参考范文,很好地展示了文章的结局和回应。

A few weeks later, when I almost forgot the contest, there came the news. My heart raced as I read the announcement on the school bulletin board—my essay had won first place! I could hardly believe it. The joy and pride that filled my chest were indescribable. My hard work, persistence, and the support of my teacher had paid off. I felt a newfound sense of confidence and accomplishment, knowing that I had overcome the challenges of writing in my second language. I couldn't wait to share the news with my family and friends.

I went to my teacher's office after the award presentation. My eyes were brimming with tears of gratitude. As I entered, he looked up from his desk, his face beaming with pride. "I knew you could do it," he said warmly. I hugged him tightly, unable to express just how much his belief in me had meant. It was more than just winning a contest; it was about discovering my own potential and the power of perseverance. That day, I learned that with hard work, determination, and the support of those who believe in you, anything is possible. And from that moment on, I embraced writing as a newfound passion, forever grateful to the teacher who had seen something in me that I hadn't seen in myself.

这篇文章通过拉波夫叙事原理的分析,清晰地展示了第一人称的作者在写作比赛中所经历的点题、指向、进展、评议、结局和回应过程。这个故事鼓舞人心,传达了一个重要的信息:只要付出努力、坚持不懈并得到信任和支持,任何事情都有可能实现。

例2:2022年高考读后续写。

在学生习作中出现了很多不合逻辑的接续结局,比如说,David 最终在比赛中得到了第一名的好成绩。这明显就是没有读懂、读透指向部分所给的信息。原文各段落根据拉波夫叙事原理的分析如下:

第一段：点题。通过描述大型越野跑活动的当天情景，引起读者的注意并为故事展开做好铺垫。

第二段：指向。主人公发现 David 独自站在一边的场景，并询问原因。这引起了读者的好奇心，David 为什么决定不参加比赛？

第三段到第五段：进展。揭示 David 弃赛的原因是害怕被嘲笑；教练给了他是否参加比赛的选择。这些情节推动着故事向前发展，展现了 David 的困境和面对的挑战。

第六段：评议。David 的特殊情况和普通孩子身份凸显，但同学们坦然接纳他加入越野队。这一态度彰显了他的积极参与和坚定毅力，凸显了他的与众不同。

续写第一段，仍然是故事的进展。David 回避我的目光，可知他非常沮丧，但是老师需要根据具体的行为来判断他的心情，而不是直接描写 David 自我是如何难受的。最终在"我"的劝说下，David 决定参加比赛。

续写的第二段，是故事的结局和回应。比赛中，David 虽落后，但以独特方式不懈追求，终于抵达终点，满心欢喜。这是对整个故事进行回应，以及对 David 坚持参与比赛所付出努力的肯定和鼓励。

评议部分 "David had not missed a single practice, and although he always finished his run long after the other children, he did always finish." 很关键。将 David 写成冠军的考生，必定是忽略了该句话。作者在第六段中对 David 的赞赏也早有暗示 "As a special education teacher at the school, I was familiar with the challenges David faced and was proud of his strong determination." "我"所骄傲的是 David 坚持不懈的精神，而 David 本身所看重的也是参与的过程。从 "...always finished his run long after the other children" 这一点就已经向读者传达了一个信息：David 并非能够赢得比赛的人。然而，是否能够获胜从来都不是他们所关注的焦点。

对于续写而言，逻辑自洽和情节的合理是首要的。通过拉波夫叙事原理细致分析语篇结构，可以确保考生能够准确地把握故事的方向。至于语言的质量、标点的运用以及书写的美观等，需要通过阅读和写作实践不断打磨。

第四章　说明文文体

说明文以阐释为宗旨,揭示事物的性质、特征、结构、功能、结果及发展,帮助读者深入理解事物本质,旨在传播知识,是高中英语阅读教学和各类考试中常见的文体之一。

第一节　说明文语篇类型及结构

本节主要从说明文的类型、语篇结构和说明方法等进行说明。

一、说明文的定义及类型

"说明文是以'说明'为主要表达方式,以传授知识为根本任务,介绍事物,阐明事理,说明事物运动、变化、发展规律的语篇类型"(梅德明、王蔷,2018)。

说明文是深入解析、传递信息的文体,为核心主题提供全面阐释。从操作流程到工作机制,从特性对比到成因分析,它详尽描绘事物的各个方面。它旨在向读者传达事物的形态、特性、成果及功能,应用场景广泛,包括解释客观事物、指导操作、解读抽象概念等。掌握说明文的关键在于理解事物的核心特征与本质。

说明文,尤其是科技类,以其高度的科学性和结构的条理性见长。它运用准确严密的语言,客观平实地描述事物,通过详尽的细节展示事物的特征。在结构上,说明文常运用总分、递进等手法,按照时间、空间或从现象到本质的顺序进行阐述。其显著特点在于知识性和客观性,避免个人感情倾向的介入。说明文旨在客观阐述事实,词汇选择力求准确、简洁,而非表达主观意见。

说明文由于呈现方式特别,因此题材相对固定。说明文语篇类型,大致可以分为事物型说明文和事理型说明文。事物型说明文是对客观事物作出的全面说明,包括形态、构造、性质、类别、功能等;事理型说明文是对抽象事理的阐释,包括理解概念、特点、来源、演变、异同等。

教材中的说明文语篇数量不是特别多,阅读设题主要涉及段落主题句(topic sentence)、文章结构(structure)、情感变化(emotion)、写作目的(purpose)和语篇出处(source)等。

不同类型的说明文,结构各异,学生须具备说明文语篇的结构意识,有效把握文章脉络,厘清段落层次关系,深层理解作者写作意图。说明文的语篇组织结构主要可以分为以下几种:描述模式、因果模式、问题解决模式、序列模式、比较对比模式等(Masoumeh Akhondi, Faramarz Aziz Malayeri, Arshad Abd Samad:2011)。常见的语篇模式主要是描述模式(也就是我们常说的一般—特殊模式)、问题解决模式和比较对比模式。

这些类别并非独立存在,无论按照什么标准分类,它们都存在着交叉。一篇说明文可能同时具备多种特点,不同部分的组织结构也各不相同,因此在进行综合评判时需考虑具体的文本内容和写作目的。

二、各种组织结构的说明重点及语篇结构

无论采用何种组织结构,说明文的各个段落都必定围绕着说明对象展开。组织结构将根据说明目的呈现不同的方式。通过说明文语篇的阅读,学生能深入体会和掌握说明文的文体特点、说明文的写作方法和行文框架。

描述型说明文主要通过描绘事物的外观、性质、特征或现象的方式来呈现信息。让读者对所描述的内容有清晰、生动的认识,通常运用详细的描写和具体的细节来使读者更好地理解作者想要传达的信息。描述型说明文通常以客观、中立的角度描述事物,让读者获得关于某个主题的直观印象。如图4-1所示。

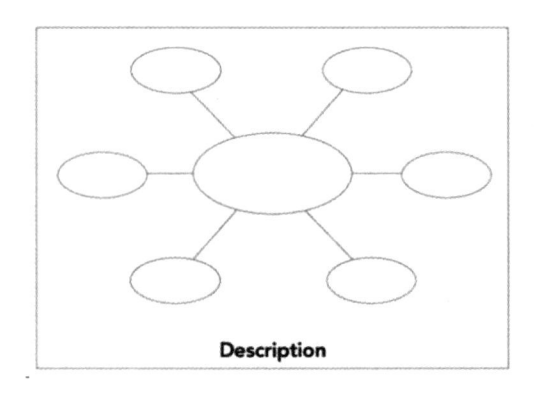

图 4-1　描述性说明文的组织结构

教材语篇中的 Longji Rice Terraces 就属于这种类型的语篇。首先以龙脊梯田的四季美景引入话题，分别从梯田的建造历史、原因、工作原理以及梯田对于当地人的重要性几个方面进行说明。

因果型说明文专注于揭示事物间的因果关系，以解释特定现象或问题。它通过阐述事件起因和结果的逻辑联系，帮助读者理解事物发展的必然性和推导过程。这种文体通常基于客观事实、数据和逻辑推理，构建出事物发展过程中的因果链条，使读者能够深入理解事件的成因及其潜在影响。在撰写过程中，因果型说明文强调论据的充分性和合理性，避免片面或主观臆测，以确保信息的准确性和可靠性。如图 4-2 所示。

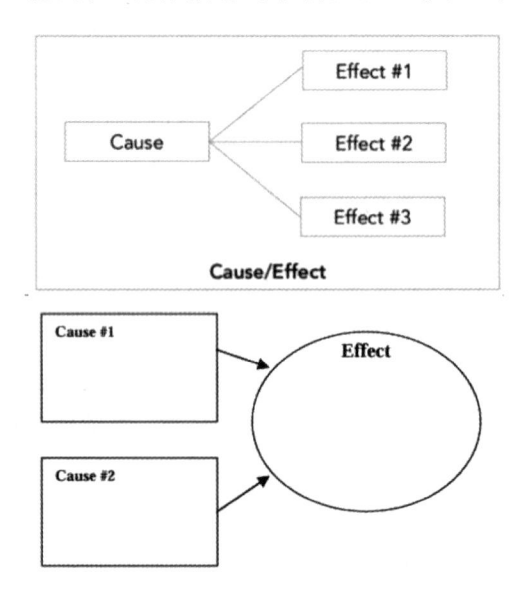

图 4-2　因果型说明文的组织结构

教材语篇 The Monarch's journey 中关于帝王蝶如何找到目的地和帝王蝶数量大幅下降的原因都是明显的因果关系。

问题解决型说明文向读者介绍某一问题或疑惑，并提供清晰、详细的解释和解决方案。这类说明文通常会从问题的背景与原因入手，逐步引导读者理解问题的本质，并通过逻辑性的论述和举例分析等方式，阐述解决问题的方法和步骤。最终目的是帮助读者全面地理解问题，并使其能够有效地应用所提供的解决方案解决类似问题。该类说明文逻辑清晰、表达准确，使读者通过阅读文本能够获得实际帮助与启发的效果。其组织结构如图 4-3 所示。

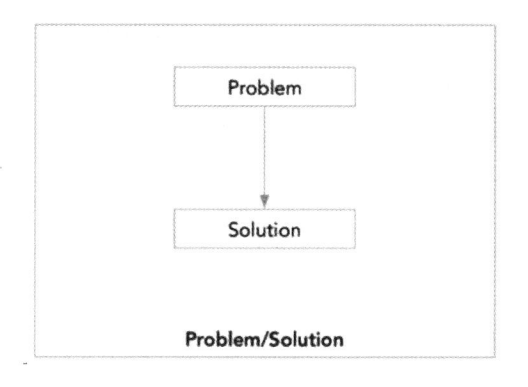

图 4-3　问题解决型说明文的组织结构

The best job in the world 教材语篇首先通过招聘大堡礁守护员的广告吸引读者，接着介绍大堡礁的生物多样性及其面临的污染和气候变化威胁。文章旨在提升保护海洋的意识，最终达到保护大堡礁、解决其问题的目的。

序列型说明文按照事物发展或事件发生的顺序组织和呈现内容，通过时间、空间或逻辑次序来清晰展示事物之间的关联和发展过程。其写作目的是让读者理解事物发展的顺序和逻辑，从而全面把握某过程或现象的内在关系。文章通常采用有条理的叙述方式，着重描述起因、经过和结果，帮助读者系统性地掌握主题内容。其组织结构如图 4-4 所示。

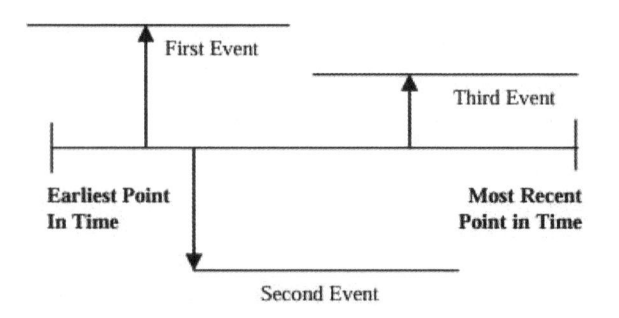

图 4-4　序列型说明文的组织结构

教材语篇 The Mysteries of the Maya 虽然从不同角度介绍曾经的玛雅文明，但基本上是按照时间线铺排开整个语篇内容。从玛雅人衰落的原因分析，现在的我们也可以得到启示：爱护自然，思考我们的过去、现在和未来。逻辑顺序型说明的组织结构如图 4-5 所示。

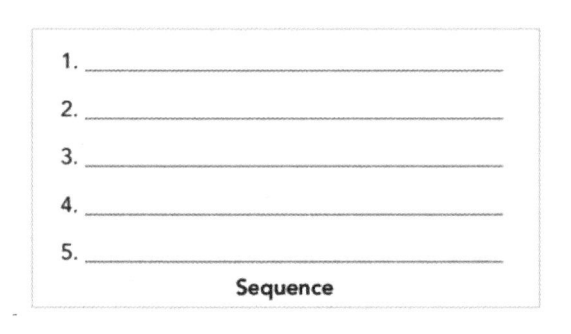

图 4-5　逻辑顺序型说明文的组织结构

教材语篇 The secret language of plants 中植物间交流的第一个途径 using chemicals 就是按照事件发生的逻辑顺序展开说明。

比较对比型说明文旨在揭示两个或多个事物、概念、现象之间的异同。通过客观全面的比较手法，呈现它们各自的特点和特征。作者会列举它们的共同点、差异点，并可能包括优缺点、适用场景等方面的比较，以助于读者深入理解这些对象之间的联系和区别。写作目的在于帮助读者辨析事物特性，促使他们在比较中获得新见解，以便更深入地理解对象，并在实际应用中作出明智选择。比较对比型说明文的组织结构如图 4-6 所示。

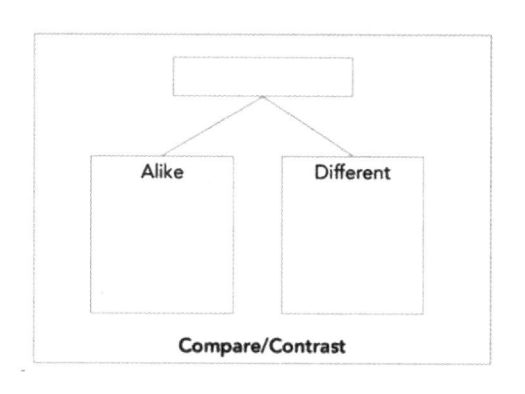

图 4-6　比较对比型说明文的组织结构

教材语篇中的 Sharks: dangerous or endangered? 对比了人们对于鲨鱼的态度变化,由原先长时间认为的 dangerous,导致人们大量捕猎鲨鱼,最终造成它们 endangered 的状况。另外,Art and technology 也属于非常明显的对比类型的说明文。虽然语篇比较长,但教材中给出了表格形式的配套练习,明确了语篇的结构类型,降低了阅读难度。

以上是说明文的基本组织结构类型,但是说明类别不同,语篇结构也不尽相同。在第二章中介绍的五种语篇组织模式中,用于说明文的主要是其中的三种,即提问—回答模式、问题—解决模式和概括—具体模式。根据高考中常考的说明文语篇,又可以细化为研究报告类、科普类、现象类、问题—解决类等,其中后三个就包含了提问—回答模式和问题—解决模式。

研究报告类说明文首先提出结论,随后阐述研究过程,包括对象、方法及结果。权威人士对结果进行解析、评价,并提出应用建议与未来研究方向。整体遵循由概括至具体的逻辑,反映出英语文本结构中的"头重"特征。研究报告类说明文的组织结构如图 4-7 所示。

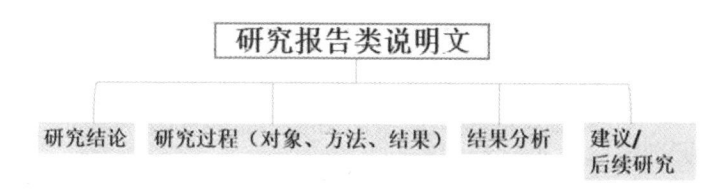

图 4-7　研究报告类说明文的组织结构

科普类说明文主要引入新事物(包括新产品或新做法),简述背景,阐明原理,强调优点并探讨改进与前景,旨在普及科学知识。其组织结构如图 4-8 所示。

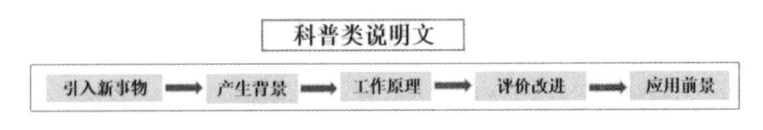

科普类说明文

引入新事物 ➡ 产生背景 ➡ 工作原理 ➡ 评价改进 ➡ 应用前景

图 4-8　科普类说明文的组织结构

现象类说明文首先描述现象，分析产生现象的原因，这种现象所产生的影响，不同领域中的人们的看法，最终提出解决或应对措施。其组织结构如图 4-9 所示。

现象类说明文

描述现象 ➡ 分析原因 ➡ 介绍影响 ➡ 观点看法 ➡ 应对措施

图 4-9　现象类说明文的组织结构

问题解决类说明文首先在情境中引入问题，阐述问题造成的后果，分析问题产生的原因，介绍采取的应对措施，以及对结构的评价。其组织结构如图 4-10 所示。

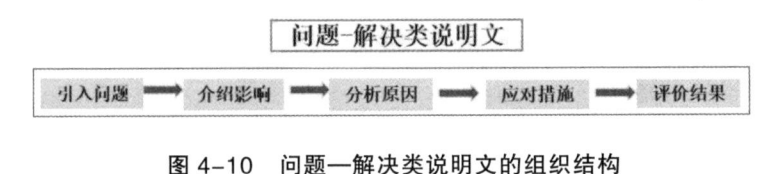

问题-解决类说明文

引入问题 ➡ 介绍影响 ➡ 分析原因 ➡ 应对措施 ➡ 评价结果

图 4-10　问题—解决类说明文的组织结构

针对不同的说明对象进行细化，便于学生在阅读中快速调动各种语篇图式，分析文章框架，进行深度阅读。

与语篇结构图形同等重要的还有各自的语篇标志词或短语。表 4-1 中分别列出了各种类型的说明文常见的语篇标志词或短语。

表 4-1　各个类型的说明文常见的语篇标志词或短语

类型	语篇标志词/短语
Description	for example, characteristics, for instance, namely, such as, be like, including, to illustrate, as a matter of fact, in fact
Sequence	first (ly), second (ly), third (ly), later, next, before, then, finally, after, when, since, now, previously, eventually, in addition, furthermore, moreover, in short

续表

类型	语篇标志词/短语
Compare/contrast	however, nevertheless, on the one hand...on the other hand, but, similarly, although, yet, while, also, in/by contrast, different, alike, the same as, either/or, in the same way, likewise, just like, just as, in comparison, whereas, yet, on the contrary, in comparison, unlike, whereas
Cause/effect	accordingly, if—then, reason why, as a result, consequently, as a consequence, therefore, because, since, so that, due to, hence, thus, for, lead to, contribute to
Problem/solution	problem is, dilemma is, because, so that, question/answer, if—then, puzzle is solved

语篇中的标志词与短语构成逻辑线索,有助于学生辨识文本结构。同时,图形化结构有助于学生理清观点层次和内在关系。通过标志词和短语,学生可以把握文本的组织脉络,并利用图形展示主要观点与支持细节间的联系。教师的核心任务是指导学生识别文本结构,并聚焦重要信息。掌握这些技能后,学生可更深入地理解说明文,学会识别不同文本结构,预测信息类型,进而提升阅读能力和长期阅读表现。

"英语说明文语篇经常受亚里士多德的演绎法逻辑思维模式的影响,突出主题句,注重分析推理,直线性、有秩序、有层次地围绕主题展开具体细节;信息安排往往采用'突显'语序:由近及远,开门见山,一语破的,头短尾长,先点出主要的或重要的判断、结论、观点、态度、要旨、结果、行为等,再追叙一些与此有关的背景、历史、条件、环境、事实、情况、情节、理由、原因、分析、例证等,语篇开头注重的是 where the argument/talk is going,也有受培根归纳法逻辑思维模式的影响,采用相反的语序,或按照时间先后、事理顺序的自然语序,或采用倒叙、跳跃、片段、意识流等表现手法。由此我们可以理解说明文的各种结构形式,其实都是遵循着以上的两种原则排布。"(连淑能,2010:272)

三、说明文常见的开篇模式

为了说清楚某个事物,英语的语篇通常会以开门见山的方式展开,一语破的,先点出关键的判断、结论、观点、态度或要点,而后逐步展开其他内容。不同类型的说明文各自具有独特的开篇模式。熟悉这些模式有助于读者迅速辨别语篇类型,快速把握语篇主题,并通过调动语篇结构来全面理解内容。

高中英语说明文常见的语篇开篇模式包括以下几种。

(一) 研究报告式

研究报告式开头,典型词汇包括 according to a paper/research/study/survey..., a paper/research/ study/ survey...show, suggest, find, demonstrate, showcase 等等(动词有时以现在时,有时以过去时呈现)。开篇揭示研究结论,为文章核心所在,能提炼出文章的说明对象、写作目的、语篇题目等,是需要重点关注的信息节点。

但研究报告类说明文的主旨不都出现在语篇的第一段,有时也出现在第二段。例如,2023 年全国新高考 Ⅱ 卷 D 篇就是典型的例子:

"As cities balloon with growth, access to nature for people living in urban areas is becoming harder to find.

Past research has found health and wellness benefits of nature for humans, but a new study shows that wildness in urban areas is extremely important for human well-being."

第一段说明在城市里很难找到自然景观,第二段才以研究报告类的结果呈现模式点明城市中的自然景观对人类的健康幸福极其重要。

在教材说明文语篇中,也有类似的例子。如语篇 The secret language of plants 的研究结果也是在第二段呈现:

"Talking plants have long been a thing of myths and legends. Many cultures have stories of talking trees that give advice as well as warnings to people.

With us long believing that talking plants are fantasy, **new research has revealed** something amazing: it appears that plants can communicate after all."

另外,高考题中让学生比较头疼的阅读 C 篇和 D 篇经常出现此类说明文。近三年全国高考题中都有此类例子。

"On March 7, 1907, the English statistician Francis Galton published **a paper which illustrated** what has come to be known as the 'wisdom of crowds' effect."(2023 全国 Ⅰ 卷 D 篇)

"The Government's sugar tax on soft drinks has brought in half as much money as Ministers first predicted it would generate, **the first official data on the policy has shown**."（2022 年全国乙卷 D 篇）

"Popularization has in some cases changed the original meaning of emotional intelligence...**Research has shown that** emotional skills may contribute to some of these qualities, but most of them move far beyond skill-based emotional intelligence."（2021 年新高考 I 卷 D 篇）

（二）问题导入式

通过提出一个富有启发性的问题来引领读者进入文章的主题，激发他们的兴趣和思考，唤起他们对问题的关注。这种开篇方式旨在吸引读者的注意力，培养他们的主动参与意识，从而引导他们深入语篇学习。此类文章通常以对这个问题的正向回答为主题展开。

教材语篇 Art and technology 的开篇就属于此种类型：

"Think 'art'. What comes to your mind? Is it Greek or Roman sculptures in the Louvre, or Chinese paintings in the Palace Museum? Or maybe, just maybe, it's a dancing pattern of lights?"

高考题中问题导入式的开篇模式也很常见。

"What comes into your mind when you think of British food? Probably fish and chips, or a Sunday dinner of meat and two vegetables. But is British food really so uninteresting?"（2023 新高考 II 卷 C 篇）

"Can a small group of drones guarantee the safety and reliability of railways and at the same time, help railway operators save billions of euros each year?"（2022 年全国乙卷 C 篇）

（三）场景描述式

通过讲述一个真实或虚构的故事或描述一个场景、一个现象来引入文章的主题，增加故事性和情感色彩，吸引读者的注意力。此类说明文常采用形象生动的语言，通过对具体的场景或情景的描写，巧妙地传递情感或态度。这种风格下的首段，甚至次段，常呈现出明显的叙事色彩，使读者能够身临其境。通过描述事件发展过程或相关背景来引导读者进入文章的主题。

无论是教材还是高考题,都有很多此类说明文开篇模式。

"We see a woman swimming at night in a dark sea. Suddenly, she is pulled underwater. She surfaces, cries in fear, then disappears forever. This is the opening scene from the 1975 film Jaws, showing a shark attack. It tells the story of a great white shark that attacks and kills swimmers."(Book 2 Unit 6, Sharks: dangerous or endangered?)

"I was about 13 when an uncle gave me a copy of Jostein Gaarder's Sophie's World. It was full of ideas that were new to me, so I spent the summer with my head in and out of that book. It spoke to me and brought me into a world of philosophy."(2023 全国甲卷 C 篇)

在这个类别的语篇开头模式之下,也有学者把动物类话题开篇的说明文单列为"物种型开篇模式"。

"Grizzly bears, which may grow to about 2.5 m long and weigh over 400kg, occupy a conflicted corner of the American psyche—we revere them even as they give us frightening dreams."(2023 全国甲卷 D 篇)

"Goffin's cockatoos, a kind of small parrot native to Australasia, have been shown to have similar shape-recognition abilities to a human two-year-old...."(2022 全国甲卷 D 篇)

(四)引语导入式

开篇以引语导入在高中英语说明文中很常见。引用名人名言、文学作品中的经典语句等来开篇,一方面吸引读者的阅读兴趣、增强文章的感染力,并可以通过引语,为文章主题铺设一个引人入胜的前奏,让读者对即将阐述的内容产生好奇心和期待感,巧妙地引出文章的主题或中心思想,增加文章的权威性和深度。另外,适当的引语可以作为外部引证来支持作者的观点或论证,增强文章的说服力。

"If you look the right way, you can see that the whole world is a garden."...

这是 A love of gardening 语篇的首段开头，整个文章以《秘密花园》中的句子开篇和结尾 "Where you tend a rose...A thistle cannot grow." 达到总结和升华的作用，使整个语篇更具有思想性和感染力，给读者留下深刻印象。

（五）对比型开篇模式

观点对比型开篇模式常见于社科类文章，包括心理学方面的内容，其难点是语篇常涉及意识形态领域，挑战观点，引发思考。对于缺乏主动思考意识的学生，这类文章难度很大。要读懂这类文章，需要有广泛的社科文阅读积累，另外还需要培养主动思考的习惯。

"...When we look at a pine cone, we might think how much it looks like the tiles on a roof. An open flower might make us think how closely it resembles an umbrella. It is natural to think in this way, but of course it wasn't the umbrella that inspired the flower or the roof that inspired the pine cone."（选必三 Unit 5, Nature in architecture）

"The United States rose to global power on the strength of its technology, and the lifeblood that technology has long been electricity. By providing long-distance communication and energy, electricity created the modern world. Yet properly understood, the age of electricity is merely the second stage in the age of steam, which began a century earlier."（2022 年浙江 1 月卷 B 篇）

说明文的常见开篇模式还有引用数据式、下定义式开篇等。有的说明文的开篇可能存在几种模式的混合运用。

"Talking plants have long been a thing of myths and legends. Many cultures have stories of talking trees that give advice as well as warnings to people. Alexander the Great and Marco Polo were said to have visited such a tree in India. And in some modern stories, such as the film Avatar, trees can communicate with animals and people.

With us long believing that talking plants are fantasy, new research has revealed something amazing: it appears that plants can communicate after all."

这两段来自 The secret language of plants 语篇开头，包含引用式和

研究报告式两类模式。

"...But why are certain sounds more common than others? A ground-breaking, five-year study shows that diet-related changes in human bite led to new speech sounds that are now found in half the world's languages."（2022年全国Ⅰ卷D篇）

这个语篇开头可以被归类为问题设问型开篇,其目的是通过一个问题引发读者思考、激发兴趣,并引出后续内容的讨论。但也包含着研究报告类说明文的标志性语言 a ground-breaking, five-year study shows。

"'During an interview for one of my books, my interviewer said something I still think about often. Annoyed by the level of distraction in his open office,' he said, 'That's why I have a membership at the coworking space across the street—so I can focus'. His comment struck me as strange. After all, coworking spaces also typically use an open office layout. But I recently came across a study that shows why his approach works."（2021全国乙卷D篇）

这则语篇开篇模式属于引语导入型开篇,通过引用他人的言论或经历来吸引读者的注意力,同时预示了接下来要介绍的研究结果或观点,但也包含着研究报告类的标志性语言 a study shows。

开篇模式多样,其功能各异：问题式启发思考,场景式增强情感,引语式赋予权威,数据式提供客观支撑。这些模式服务于文章内容和目的,以便吸引读者,引导内容展开。同时,它们也帮助读者识别文章类型,深入理解结构。

四、说明文常见的说明方式

说明文通常主题明确,逻辑清晰,结构合理,而且为了更好地说明观点或论点,常会使用不同方法介绍说明对象。基本说明方法包括下定义、举例子、作比较（对比说明异同/类比说明相似）、分类别、列数字、作引用、析因果、看图示、析表格等等。在说明文教学过程中,学生应该学会辨识语篇中所采用的说明方法,分析这些方法如何使说明更加清晰、准确和易理解,并能在口头或书面表达中学以致用,使自己的表述逻辑更加清晰,说明更精准。

前面章节中针对语篇的宏观和微观分析时,以 The Longji rice terraces 语篇为例进行过分析。本章就不再针对说明文进行语篇分析,接下来的两节会针对高考英语说明文常考的两个题型:阅读理解和七选五进行分析和做题技巧的说明。

第二节 高考说明文阅读及解题技巧

本节课将基于对说明文语篇结构的了解,围绕高考阅读理解对说明文的考查要点进行分析,并介绍针对性的解题技巧,以期达到教考衔接。

一、高考题中的说明文阅读理解

说明文在实际生活中使用非常广泛,无论是介绍最新科技发现,还是弘扬中华优秀文化成果,都离不开作为文本载体的说明文。高考中对于说明文的考查涉及"人与自我""人与社会"和"人与自然"三大主题语境,涉及所有题型。

高考说明文选材丰富,涉及社会现象、科技发明、科学实验、生态环保、天文地理、人文艺术等各个领域,主要分为对社会现象的解释和介绍最新科研成果两大类。近几年,高考选材范围已经扩展到全球而不再局限于英美主流国家,但选取的是各国主流媒体使用的地道、原汁原味的语料,篇幅一般在 350～500 字,包含许多生词和长句。

根据近年来全国卷和各地高考试卷的命题动向,高考说明文注重文章结构分析,结合说明对象考查学生说明和写作技巧。近年科普类说明文常涉及专业话题,句式复杂且生词多,多见于阅读 C、D 篇。它们客观陈述事实,常用被动语态,凸显信息要点,强化客观性和逻辑性。此外,这类文章倾向于使用名词短语结构,简洁而内涵丰富,但无疑增加了阅读理解的难度。

许多优秀学生在Ⅰ卷几乎都可以得满分,但往往最拿不准的就是阅读理解题型中的说明文 C 篇和 D 篇。说明文之所以能成为学生的难点,主要表现在以下几方面。

（1）说明文中涉及的陌生对象，特别是社会现象，心理学及新事物的介绍，常超出学生的认知范围。这些文本中充斥着大量专有名词和术语，超纲词汇多，且同一词汇的不同词性，用法交替出现。即便附有中文解释，学生也往往难以理解。在阅读说明文时，学生常常因生词和难词而受阻，不得不反复阅读，耗费大量时间，这极大地影响了他们对文本的整体理解和语篇分析的效果。当遇到阅读理解问题中某些选项难以理解时，学生常感无从下手，这种阅读困难导致许多学生对说明文产生畏难情绪。

例如，2022年新高考Ⅰ卷D篇对唇齿音的演化研究，文章中对 labiodental 没有直接的标注，第二段和第三段中含有 labiodental 的句子分别对 labiodental（唇齿音）给出了 such as "f" 和 "v" 和 which are formed by touching the lower lip to the upper teeth 的说明，但是相信很多学生仍然难以理解。另外，文章中还出现了 Neolithic period 这样的专业术语。出题专家可能认为这个词不影响做题，所以没有加注汉义，但是考生短时间内未必判断得出来是否会影响他们做题，也可能会花时间纠结，导致拖慢做题速度。

（2）长难句多，往往从句套从句，甚至一句话就是一个段落，学生解构句子的过程难度较大。例如，2023全国Ⅰ卷C篇中的"In part one, I describe the philosophical foundations of digital minimalism, starting with an examination of the forces that are making so many people's digital lives increasingly intolerable, before moving on to a detailed discussion of the digital minimalism philosophy."主句是"主谓宾"结构的 I describe the philosophical foundations of digital minimalism，现在分词 starting with... 和 moving on 短语作状语，before 说明两种方式的先后，即"先从对这些 forces 的检查开始，再到更详细的数字极简主义哲学的讨论"，其中 the forces 后面跟了一个由 that 引导的定语从句，说明了前面的 forces 已经让很多人的数字生活越发难以容忍。

这样的长难句在事理性说明文中较常出现，在本就超出学生认知的话题面前，额外增加了理解难度。然而，长难句所在的位置又往往是出题点，所以学生必须学会解构和理解长难句的句子结构。比如2022全国新高考Ⅰ卷的D篇，最后一段中"The set of speech sounds we use has not necessarily remained stable since the appearance of human beings, but rather the huge variety of speech sounds that we find today is the product of a complex interplay of things like biological change and cultural evolution."对应了第 35 题"What does Steven Moran say about the set of human speech sounds?"的观点态度问题。这个句子的内在结构是由 not...but 构成的转折,否定了前者,肯定了后者,可以提取的关键词是 not stable(=dynamic)和 complex interplay,对应了选项 C 中的 a complex and dynamic system。

（3）学生普遍在整体把握语篇方面存在不足。根据课程标准,学生应具备全面理解语篇的能力,而近年来的高考试题也着重考查这一点。阅读理解题目不仅检验学生对语篇基本信息的理解,还逐步增强了对他们推断、归纳和概括等高级思维能力的考查。这类题目鼓励学生运用批判性和辩证思维,基于语篇内容进行逻辑推理,并据此作出回答。科普说明文,以精练的语言和清晰的逻辑,向读者普及科学知识,对学生的语篇分析能力提出更高要求,包括规范的表述,清晰的条理和严密的逻辑。因此,阅读科普说明文需要深入思考和掌握相关阅读技巧,以提升学生的思维能力和理解能力。

说明文语篇分析的重点是逻辑关系的理顺,理解内容并为后续推理和深入分析作铺垫。但由于其内容超出学生认知,使学生很难把握英语说明文的逻辑关系,很难建立逻辑思维框架,导致学生对内容的解读片面,无法充分理解主旨和内涵,进而在英语阅读理解题上失分。

二、高考阅读理解对说明文考查

高考说明文通常考查学生理解语篇能力和运用各种阅读策略提取、归纳、转换信息的能力,侧重考查考生对整体语篇把握和领悟的能力,以及对特定细节的识读和处理能力。

当我们确定了一篇说明文后,首先需要根据该文的开篇模式来识别其所采用的基本结构。在明确了语篇的结构图式后,可以找出文章的主题句和每个段落的主题句,从而确定文章所要说明的具体对象或主题。

从课程标准中的语篇分框架 What, Why 和 How 的角度来看,高考阅读理解中的设题都围绕说明对象,从不同角度、不同思维层次进行考查,且分别对应了不同的考查方向:What 通常对应的是事实性的知识,包括 What, When, Where 等事实理解性问题;文体特征的 How 对应了 structure，theme 和 writing purpose 等方面的问题；体现人文价值的 Why 通常对应 value，culture 和 emotion 等方面的问题。

"不同话题有不同的测试重点和命题规律，但无论是哪一话题的文章都遵循说明文的说明层次，即：是什么；为什么；怎么样；怎么办。"（种秀娟，2015）

根据对近几年高考说明文的分析，说明文阅读设题以考查细节理解题、推理判断题为主，词义猜测题、主旨大意题、观点态度题为辅。虽然各题型考查的侧重点不尽相同，但都是用真实的语篇考查课程标准中要求学生掌握的相关技能。通常有四个问题，彼此呈逻辑递进关系。这种方式促使学生不仅停留在表面理解，而是更注重学生在概括、归纳、推理和判断等方面的综合能力。

下面呈现几幅图片，展示高考说明文语篇的结构、段落主旨及对应的出题点。

2023全国新课标I-C篇
Para.1 writing purpose：make the case for+ how to adopt
Para.2 philosopical foundation
Para.3 suggested method
Para.4 why it works
Para.5 help you cultivate a sustainable digital minimalism lifestyle.

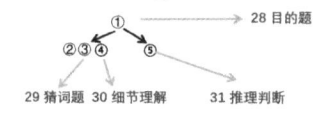

① → 28 目的题
②③④　⑤
29 猜词题　30 细节理解　31 推理判断

2022全国新课标I-A篇
21 文章来源题-推理判断
Grading policies for introduction to literature
grading scale → essays (60%) ← late work
group assignments(30%)
daily work/in-class　23 晚交作业的结果-
writings and tests/group　细节理解
work/homework (10%)
22 评分构成-细节理解

2022全国新课标I-B篇
24 个人经历说明的问题-推理判断
my story of wasting food(para.1)　phonemenon
food waste problem(para.2)
food waste　environmental problem related　problem
to food waste(para.3)
　　　　　　25 浪费后果-细节理解
methods of reducing　solutions
waste(paras 4-5 公司+个人)
26 公司做法-细节理解　27 个人做法-细节理解

图 4-11　高考说明文语篇的结构、段落主旨及对应的出题点

从图 4-11 可以看出，语篇设题都设置在语篇结构的主干上，而且，除了主旨大意题以外，其他题目基本做到了"题文同序"。

（一）高考说明文设题及解题策略

下面从语篇结构方面分析高考题中的设题及解题策略。

（1）选择合适的标题。常见的提问方式有"What would be the best title for the text? Which of the following is a suitable title for the text?"等。表面上是评估学生归纳和概括主旨大意的能力，实际上深入检验学生对说明文篇章结构知识的掌握与运用。

例如，2022 年全国新高考 II 卷 C 篇，针对美国居高不下的开车用手机现象推出的新检测设备 Textalyzer。语篇前两段说明之前针对开车用手机的现象进行的所有努力都没有效果，交通事故数量甚至不降反升。第三段权威人士分析了原因，到第四段，决心采取严厉措施"They want to treat distracted driving like drunk driving"。后面的两个段落分别从设备和法律角度确保 Textalyzer 的有效性进行深度说明。第 31 题的题干是 What is a suitable title for the text? 而 B 选项 Texting and driving? Watch out for the Textalyzer 跟语篇结构相关，问号前是说明问题，跟语篇的前三段有关，问号后是警告开车人要小心 Textalyzer，跟语篇的后三段有关。

再如，2021 年新高考 I 卷 C 篇，全文三个段落，第一段以水禽数量减少及背后的原因做背景，第二段作为语篇主题段落提出了说明对象 the Federal Duck Stamp，第三段说明了鸭票的成功，语篇中的二三段多次提及 the Federal Duck Stamp。对于尽可能避免重复的英语而言，多次重复的内容就是为了强调文章的核心说明对象。第 31 题的题干是"Which of the following is a suitable title for the text?"选项 B，C，D 的关键词都有以偏概全的问题，只有 A 选项 The Federal Duck Stamp Story 与语篇结构呈现的主要内容一致。

在归纳标题时，要牢记标题的特点，即短小精悍，多为短语，且能快速抓住读者眼球；概括性强，能涵盖语篇的全文主要内容；精确性强，表达客观，不随意改变语意程度，感情色彩要跟文意搭配。

（2）选择文章主旨大意。常见提问方式有"What is the passage mainly about? What does the passage mainly talk about?"等，主要关注

读者是否能够借助说明文的篇章结构，准确地把握和定位文章的核心主旨。例如，2018 年高考英语全国卷 I 阅读理解 C 篇第 31 题的题干为 "What is the main idea of the text?" 该语篇为说明文，以时间顺序说明语言多样性减少的问题，主题句在文章第一段 "Languages have been coming and going for thousands of years, but in recent times there has been less coming and a lot more going." 重点是 but 之后，对应选项 C 中的 results in fewer languages。

（3）选择段落大意。常见提问方式有 "What is the...paragraph mainly about? What does the...paragraph mainly discuss?" 等。同样检验读者运用说明文的篇章结构知识定位并理解主旨句的能力。例如，2023 年高考英语全国卷 I 阅读理解 D 篇第 32 题的题干为 "What is paragraph 2 of the text mainly about?" 该语篇判断为研究报告类说明文，语篇主旨在第一段。

第一段对群体智慧进行了定义和解释：in some cases, the average of a large number of independent estimates could be quite accurate 是结论。第二段总共六句话，句子间的逻辑关系如图 4-12 所示。

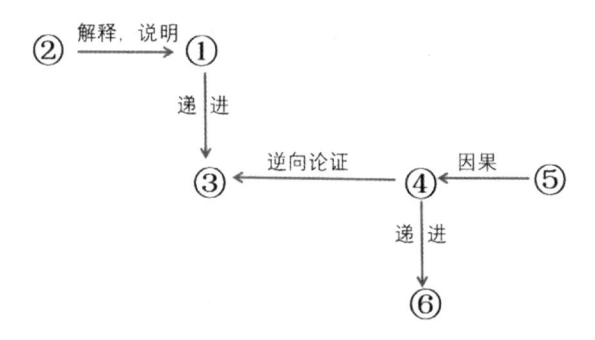

图 4-12　句子间的逻辑关系

段落的核心是第三句话，回应第一段中的主旨。第二句话解释第一句话，人们犯的错如何不同，而第一句话递进得出第三句话这个结论。第四句话是对第三句话的逆向论证，但跟第五句话之间是因果关系，第六句话是在第四句话的基础上进一步解释和强调可能的结果。由句子间的关系可以得出段落主旨是"群体智慧"的底层逻辑。也就是 B 选项 The underlying logic of the effect。

在解答主旨题型时，首先确定文章的文体，再利用对应文体的篇章结构知识定位主题段或主题句，结合关键词，通常能得出正确答案。

但有些段落的主旨要根据上下文来判断。例如，2022 全国新高考 I 卷 D 篇 34 小题的题干是"What is paragraph 5 mainly about?"本题的解答要跟上一段结合起来判断。第四段中提到了咬合方面的改变跟新石器时代农业的发展有关。第五段开头句中的 also confirmed 对应了选项 A 中的 supporting evidence for the research results。

还有的段落中的主旨需要通过说明方法来判断。例如，2019 年浙江 6 月高考题 C 篇中的第 7 题的题干是"What is the second paragraph mainly about?"主题句以研究发现的结果呈现"The number of trees larger than two feet across has declined by 50 percent on more than 46,000 square miles of California forests, the new study finds."段落中除了 50% 的大树损失，还有数字 55% 和 75% 就更凸显问题的严重性。A 选项 The seriousness of big-tree loss in California 中的关键词 seriousness 就是通过列数字的形式得出的结论。

（二）语篇的显性衔接手段是解细节题的关键

阅读中的细节题，不限于说明文设题，考查的是对细节信息的筛选查找，包括单细节题和多细节题。单细节题的题干中心词非常明确，涉及的内容比较单一，通过关键信息定位，可以相对容易地找到答案。多细节题一般不能直接通过题干信息定位答案。

例如，2021 全国甲卷 B 篇阅读的 26 题，题干是"What similar experience do Solio and Kisima have?"题干中提及的是两个黑犀牛妈妈的名字。这个题目的答案涉及三个段落的细节内容。在第一段中，提到了小黑犀牛的出生"When the tiny creature arrived on January 31, she became the 40th black rhino to be born at the reserve."第二段中提到"Her mother, Solio, is a first-time mum and she is doing a fantastic job."第三段中提到了另外一头小黑犀牛的诞生"The first rhino to be born at Port Lympne arrived on January 5 to first-time mother Kisima and weighed about 32kg."根据这三个句子的信息，可以跟选项 A 进行匹配 They had their first born in January。对于多细节题，解题方法与单细节题相似，关键在于深入研读相关段落并逐一核对信息。若熟悉文章结构及各部分要点，定位答案将更加便捷。

下面主要针对单细节题进行方法和策略的介绍。

细节题的解题策略涉及几个关键步骤。首先,根据文章的语体特征和结构,明确每段的主旨。其次,识别题干和选项中的关键词,并与段落主旨对照,初步确定答案所在段落。接着,对比选项与原文中的关键词句,选取意思相近的正确选项。值得注意的是,答案往往不直接呈现原文词汇,而是通过同义词、近义词、句型转换或上下义归纳概括来设置。此外,答案还可能涉及语法衔接、语法或标点符号的使用。因此,运用语篇衔接手段辅助筛选是解答细节题的有效方法。

很多学生因为词汇或语篇知识方面的问题,对有些答案模棱两可,甚至总在两个答案之间纠结,那就有必要首先了解一下细节题中主要的错误答案的设置方式,主要有以下几种。

扩缩范围:旨在通过精确控制词汇的使用来严格界定文章内容的范围。题目有时会通过加上 almost, all, nearly, more than, generally, normally, usually 等词汇,用以限制和明确文义的边界,以确保精准、达意。也就是在选项中改变或省略这些词汇,进而改变信息的涵盖范围、程度以及情感色彩,对考生造成困惑和干扰。

偷梁换柱:整个干扰项和原文在表述上差异不大,但是在考生易忽视的地方换了几个单词,造成句意的改变。

答非所问:干扰项表述在原文中出现,但是该表述不能对提问进行回答。

无中生有:干扰项往往是基本的生活常识或普遍认可的观点,但选项表述在原文中没有依据,属于作者根据自己的人生阅历等主观臆测编造而出的。当然,干扰项也有可能与设置的问题毫不相干。

移花接木:答案部分准确,但还会把其他不相干或不准确的信息嫁接到一起,这一点对于不仔细读题的学生很致命。

鱼目混珠:在词句理解类的试题中,干扰项错误地将某个词句的表面意思作为其在特定文章语境中的真实含义。

其实,阅读理解题目的答案所有都在文本中,仔细读懂语篇是做对题的前提和关键。把答案选项和语篇看成一个整体,利用语篇衔接手段来解题,常见的有以下几个方面。

1. 语法衔接

（1）指示照应

答案的确定要靠指示代词，如 this，that，these，those 等有指示功能的词来确定。如 2022 全国新高考 I 卷 D 篇第 32 小题，题干是 "Which aspect of the human speech sound does Damián Blasi's research focus on?" 根据人名定位到原文第二段。题干中的关键词跟原文中的对应有偏差，通过指示代词的回指功能，可以准确定位关键细节是前面一句中的 speech sounds...were common in the languages of societies that ate softer foods 指的是语音的发展，对应选项 D。

（2）比较照应

答案的确定需要通过形容词或副词的比较级或最高级。如 2021 年新高考全国 II 卷 D 篇 34 题的题干是 "Why does Pete Bonds still hire cowboys to watch cattle?" 题干问雇佣牛仔的原因，原文中 Pete Bonds 认为牛仔放牛是 the best way，跟 B 选项中 He thinks men can do the job better 匹配。

再如，2021 全国乙卷 D 篇 33 题，题干是 "Which level of background noise may promote creative thinking ability?" 原文以 similar to 形容词和 outperformed 派生动词两种形式表达了比较的概念，极大地超出其他几个对照组，也就最有可能提升创造性思维能力。

2. 词汇衔接

细节题答案多数时候都可以依据语篇结构关键词和词汇衔接手段锁定。词汇衔接在阅读理解细节题的解题中主要涉及词汇复现。

（1）同词复现

同词复现可以指同一词根之下的名词、动词、形容词、副词等变体，这是词汇衔接中最容易定位匹配的。如 2023 全国新高考 II 卷 C 篇第 29 题，题干是 "What are the selected artworks about?" 原文第一段出现 book lovers，the book，the image of reader，books and reading 等，与 C 选项 Books and reading 是同词复现。

（2）同义词解释

词汇衔接手段在定位细节题答案时最常见的就是同义词解释，连续四年在高考说明文语篇都用了这种设题方式。例如，2023 全国乙卷 C 篇 28 题，题干是"What do people usually think of British food?"原文与英国饮食直接相关的形容词是 uninteresting 和 less-than-impressive，对应选项 A 中的 simple and plain。

再如 2022 全国新高考 Ⅱ 卷 C 篇 28 题，题干中心词是 the ban on drivers' texting，原文第二段有关于禁令的结果，其中，The problem...appears to be getting worse 说明禁令效果不佳，对应选项 A 中的 ineffective。

2021 全国新高考 Ⅱ 卷 D 篇 32 题，题干是 "What is a problem with the cattle-raising industry?" 原文中面对的问题是 a labor shortage，B 选项中的 lack of workers 是其同义解释。

2020 全国新高考 Ⅰ 卷 D 篇 12 题的出题模式相同。题干是 "What is the recent study mainly about?" 该语篇是研究报告类的说明文，答案在第一段 According to a recent study in the *Journal of Consumer Research* 后面，也就是我们一起吃饭的同伴的体重和 consumption habits 对我们的食物摄入有影响，其中 consumption habits 与答案 D 中的 eating behavior 构成同义解释的关系。

（3）上下义词

常见的上下义词形式的细节定位，一般是语篇中运用下义词，但是答案限于篇幅，常会选用文章中相应词汇的上义词进行概括。

如 2022 全国新高考 Ⅱ 卷 C 篇第 9 题，题干是 "What can the Textalyzer help a police officer find out?" 原文中的 texted, emailed or done anything else that is now allowed 与 recent activity 是上下义关系，跟选项 B 中的 used their phone 也构成了上下义关系。

再如 2022 年全国新高考 Ⅱ 卷 D 篇 13 题，题干是 "In which aspect were the two groups different in terms of research design?" 语篇中的 nonaerobic exercise 和 high-intensity aerobic exercise 是具体类型的运动方式，而选项 C 中 exercise type 是更加宽泛的概念，它们之间构成了上下义关系。

有时在解答一个题目时，可能运用不止一种词汇复现手段。如 2020 全国新高考 Ⅱ 卷 D 篇 32 题，题干是 "What can we learn about rainforests from the first paragraph?" 关键信息是 rainforests，原文中

的 a rich variety of plants, food, birds and animals 对应了 D 选项中的 rich in wildlife，其中 rich 是同词复现，而 wildlife 与 plants, birds and animals 构成上下义关系。

3. 语法手段

阅读理解细节题的解答，有时还需要利用语法知识来判断。从这一点上就更加可以理解课标中关于语法的阐述"在语言使用中，语法知识是'形式—意义—使用'的统一体，与语音、词汇、语篇和语用知识紧密相连，直接影响语言理解和表达的准确性和得体性。""语法参与传递语篇的基本意义，语法形式的选择取决于具体语境中所表达的语用意义。"（中华人民共和国教育部，2020：23，25）

（1）可以利用时态解决细节问题。

2016 年全国 Ⅱ 卷 D 篇 34 题，题干是"Who reached the South Pole first according to the text?"因为语篇中涉及的外国人名比较多，学生在选择时很费劲。但是如果能读懂原文中"Captain Scott had reached the South Pole early in 1912 but had died with his four companions on the march back."就可以根据过去完成时判断，Captain Scott 虽然没能安全返回，但他是最早到达南极的人，由此锁定答案 C。

（2）在抓句子主干信息时，定语从句，特别是非限定性定语从句，应该首先去掉。

例如，2012 年四川卷 E 篇 57 题的题干是"What is the key information the author wants to give in Paragraph 1?"要求找出作者要表达的关键信息。因为该语篇是研究报告类，看似总结段意，其实是要找语篇主旨。第一段只有一句话"Plants are flowering faster than scientists predicted in reaction to climate change, which could have long damaging effects on food chain and ecosystems."这个题目的 A 选项是"Plants' reaction to weather could have damaging effects on ecosystem." B 选项是"The increasing speed of flowering is beyond scientists' expectation."非限定性定语从句常用来对主句中的先行词进行补充说明，以丰富和生动句子，而非其关键内容，很多学生因不理解其功能而错误选择了 A 选项。而 B 选项中的 beyond scientists' expectation 对应了原文中的 flowering faster than scientists predicted。

其他从句也能影响对语篇的理解。如 2023 全国新高考 Ⅱ 卷 D 篇 35 题，题干是 "What should be done before we can interact with nature according to Kahn?" 问 Kahn 认为在与自然互动之前需要做什么。从原文中 so that 引导的结果状语从句反向推，达到这个目的 we also need to protect nature 匹配选项 B 中的 environmental conservation。

（3）英语标点符号功能强大（后面有专门的章节进行介绍），阅读中可以用来定位细节答案。

如 2021 年全国乙卷 D 篇 32 题，题干是 "Why does the interviewer prefer a coworking space?" 问采访者为什么喜欢 coworking space，原文中 "That's why I have a membership at the coworking space across the street—so I can focus." 破折号的解释功能在这里明确表达了说话人可以保持专注，对应答案 A 中的 help him concentrate，同义词解释。

掌握以上几种方法，考生在高考细节题目的作答中会更加得心应手。

（三）推理判断题的解题策略与技巧

高考中的推理判断题是一种颇具挑战性的题型，不仅考验考生对文章具体事实的把握，还要求结合常识进行逻辑分析，以洞察作者的深层意图、动机、人物特性，以及事件的演变逻辑。这类题目在近年来的高考中题量保持相对稳定，重要性仅次于细节理解题，且与文章的事实细节紧密相连。解答时，考生需从整体上把握文章的核心，构建表层与深层意义间的桥梁，将已知与未知相互映照，进而领悟作者隐含的深意。

英语推理判断题通常涉及 assume, attitude, conclude, imply, infer, intend, mean, purpose, suggest 等词汇或短语，以及 can, could, might, would 等推测性情态动词，或 probably, most likely 等表示可能性的副词。解答时，需依据原文内容一步推断出答案，避免使用 only, never, all, absolutely 等绝对性词汇。正确答案往往包含 can, could, may, might, often, possibly, probably, some, sometimes, usually 等非绝对性词汇。

推理判断题旨在深入理解和超越语篇的表层含义，其核心要求考生全面把握原文的基本含义，通过解析文本内部的逻辑关联和细节，揭示文本的深层与隐含信息。此题型强调对语篇内容的深度理解和合理推断，测试学生的高层次阅读技能，包括厘清上下文逻辑关系、细节识别与理解能力。正确答案须对原文信息进行同义改写或综合阐述,不可直接选用原文原句或引入个人观点。在做题时,学生应围绕文本细节、事实,并考虑作者的措辞、态度和语气,结合相关知识,进行精确、逻辑严密的推理判断,从而得出与文本相符的结论。

高考推理判断题主要包括推断写作目的/意图、文章出处、作者观点/态度、隐含意义以及下文内容等方面。预测事件发展趋势或推断下文内容的题目,超越单纯语篇理解,很有挑战性。要求考生结合自身知识、经验以及对世界的认知,对文章中未明确提及但可通过逻辑推理得出的信息进行判断,展现其高层次的语言运用能力和思维深度。

在解答推理判断题时,正确答案往往不是原文的直接表述。因此,与原文直接相符的选项通常不是答案。解题时,需要精准地理解原文,同时结合语境和常识进行推理,洞察作者的隐含意图。避免主观臆断和武断解读,要警惕几种常见的误区:简单复述原文不能构成结论,片面或无关紧要的结论不可取,与文章内容相悖或逻辑不符的推断亦需排除,即使某个结论符合常识,但若文中无相应支持也不能采纳。考生需全面审视所有信息,避免片面思维,要忠实于原文,以已知信息为依据推断未知。

推理判断题是阅读理解的重要部分,同时也是考生容易失分的题型。面对不同类型的推理判断题,尽管解题方法各异,但清晰地说明方法在解题过程中都至关重要。以说明文为例,常用的例证法能够生动地解释观点,而文章开头的人或事物则常用来引出话题,吸引读者的注意力,从而激发他们的阅读兴趣。

例如,2022 年全国新高考 I 卷 B 篇第 24 题,题干是 "What does the author want to show by telling the arugula story?" 原文第一段中的 try to be mindful of food, unthinkingly bought way too much 对应了选项 B 中的 wasted food unintentionally at times,由此引出食物浪费的主题,进而呼吁大家珍惜粮食,减少浪费。

段落中以人或物为例,常用于佐证前述观点。

如 2021 全国新高考 I 卷 D 篇 33 题,题干是 "Why does the author mention 'doctor' and 'cheater' in paragraph 2?" 原文第二段主旨句说明情商作为一系列技巧,可善可恶,随后举医生和骗子的例子,最终得出结论,高情商的人未必是有道德的人。这里的两个例子就是为了厘清前面的概念,对应了 B 选项中的 clarify a concept。当然,还可以表述为

To prove/explain a (n) concept/idea。

有的时候，例子和需要例证的内容相隔较远，理解起来难度比较大。例如，2022 年北京卷 C 篇，语篇主题是系统思维。第 29 题的支撑信息与结论相隔较远。

29. What can be inferred about the field of nutrition?

A. The first objective of systems thinking hasn't been achieved.

B. The relationships among players have been clarified.

C. Machine learning can solve the nutrition problem.

D. The impact of nutrition cannot be quantified.

第三段开头 Take nutrition 举例证明或厘清上一段中的某些内容。分析第二段可以看出，前半段说的是系统思维的重要性。后半段说明，要改变包括饮食系统在内的所有系统，需达成三个核心目标：首先，全面认知系统中的相关因素；其次，明晰这些因素间的相互关联；最后，量化这些关联对系统内部及外部环境的具体影响。最后第三段提到，在饮食系统中存在至少 26,000 种生物化学物质，但大部分仍未知。对应了选项 A 中的 The first objective of systems thinking hasn't been achieved.

下面结合说明方法和具体的解题技巧针对不同类型的推理判断问题进行介绍。

1. 推断写作目的 / 意图

阅读理解中的推断作者意图或目的题，考查学生对英语语篇整体感知和理解能力。解这类题的关键在于理解文章的体裁、题材、把握其主题思想。另外，可以从写作手法角度推断作者的写作目的 / 意图，如：语篇开篇模式中的设问、引入案例或社会现象等，常用来引出主题或提供背景信息。此外，举例、引语、列数据等手法也能有效地支持或说明文章中的某些观点或主题。

英语语篇功能主要有四种，分别是信息功能、表情功能、劝说功能和社交功能。对应于高考常考题型粗略分类，分别是说明文、记叙文、议论文和应用文。每种文体对应的功能词也不尽相同，如体现描写功能的说明文和记叙文，主要目的是 to entertain readers 或者 to tell an experience，正确答案中的标志词主要有 describe, show, express 等。

对于描述功能的说明文和新闻而言，主要是告知，正确答案标志词主要有 analyze, demonstrate, explain, inform, report, tell 等。对于劝说和论辩功能的议论文，其正确答案标志词有 advise, argue, comment, praise, convince, prove, persuade, clarify, evaluate, assess, criticize 等。应用文主要是用来告知或销售（产品或服务），即 to persuade readers, to sell a product or a service, to attract readers or visitors 等，所以其正确答案标志词主要是 advocate, encourage, tell, persuade, attract 等。

有些语篇，作者的写作意图有非常明显的表述，虽说是推理判断题，但更接近于细节题，如 2023 全国新高考 I 卷 C 篇 28 题。题干是"What is the book aimed at?"原文开篇句的核心词是 make the case for 和 teach，包含两个层次：解释概念和告知如何做，对应了选项 B 的 advocate a simple digital lifestyle。

在多数情况下，作者并未直接阐述其写作意图。因此，读者需要全面阅读并深入理解文本，通过探究字面含义、逻辑关系以及细节中的隐含信息，来推断并领会作者真正的写作目的。

除了根据语体推断写作目的/意图，还可以根据文章或段落主旨的归纳判断。例如，2020 年全国新高考 I 卷 C 篇 11 题，题干是"What is the purpose of this text?"本题需要综合各个段落的主旨内容，进行推断。第一段汤姆·比塞尔原计划回到 Uzbekistan，撰写一篇关于咸海消失的文章。第二段说明他的访问涉及了更多内容，最终写成了一本书。接下来的几个段落分别介绍了书的概要、主要内容和对其评价。四个选项中只有 A 选项跟书有关，目的是向读者介绍并推荐这本书。

还有的时候，考察作者写作目的或意图以比较隐蔽的形式提问。例如 2022 年全国乙卷 27 题，题干是"What is the text?"看似是询问语篇类型，其实也是在考查写作目的/意图，根据语篇第三段的"The book ends with ..."和第四段第一句话"Wickenden is a very good storyteller. ... move her to some beautiful writing"可以判断这是一篇书评。书评的目的是促进阅读，推广优秀作品，促进文学交流与发展，当然也就是语篇的写作目的/意图。

2. 推断文章出处

文章出处及读者读象类题目题干中通常含有 be from, come from, be taken, appear 等词汇。文章出处要从文体特征、文章内容、语言特色和标志性信息着手,结合文章的具体内容来断定。

文章的第一段出现日期、地点或通讯社、报纸的名称,通常就可以判断为新闻,主要来自 newspaper 或 website。而且,新闻的客观性和严肃性较强,文章风格严谨、客观,通常不带有个人倾向的观点,但会客观呈现不同消息来源的观点或评论。

Advertisement 的格式特殊,容易辨认。产品和服务广告通常包括对产品和服务的介绍、推广、价格等,招聘广告包括对招聘人员的要求及职位描述等。

营养或健康饮食等内容通常来自 magazine 或 health section of a newspaper。

文化教育类的文章,通常是 education section of a magazine or a newspaper。

研究报告类文章,通常跟 science, report 或 medical journal 等专业杂志、网站有关。

人物类的有可能与 biography 或 autobiography 有关,艺人或体育明星等可能出现在 entertainment, sports section 等。

文中出现链接或 online, web, website, click 等字眼可轻松判断出文章源于网络。

例如,2023 全国Ⅱ卷 C 篇 28 题,题干是"Where is the text probably taken from?"根据文章第一段"*Reading Art: Art for book lovers is a celebration of an everyday object—the book, ...*"和第二段"In this 'book of books', ..."可知,这是一本介绍艺术作品的书籍。

再如,2022 年新高考Ⅰ卷 A 篇 21 题,题干是"Where is this text probably taken from?"根据文章标题 Grading Policies for Introduction to Literature 以及 Essays(60%)下的 the grade for this course 和 Group Assignments (30%) 下的 ...Blackboard, our online learning and course management system 可知,本文是对一个文学导论课程评分规则的详细介绍,应该是选自课程方案 a course plan,故选 C。

考生需结合常识与文章内容做出准确判断,并注重学习不同文体的结构、语言特色和专用词汇。答题时,依据文章风格与词汇迅速定位答案,提高效率。

3. 推断人物的观点或态度

推断作者或文中人物的态度题是"评价类"推理判断类题目,需要读者从字里行间揣摩作者或文章中主人公等的观点态度。可以是对文章中涉及的人、事、物的分析和评价,即作者或者读者认为某人、某现象、某物怎么样?

询问语气态度的题,选项里常出现的词如表 4-5 所示。

表 4-5 询问语气态度选项中常出现的词

Positive	sympathetic, satisfied, positive, supportive, optimistic, favorable, hopeful, promising, caring
Neutral	neutral, uninterested, indifferent, objective
Negative	critical, disappointed, doubtful, disapproving, puzzled, concerned, pessimistic, unfavorable, suspicious, skeptical

注意:

(1)说明文一般是客观叙述,所以态度题里,subjective 一般不是答案。

(2)既然有兴趣写出文章,indifferent 一般也不是答案;同样地,介绍新产品或新事物的文章,即便提出其各种不足,但态度题也多是褒义选择。

人物的观点和态度需读者细读文章,准确理解主题和文意,在作者构建的语义场中,通过实词和修辞手法分析辨别人物的观点和态度。

首先辨识文体及结构,确定文章主题,根据文中语言的情感倾向对文章整体的情感走向有初步的了解。特别关注主题段或出题段落中的转折词,包括 but, yet, although, as a matter of fact, however, in fact, now 等,其后的内容更能表达作者或文中人物的观点。同时,注意作者的引语或例子,判断人物的态度倾向。做这类题目时要注意客观,不要将个人的好恶掺杂到作者或文中人物的态度和情感判断上。

推断人物观点或态度题,通常在设题中可以看到,有一些题目的设置角度是作者角度,也就是 "What does the author think of …? What's the author's attitude towards…?"

如 2023 年全国新高考Ⅰ卷 D 篇 35 题,题干是 "What is the author's attitude toward Navajas' studies?" 询问作者态度。定位到原文最后一段,从作者的用词中可以判断其态度,首先是 resulted in a global reduction in error,这是优点。后面 although 引导让步状语发生转折,但是说的是 limitations and many questions,主句 the potential implications are enormous 仍然是优点。所以,作者的态度非常明确,明显是褒扬。四个选项中有三个中性或负面的:unclear, dismissive 和 doubtful,只有一个 approving 是褒义,当然还可以引导学生提供其他可用的词汇,如 supportive 等。

再如,2023 年全国甲卷 C 篇 31 题,题干是 "What does the author think of Weiner's book?" 定位到原文第五和第六段,由第五段的 humor 和第六段的 simplicity 可以判断作者的态度是 humorous and straight forward。

另一类设题询问文中人物对人、事、物等的看法。这类题目根据题干中提及的人物,可以比较容易地定位答案的位置,根据用词,直接判断态度。例如,2022 年全国甲卷 D 篇 34 题,题干是 "What does Shirley Fitzgerald think of Sydney?" 定位到原文 "... Sydney swept aside much of its past, including many of its finest buildings." 可知,Shirley Fitzgerald 认为在奔向现代化的过程中,悉尼摒弃了许多自己过去的东西,包括那些精美的建筑物。A 选项 losing its traditions 与 swept aside much of its past 构成同义解释。

但有时候,对文中人物态度题问得比较巧妙。例如,2023 年全国新高考Ⅱ卷 B 篇 25 题,题干是 "What was a problem facing Jaramillo at the start of the program?" 本题虽然没有直接问人物的态度,但在第二段中作者运用了重复的修辞手法,连用三个 awful,强调孩子们对项目的最初反应,匹配 C 选项中的 Some kids disliked garden work。

还有一类态度题的设题中不出现 author 或其他人物的姓名,提问方式如 "Which of the following best describes the impact of the program? Which best describes ...?" 等,更强调读者对人、事和物的分析和评价。例如,2023 年全国乙卷 29 题,题干是 "Which best describes cookery programmes on British TV?" 定位到原文第二段和第三段。第二段最后一句话总结段意 "... TV programmes have helped change what people think about cooking." 第三段开头 "..., 1 in 5 Britons say that watching cookery programmes on TV has encouraged them to try different food."由此可以判断节目的成功就在于影响了英国人对饮食的看法和做法，匹配 D 选项的 influential。

4. 推断隐含意义

在解读文章时，考生应聚焦于文本的篇章结构、内在逻辑链条，以及细节信息，如时间脉络、地点描述、人物关联、角色身份和事件等。通过分析文本中的明确信息和上下文逻辑联系，以及事物随时间的发展变化，来洞察作者未直接表达的深层含义或意图。此外，解答推理判断隐含意义时，考生还需结合生活常识和经验，通过逻辑推理揭示文本的内在含义，而非仅仅停留于句子层面的理解。

设问中常涉及 imply, infer, conclude, indicate, suggest 等词汇，旨在引申理解特定人物、物体或现象。正确选项往往是对原文的巧妙"同义转述"，而非直接复述，这极大地考验了学生的阅读理解能力。在日常词汇教学中，坚持进行英英释义对学生应对此类题目大有裨益。在解答涉及隐含意义推断的题目时，考生应首先识别题干关键词，然后在文中定位相关细节，并进行深入分析和推敲，如人物感受或措施效果等。

例如，2023 年全国新高考 Ⅰ 卷 C 篇第 31 题，题干中的关键词 suggest, practice, part two, 定位到语篇最后一段 "You can view these practices as a toolbox meant to aid your efforts to build a minimalist lifestyle ..." 句子的核心结构 view these practices as a toolbox 跟 A 选项中的 use them as needed 匹配。

有时，答案的推断跨越段落，需要关注语篇信号词，分析段际关系。例如，2023 年全国新高考 Ⅰ 卷 D 篇第 33 题，根据题干中的关键词 Navajas' study, accuracy, increase 定位答案到第三自然段。段首句以 But 开始，说明本段跟上一段之间构成转折关系。回到第二段，其中 "..., the wisdom of crowds requires that people's estimates be independent." 也就是各个参与者需要独立作答，群体智慧才会准确。比对各选项，D 选项中 estimates were not fully independent 对应原文中的 have a discussion，由此选出答案。

有时，隐含意义推理题的答案需要借助说明方法来精准判断。如

2023年全国新高考Ⅱ卷C篇第31题,题干是"What does the author want to say by mentioning the e-reader?"前文提到,在文中提到具体的人或事,在语篇中间,主要是为了例证的作用,但这里显然不是。根据关键词 e-reader,定位答案到语篇最后一段。段首句用了过去时态,而且加上 once believed to make the printed page outdated 只是过去的看法,根据信息推进模式,这是先抑后扬的手法,下文通过两个对比 as interactive as 和 in contrast to,突出传统书籍的互动性、隐秘性的传统阅读体验,甚至优于 e-readers。匹配选项 A 中的 The printed book is not totally out of date。

5. 推断下文内容

推断下文内容要求考生对接下来的故事情节或文章内容进行推断。解答该题型时,考生要把握作者的写作思路,分析语篇结构,段落之间的联系,关注语篇的最后一段,特别是尾段的最后一句,常常是承上启下的过渡句,继而作出合理的推断。常见命题形式有"What do you think will happen if/when...? What will the author continue to talk about?"等。

例如,2023 年全国乙卷 C 篇 31 题,题干是"What might the author continue talking about?"回归语篇,主要介绍电视饮食节目对英国人饮食看法和行为的影响,第一段介绍话题,第二、三两段介绍影响。第三段最后一句话"..., it's no longer 'uncool' for boys to like cooking."也就是说,文章的走向由对英国大众整体的影响转到男孩子群体的影响,指出他们对做饭的态度发生了变化,并预示接下来的内容将涉及电视上的男厨师或实际生活中男孩子对做饭的新喜好。给出的四个选项中,只有 B 选项 Male chefs on TV programmes 匹配。

再如,2022 年全国甲卷 B 篇第 26 题,题干是"What does the follow-up test aim to find out about the cockatoos?"该语篇是研究报告类文章,第三段重点说今后的研究方向"to try and work out whether the cockatoos rely entirely on visual clues, or also use a sense of touch in making their shape selections",也就是看凤头鹦鹉对形状的选择能力到底是靠哪些感官而来的。只有 D 选项 Whether they use a sense of touch in the test 跟原文匹配。

只要做题思路清晰,根据文章脉络和最后一段就能判断出下文的内容。

准确解答任何设题的前提在于对语篇的深度理解,包括透彻理解主题、掌握框架结构和说明方法。在日常学习中,广泛涉猎多领域内容、拓展认知,并在理解语篇内容的基础上,通过问题链锻炼逻辑思维和批判性思维,将有助于提高阅读理解能力。

第三节 高考七选五解题策略

七选五题型出现在全国高考题中已经有十多年的时间,主要考查的是学生对结构严谨、逻辑层次清晰的说明文的深度理解能力,记叙文和议论文比较少见,因此解题策略主要围绕说明文语篇的特点和分析展开。本节将详细介绍高考七选五的解题策略,侧重于语篇特征及其分析方法。

一、高考真题中的七选五

高考七选五题目选材以"人与社会"和"人与自我"两大主题为主。这些语篇话题贴近学生生活,但内容又具有一定的新颖性和时代感,体现了高考对新材料和新情境的重视。阅读七选五题型要求考生深入理解文章主旨,结合篇章架构和内容,从七个选项中选出五个与上下文契合的句子,恢复文章连贯性和完整性。此题型受格式塔心理学的影响,不仅考查考生词汇、语法和语篇知识,更检验考生分析、归纳和推理能力。特别侧重于评估考生对文章基本结构的理解,要求他们从宏观篇章和微观段落层面精准把握结构层次,检验对文章整体内容、结构以及上下文逻辑关系的理解和运用能力。其不仅检验考生的语言能力,还关注其核心价值与情感价值的培养。

七选五的考点分布广泛,包括段首、段中和段末的设空位置,涉及的句间逻辑关系多样,涵盖总结、结构、因果、解释、对比和过渡等。主要考查方式为句间逻辑关系、语法(如照应)和词汇(如复现、同现)手段。

重点仍在于语篇的表层衔接。测试内容不仅限于对语篇内容和背景知识的理解,还包括总结文章主旨、分析结构、把握文脉、理解细节和推理判断等能力。由于说明文通常围绕一个核心说明对象展开,因此识别并理解该对象有助于把握文章中心和各段落内容。

近两年的七选五题目难度在逐渐提升。首先,语篇中提供的显性信息如标题、小标题等有所减少,尽管仍以 how-to 类建议内容为主,但考生需仔细阅读以理解信息呈现模式。其次,语篇结构有所转变,除了传统的总分、分总、提纲式结构外,还出现了递进式结构,其逻辑关系更为复杂,考生需仔细分析段落及整个语篇的逻辑关系。此外,备选项设计更为科学,错误选项干扰性增强,正确选项间也存在干扰,增加了试题难度。试题中减少了对显性词汇衔接的考查,而更多地聚焦于隐性逻辑衔接和语篇层面的分析,这要求考生具备更高的思维水平,全面深入地理解语篇内容,经过仔细斟酌才能作出正确选择。

二、根据句间逻辑关系判断七选五选项

七选五解题过程实质是语篇分析的过程。教师要引导学生基于语篇主题,有意识地引导学生从整体上理解语篇的内容和宏观、微观结构,分析句内、段内、段落与语篇主题之间的逻辑关系,多关注语句与语篇的衔接和连贯。语篇宏观组织结构在七选五中,主要体现在段首句或者小标题的选择。本章第一节中介绍了说明文的五种语篇类型,即描述型、因果型、问题—解决型、序列型和比较对比型。考生需要在阅读中体会和掌握说明文的文体特点、说明文的写作方法和行文框架,对于判断段首句比较有利。

但是,句子在段落中的位置不同,起到的作用也不同。七选五分别在段落开头、中间和结尾设空,目的是利用空白位置的提示和上下文的线索,考查考生的逻辑思维能力。段首设空,一般为段落的主题句,学生应阅读全段,通过对段落整体的理解确定段落的主题。段中设空,学生应根据段落的主题、空前句和空后句与设空句之间的逻辑关系来决定。对于段尾设空,学生应根据设空前的内容来判断设空句是否是段落的总结句或段落主题句。

在解答七选五题目时,首要步骤是细致阅读文章标题,快速浏览文章的开头、结尾以及每段的首句,从而明确文章的主题和整体结构。小标题和段首句在这一过程中显得尤为重要。当涉及段中和段尾句子的逻辑关系时,应深入分析段落内部的逻辑链条,甚至考虑相邻段落间的连贯性作为判断依据。因此,理解句子间的逻辑联系至关重要,这就要求考生熟悉并掌握常见的逻辑关系词。

常见的彰显各种句际关系的逻辑关系词,不仅包括连词,还有副词以及常见的短语。

表示并列关系的逻辑关系词:and, or, also, further, moreover, what's more, either...or, neither...nor, not only...but also..., too, as well as, similarly, likewise 等。

表示次序关系的逻辑关系词:

顺序关系:first (ly), second (ly), last (ly), eventually, finally, next, then, later, after that, in the first place, in the second place, first of all, for a start, afterwards, at last, meanwhile, at the same time, since then, following this, last but not least, to begin with 等。

平列关系:for one thing, for another, to begin with, to conclude, some... other... still others 等。

递进关系:and, also, further, further more, likewise, besides, additionally, next, similarly, moreover, in addition, what's more, too, either, neither, not...but, not only... but also, more importantly, most important of all 等。

表示概括与例证的逻辑关系词:such as, example, take... for example/ instance, that is to say, let's say, suppose that, namely, including, in this case, to illustrate, in fact, in other words, or rather, for example, for instance, actually, as a matter of fact, put it simply, and so on, to name just a few 等。

表示转折和对比关系的逻辑关系词:

表达相似点的关系词:similarly, also, in the same way, all the same, as, like, likewise, both, in common, the same is true of, in comparison with, compared with, similarly important 等。

表达不同点的关系词:although, anyhow, despite, though, for all that, or, or else, otherwise, meanwhile, instead, however, but, still, yet, unlike, rather, rather than, nevertheless, whereas, while, in contrast to, contrary to..., conversely, (as) opposed to, in contrast (to), on the contrary, different from, on the other hand, regardless of, even if (though), and yet, even so, luckily, fortunately 等。

表示因果关系的逻辑关系词：because, for, as, so, since, because of, owing to, due to, therefore, thus, hence, consequently, accordingly, contribute to, cause, lead to, only to do, thanks to, for this reason, another reason for…, as a consequence, in that, as a result, so/such...that, result in, result from 等。

表示条件关系的逻辑关系词：if, unless, as long as, on condition that, once, providing that, if possible, if necessary, if so, if not all, if anything 等。

表示强调关系的逻辑关系词：above all, certainly, indeed, it is true that…, really, truly, of course, sure, surely, in particular, especially, actually, totally, obviously, particularly, definitely, undeniably, undoubtedly, in fact, as a matter of fact, without doubt, not to mention, to be exact, for sure, for certain, it's certain that 等。

表示目的关系的逻辑关系词：with this object, for this purpose, in this way, in order that, so that, in case 等。

表示归纳总结的逻辑关系词：altogether, overall, then, thus, in a word, in short, briefly, to sum up, in summary, on the whole, in conclusion, all in all, in general, generally speaking, in a broad sense, fortunately, therefore, hence, in brief, in sum, to conclude, to summarize 等。

如上所示，有些逻辑联系词可以表示不止一种语义关系。比如，and 既可以表示增补，又可以表示对比、结果、转折、让步等。在构建语篇的过程中，多种联结方式交织使用，共同起着衔接句子的作用。

下面是近几年高考题中根据逻辑联系词就可以判断空格答案的例子。

（一）利用因果关系逻辑联系词解题

例如，2023 年全国新高考 I 卷第 39 题："You could ask a friend or family member to help add to your list. 39. That way, you could exchange thoughts on what makes each of you special and the aspects of your personality that shine through."

本段中有非常明显的逻辑提示词 That way，空格处应该是后面 you could exchange thoughts 的前提或原因。而且，这里的 you 跟首句中的 you 所指并不相同，因为后面句子中提到 each of you，由此可以推断空格处的句子中应该有 friend，family member 或其指代词 they，而且是要做某事来彼此交流想法。七个选项中满足条件的只有 C 选项 They might even like to have a go at doing the exercise。

再如，2023 年全国甲卷 40 题："So many of us have the belief that being comfortable is the only state we will tolerate, and when we experience something outside of our comfort zone, we get impatient about the circumstances. You should learn to say to yourself, 40 You'll then gradually become more patient."

空格后的句子中 then 表明了因果关系中的果 become more patient，加上空前句子中的 outside of our comfort zone, get impatient 等词汇，所以空格处的句子定是有针对性地鼓励或安慰自己。在 F 选项 This is merely uncomfortable, not intolerable 中，可以看到对前句进行解释的 uncomfortable，另外，not intolerable 的双重否定跟 tolerate 同义。

(二) 利用递进关系逻辑联系词解题

例如，2023 年全国乙卷第 36 题："Indoor plants might look as if they just sit around not doing much, but in many ways they are the unsung heroes of the home. 36, but studies have shown that they can promote people's well being by improving their mood, reducing stress and helping their memory. What's more, indoor plants are easy to look after and are not very expensive."

根据第一句中的 in many ways they are unsung heroes of the home 可知，下文应该说 indoor plants 的优点，所以空格后的 but 不表示转折，而表示递进关系，初步判断是 not only...but (also)，对照选项，B 选项 Not only do they look beautiful 匹配。

(三) 利用转折关系逻辑联系词解题

例如，2023 年全国乙卷 37 题："Indoor plants, also known as houseplants or pot plants, are plants that like to grow indoors. Many of these species are not ideally suited to growing outside in the UK, especially in the winter. 37."

本段话需要回答 What are indoor plants? 这个问题。第一句话对其定义是 like to grow indoors，37 题空格前说 many...not ideally suited to growing outside，由概括到具体。句中的逻辑信号词 not，常跟 but 转折连用。D 选项 Instead, they grow better inside, where it is warmer 中的 instead 表示转折，且 inside 和前句的 outside 构成反义词同现关系。

再如，2022 年全国甲卷 38 题："People in France expect you to eat with a utensil in each hand. 38, instead preferring to use their hands."

38 空后有转折词 instead，后面是喜欢用手吃饭，所以空前应该是不用工具吃。符合条件的只有 C 选项 Mexicans consider it inappropriate to eat with utensils 符合条件。

（四）利用对比关系逻辑联系词解题

例如，2020 年全国甲卷 39 题所在段落：
Making Requests
39. In Portugal, this would be a serious mistake, because it shows the chef that you don't like their seasoning skills. Similarly, in Italy, never ask for extra cheese to add to your food.

本篇文章探讨的是外出用餐时的重要礼仪，特别是在"提出要求"这一环节。段首需要填写的句子不是主题句，但与其后内容相关。通过上下文中的 similarly 和具体的要求 "never ask for extra cheese..." 可以推断，前面句子应是一个提出的要求，暗示用餐者对厨师厨艺的不满或特定偏好。对比选项，只有 G 选项 It may seem like a simple request to ask for salt and pepper at a meal 符号前面的分析。

再如，2021 年北京卷第 38 题所在段落："...In one European study, participants listened to music as the researchers monitored their heart rates and blood pressure. 38. On the other hand, when the music slowed, the participants' stress and anxiety levels became lower and the effects on heart rates appeared to follow suit."

本段中间 on the other hand，形成前后情况的对比。后面是当音乐放缓,参与者的压力、焦虑水平和心跳都会降下来,情况相反的只有 G 选项 Interestingly, the more cheerful the music was, the faster their heart rates were。

逻辑关系词不仅用于句子间的连接,也适用于段落间的衔接。七选五的文章主要采用总分或分总结构的说明文,且部分文章配备小标题,因此结构明晰。根据其五种常见形式,段间逻辑较易识别。如果有逻辑联系词,段落间的关系会更清晰,有助于判断句首空格的正确答案。

例如,2021年全国乙卷38题答案的判断:

"38. If you can't take their wine away, you should certainly try ... If you're the host, you can ask them to help you in the kitchen...39.

And what about that other dinner-party killer: awkward silence? If you're faced with ...40. Just quickly turn around and say, 'This cake is extremely delicious and you have to tell me all about it.'"

38空的答案可通过段落衔接判断,但通读全文更便捷。下一段开头用 and 与 the other dinner-party killer 暗示了讨论两个 dinner-party 上的 killers,其中一个是 awkward silence。由于两段结尾均为问号,表明它们并列讨论同一主题。先寻找结构相似的问句,再结合段落内容确认答案。F 选项 "What about that person who has had too much to drink or won't stop talking." 符合条件。也就是说,这个 killer 是有人喝多了说太多话,可以归纳为 too much drunk talking。

七选五中的基本单位是句子,句间逻辑是基本逻辑关系。各种句间逻辑关系在高考题中都能找到事例,下面的主位推进环节中会进一步分析。

三、主位推进理论在七选五中的应用

"由语言形式实现的意义可以通过对形式的直接解码来实现。……语篇中句子与句子之间的连接则需要利用其间的形式衔接机制来完成。语篇的衔接机制在语篇外部实际上起着将语篇固定在情景语境中一定位置上的作用。"(张德禄,2000)。

逻辑关系词为分析句际关系提供了明显的路标,但有的句际关系没有显性的逻辑词连接。"虽然语篇是层级性的,但在其体现中它是线性的。语篇的线性特征是语篇的表层特征,因为无论语篇内部的层次和成

分与部分之间的语义关系多么复杂,都必须编码成为线性才能在实体上得到体现。每个项目本身显然也具有层级性项目,也具有包含关系和从属关系等。这些都要在项目序列中进行描述。"(张德禄,2003)

除了根据语篇主题和结构,从语篇及段落层面分析,还要看信息如何推进,也就是需要从段落信息的主位推进去考量。

Mathesius 在深入探究句子中不同元素在语言交流中的独特作用时,察觉到了一个显著的现象:句子开头的元素在交际中承载着独特的职能,为后续的对话或叙述设置了议题或主题。他将这种起话题作用的元素定义为"主位",而将其余的叙述内容称作"述位"。Mathesius 认为,主位通常承载的是已知的信息,而述位则负责传达新的信息内容。

"信息单位的构成形式是:(已知信息)+ 新信息。就是说,在每个信息单位中,都必须有一个新信息,没有新信息的单位是不完整的,也往往是不能成立的。而已知信息则是可以取舍的。'已知信息 + 新信息'是最常见的信息单位结构。已知信息先于新信息,新信息的最高点即信息中心往往是信息单位的最后一个位置,更确切地说,是最后一个'实义词项'"(胡壮麟等,2008:173)。

把句子按照交际功能角度划分为主位和述位的切分方式叫作实义切分法。"实义切分法着眼于词语在句子中的交际功能和信息的分布情况,它对于研究连贯性语篇的结构,分析语篇中句与句之间的内部联系具有重要的意义。在无标记的句子中,主语常常表示已知信息,并作为叙述的出发点,因此主语常常充当主位。"(黄国文,1988:76)

在构建语篇时,通常需要至少两个句子相互关联。这些句子间的主位、述位存在动态变化又相互关联的关系,体现为相邻句子间信息的重叠或延续,即"推进"。通过这种主位的推动与延续,整个语篇逐渐扩展内容,形成完整、连贯且意义明确的整体。

"捷克语言学家曾经指出,从句子成分的叙述价值看,述位起着重要的作用,因为它传递新信息。但是,从篇章结构来看,重要的还是主位。主位担负着少量的信息负荷,这就使它成为语篇的重要构造手段。因此,每个语篇及其段落都可以看成一个主位的序列。篇章的真正主位结构是指主位的连接和衔接,它们的相互关系和领属层次,以及跟段落、整个语篇和情景的关系。这些复杂的主位关系称为主位推进模式。"(黄国文,1988:80)

不同的语言学家对主位推进模式有不同的划分,他们的划分有交叉,也有不同,我们就选取黄国文教授的六种主位推进模式进行介绍。

(1)平行型。以第一句的主位(T)为出发点,以后各句均以此句的主位为主位,分别引出不同的述位(R),从不同的角度对同一个主位加以揭示、阐释。(黄国文,1988:81)这个模式可以表述为:

$$T1 \longrightarrow R1$$
$$T1 \longrightarrow R2$$
$$T1 \longrightarrow R3$$
$$\vdots$$

例如,2022年全国甲卷38题所在段落是典型的平行型主位推进:

"In India and the Middle East, … People in France expect you to eat … 38, instead preferring to use their hands. In Chile, you may never touch … People in Thailand generally use their forks …"

本段话的主位相同,分别是国家或国家的人作主位、述位交错陈述,所以38空,主位一定是国家或国家的人,只有C选项Mexicans consider it inappropriate to eat with utensils 符合条件。

再如,2016年全国Ⅱ卷37、38小题所在段落也属于平行型主位推进:

· 37.

Some people may think that a garden is no more than plants, flowers, patterns and masses of color. Others are concerned about using gardening methods that require less water and fewer fertilizers. 38. However, there are a number of other reasons that might explain why you want to garden. One of them comes from our earliest years.

首先根据语篇的结构和段落项目符号,37应该是一个祈使句。符合条件的是A选项Know why you garden 和B选项Find a good place for your own garden,根据段落后面a number of other reasons 可知,本段在讨论原因,故锁定答案A。另外,38空后有However 转折,也就是其前的几个句子都是一个走向,根据前面两个句子的主位some people 和others,推断这是平行结构,根据逻辑联系词,推断有可能会有still others。对照选项,E选项Still others may simply enjoy being outdoors and close to plants 中的Still others 跟前两个构成平行关系。

(2)延续型。第一句的述位或述位的一部分作为第二句的主位,这个主位又引进一个新的述位,该述位又充当下一句的主位,如此延续下去,带出新信息,推动思想内容的表达。(黄国文,1988:82-83)这个模式可用表示为：

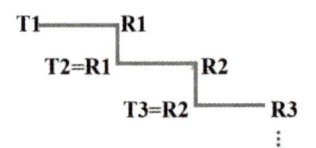

```
T1──────R1
   T2=R1──────R2
       T3=R2──────R3
                 ⋮
```

例如，2020年北京卷46题所在段落是典型的延续型推进方式：

"Many people think that positive thinking is mostly about ... In reality it has more to do with the way an individual talks to himself. Self-talk is a constant stream of thoughts of a person, ... 46. Meanwhile, positive thinking can help to stop negative self-talks and start to form a positive view on an issue."

首句述位中提到 positive thinking，第二句的主位是 it，回指 positive thinking；第二句的述位中含有 talks to himself，第三句话的主位是 self-talk，同义解释；要填的是第四句话，根据主位推进模式，第四句话中的主语应该跟上一句话中的述位中的部分词语有关，加上第五句话以 meanwhile 构成转折，且句中出现 positive thinking can help...，第四句话一定含有 negative 这个词，由此可以比较容易地锁定 B 选项 Negative self-talk damages self-confidence and decreases self-respect。

（3）集中型。第一句的主位、述位做了基本叙述以后，第二、三……句分别以新的主位开始，各句不同的主位都集中归结为同一述位（或述位的一部分）。（黄国文，1988：83）这个模式可以表示为：

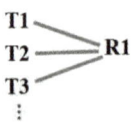

```
T1 ╲
T2 ──R1
T3 ╱
 ⋮
```

例如，2019年北京卷第46题所在段落是典型的集中型推进模式：

"Much of the work in today's world is accomplished in teams. Most people believe the best way to build a great team is to gather a group of the most talented individuals. 46. Companies spend millions hiring top business people."

段落首句强调团队的重要性。第二句话中的述位含有 the most talented individuals，第四句话中有 top business people，两者属于同一类型的述位，由此可以判断段落的信息推进方式是集中型，中间句应该也是同一模式，B 选项中的 top talent 与 the most talented individuals

和 top business people 构成同义、近义复现。

（4）派生型。第一句的主位、述位作了叙述后，以后各句的主句均从第一句的述位的某部分派生出来。（黄国文，1988：85）这个模式可以表示为：

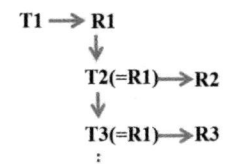

$$T1 \longrightarrow R1$$
$$\downarrow$$
$$T2(=R1) \longrightarrow R2$$
$$\downarrow$$
$$T3(=R1) \longrightarrow R3$$
$$\vdots$$

例如，2022年全国乙卷的第三个小标题所在段落：

· Practise empathy

38. The friend who is remaining needs to be sensitive to all the additional time demands placed on the friend who has moved. The one in the new environment should be sympathetic to the fact that your friend may feel abandoned.

这个段落三句话，后面两句话的主语也是句子主位，分别是 the friend who is remaining 和 the one in the new environment，其中 the one 是代词指代 the friend，后面两个句子是分情况说明该如何实现共情：be sensitive to...time demands 和 be sympathetic to...feel abandoned。查看所给的选项，G 的述位里提到了 who left...who was left behind，对应下面两个句子中的主位，属于整体叙述，后面两句分述。

再如，2018年全国 I 卷38空：

"But good news is that there are really only three kinds of decisions you need to make about color in your home: the small ones, the medium ones, and the large ones.

38. They're the little spots of color like throw pillows, mirrors and baskets that most of us use to add visual interest to our rooms...

Medium color choices are generally furniture pieces such as sofas, dinner tables or bookshelves.

The large color decisions in your rooms concern the walls, ceilings, and floors."

如果能够看出信息的推进模式，就会发现上一段结尾处的三个词中有两个跟后面段落的首句构成了同词复现，那么38空处一定要出现

small,选项中只有 D 选项 Small color choices are the ones we're most familiar with 匹配。

以上四种为常见的主位推进模式,下面两种比较少见。

(5)交叉型。第一句的主位成为第二句的述位,第二句的主位成为第三句的述位,第三句的主位又成为第四句的述位,如此交叉发展下去。(黄国文,1988:84)这个模式可以表示为:

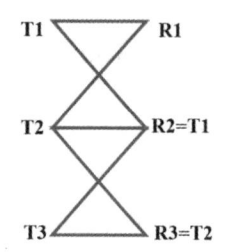

```
T1      R1
  ╲  ╱
   ╲╱
   ╱╲
  ╱  ╲
T2      R2=T1
  ╲  ╱
   ╲╱
   ╱╲
  ╱  ╲
T3      R3=T2
```

新概念英语中的这一段话是典型的交叉型主位推进的模式:"The play was interesting, but I didn't enjoy it. A young man and a young woman troubled me. I turned round and looked at them, but they didn't pay any attention to me."

第一句的主位 The play 是后一句中的述位 it,后一句的主位 I 是第三句中的述位 me,第四句中 I 又成为主位。第三句中的主位 a young man and a young woman 是下一句的述位 them,到最后一句中又成为主位 they。

(6)并列型。第一、三……组句的主位相同,第二、四……句的主位相同。(黄国文,1988:84)这个模式多用于表示对比,可以表示为:

T1 → R1
T2 → R2
T1 → R3
T2 → R4
⋮

下面的语段属于并列型的主题推进模式:"Americans eat with knives and forks; Japanese eat with chopsticks. Americans say "Hi" when they meet; Japanese bow. Many American men open doors for women; Japanese men do not."

2021 年全国新高考 Ⅱ 卷第三段的后半部分,勉强也能算并列结构:"A history book which may contain the facts in story form will be easier to read than one dealing with scientific subjects. In the former case you may be able to read a chapter. In the latter you may only be able to read one page."

无论空格处在什么位置，都涉及新信息的推进，可以从主位推进的角度分析。

（一）小标题或段首空

小标题设空，需关注语篇整体结构，参考其他小标题形式，选择符合条件的句子，并基于段落主旨，确保语义连贯性，选出最佳答案。

例如，2023年全国新高考Ⅱ卷七选五。语篇的首尾段和各段小标题如下：

"As an artist who shares her journey on social media, I'm often asked by curious followers how to begin an art journey... So I've put together some good tips for starting an art journey.

• Start small.

• Paint often and paint from life.

• Continually challenge yourself to try something new.

• 39. Seeking and accepting constructive feedback is crucial to growth. ...

The journey you're on won't follow a straight path. 40 Push through, give it time and put in the effort. You will harvest the rewards of an artistic life."

根据首段中的最后一句可知，这是一篇 how—to 的建议类说明文，文章结构是总分总。39 小题是小标题，根据前面三段的小标题，遵循平行结构，也应是祈使句。选项中符合条件的有四个：

A. Get out of your comfort zone.

B. Make career plans and set goals.

D. Share your work if you feel comfortable doing so.

F. Evaluate your performance and, if needed, redefine your role.

根据对所在段落的分析，空后句中心词是 feedback，加上后面以作者自身经历举例证明自己的观点。所以，答案选定为 D，只有分享才能获得反馈。

再如，2023年全国甲卷七选五。语篇有题目和段落项目符号，结构和内容清晰。Tricks to become a patient person 是典型的 how—to 类型的说明文,整个语篇是总分结构,前两个小标题分别是 practice gratitude 和 make yourself wait,39 小题也应该是祈使句。

·39.

So many of us have the belief that being comfortable is the only state we will tolerate, and when we experience something outside of our comfort zone, we get impatient about the circumstances. You should learn to say to yourself, "40." You'll then gradually become more patient.

符合条件的选项有三个,分别是:

A. Find your causes

B. Start with small tasks

C. Accept the uncomfortable

根据本段第一句话可知,本段提到了舒适是我们唯一能容忍的状态,也就是本段主旨与接受不舒适相关,C 选项中 uncomfortable 跟文段中的 comfortable 构成反义同现关系。

段首句除了作小标题外,通常是段落主旨,也可能是承上启下的过渡句。若段落使用演绎法构建,其核心通常位于开头,即首先明确主题,随后围绕该主题进行深入展开和说明。要判断段首句是否为主题句,关键在于分析它与随后句子之间的逻辑联系。若后续句子是对首句内容的详细解释、论证或具体描述,则首句即为该段落的中心思想。

另外,有些段落有明显的信号词,如 also, besides, finally, first, for example, next, second, to begin with 等,会有助于确定主题句的位置。当然,段首设空也可能是过渡句,可以根据语篇结构或前段尾句信息和空后句子的信息来锁定答案。

例如,2021 年北京卷中出现两个段首设空。各段主题句及设空句如下:

Para 1 Music could also be helping you with many other health problems behind the scenes.

Para 2 36. However, for the same reason, music can be very beneficial if one is in pain.

Para 3 Many people enjoy relaxing music in the evening prior to going to bed.

Para 4 When it comes to heart health, there is speculation that it's not the style of music, but rather the tempo that makes it so good for your heart health.

Para 5 39. But there is a whole range of other health issues that turning up the radio could be beneficial for, which is what makes music so valuable.

本篇文章采用总分总的结构，重点阐述音乐对身体健康的积极影响。第二段至第四段分别探讨了音乐在缓解痛苦、改善睡眠和增强心脏健康方面的益处。对于36空，尽管不是直接的主题句，但通过however的对比手法，其后是音乐可能带来的正面效果，其前则是对立信息，B选项中的harmful跟beneficial构成反义词同现。对于39空，作为总结段落的开头，强调了音乐在解决一系列其他健康问题上的益处，but表示递进，而非表示转折。E选项"The implications of music on overall well-being are really impressive."符合要求。

再如，2020年全国Ⅱ卷40空是典型承接前段尾句的过渡句：

"…Emoji can help communication feel friendlier, and even a serious note can be softened with an encouraging smile.

40, and emoji can contribute directly to that positive outcome. And when your employees begin adding smiling emojis to their business communication, you'll know you have succeeded in improving your work culture."

根据空后信息that positive outcome，空内信息一定积极正面，且下一句话中从句出现了smiling emojis，跟前段尾句内的an encouraging smile构成同义词复现，主句中心信息是improving your work culture，跟F选项Studies show that friendlier communication leads to a happier workplace中的a happier workplace构成同义复现，而且F选项中friendlier communication跟前段尾句communication, friendlier构成同词复现。由此可知，40空就是承接前段的过渡句。

（二）段尾句

在某些段落中，作者常先列出事实，随后逐步通过论证手法深化内容，直至揭示核心论点。若段落起始句不具概括性，则主题或总结句常见于段尾，用以强调或归纳。当观点难以解释或接受时，主题句或总结句常置于段末,起到画龙点睛或引入高潮的特殊效果。此类句子前常有逻辑连接词,如 consequently、hence、in conclusion, thus, therefore 等,或显性的词汇、语法衔接手段。段尾句也可能为过渡或细节句,需要关注逻辑关系词和词汇的复现来判断。

2023年全国新课标Ⅰ卷38题就是典型的段末总结句:

"At the top of a second page, put the heading 'Acts of kindness'. On this one, list all the positive things you've done for others. It might be the time when you helped …, when you did the ironing…, or when you baked cookies … 38.

You could ask a friend or family member to help add to your list."

38空所在段落的要求列出所有为他人做过的好事,下一段是朋友或家人添加列表,这样可以确定的是38空跟下段无关,只是段落总结句。其前的三个 when 并列句中列举的内容跟 F 选项中的 no matter how small 构成了上下义的关系,write down 跟 list 构成同义复现。

2023年全国新课标Ⅱ卷37题也属段末总结句:

• Paint often and paint from life. … to put in those brush miles…, paint from life as much as possible. 37.

• Continually challenge yourself to try something new.

本段主题句包含两个层面的信息 often, from life。本段的主题推进模式是派生型,二、三两句分别针对这两个点进行说明。最后是对整个段落的总结,G 选项中的 repetition 和 often 构成近义解释。

2020年海南高考卷第36题是典型的过渡句:

Talking freely with your doctor … Don't be afraid or embarrassed to discuss something that is bothering you. 36.

• Stay positive.

• Keep track of how you are feeling.

• 39.

• Ask questions.

根据文章结构可以看出,语篇是总分结构,在总和分交界的句子通常是过渡功能。给定选项中,只有 B 选项 "Here are some tips for talking with your doctor." 满足条件。

2023全国甲卷的36题是典型的承接上文的细节句:

"Here's a riddle:What do traffic jams, long lines and waiting for a vacation to start all have in common? There is one answer. 36."

根据题目 Tricks to becoming a patient person, 语篇是 how—to 类型的说明文。段首以谜语的形式提供了没有耐心的场景,引出下文的建议。36 空是对前文的回答,跟下文无关。F 选项中的 they all 代词指代前面提到的三种情况,且 use a little extra patience 跟文章主题相关。

2023 全国乙卷 39 题通过举例说明前一句话,也是承接上文的细节句:

Why are indoor plants good for you?

…They also remove some harmful chemicals from paints or cooking. 39.

Which plants can you grow?

这两个段落分别谈论不同的话题,39 空与下文无关。E 选项"Plants like peace lilies and devil's ivy are among the best."是对前一句举例说明。

四、利用语篇显性衔接手段判断七选五选项

对于七选五设空问题,可以利用句际逻辑关系和信息主位推进模式,当这些关系不明显时,可依赖语篇的显性衔接手段如代词指代、词汇同现和复现来判断。

"词汇衔接与指代是衔接机制的最明显的,也是最有效的衔接手段,两者结合可以组成衔接链,可以表达语篇的主要内容,特别是由中心标记组成的衔接链,可以直接反映语篇的中心内容和中心主题。"(张德禄、刘汝山:2003:207)

值得强调的是,词语复现策略虽高效,但非判断选项的唯一标准。实际上,应优先考虑含复现词的选项,但最终判断其正确性还需通过将其代入原文,检验其语境连贯性。

(一)利用代词照应关系进行判断

例如,2022 年全国新高考 I 卷 39 题:

"My partner posted her request … Her notice included what kind of training …, how many days … how many hours …, and her age. It also listed ... 39."

本段的信息主位推进模式是平行结构,第一句中的 request 跟后面的 notice 在该语境中同义,后面两句话分别以 her notice included 和 It also listed 开头,属于平行结构,末句要么是平行,要么是总结。比较选项,G 选项"Any notice for a training partner should include such information."中的 such 是典型的代词指示照应,回指上面两个句子中提到的信息。

再如,2021 年浙江 1 月高考第 34 题:

"Researchers have a good way to deal with this problem. Make all customers stand in one long, snaking line called a serpentine line—and serve each person at the front with the next available register. 34. This is what they do at most banks and fast-food restaurants."

34 空后面的 this 可以指代安排顾客以蛇形队伍接受服务这件事,整个句子是对前面做法举例解释。F 选项中的 registers 跟空前的 register 构成同词复现,this method 回指前面的做法,跟后面的 this 同时构成同词复现。

（二）利用词汇的同现和复现关系进行判断

1. 利用同词复现和反义词同现关系判断选项

例如,2023 年全国新高考 I 卷第 40 题:

"... most people learn not from their successes but their mistakes. The thing is, it's true. 40. We're all changing and learning all the time and mistakes are a positive way to develop and grow."

段中句要么是承上启下的过渡句,要么是跟上下文构成逻辑关系的细节句。空格前和后都出现了 mistake,根据信息推进,很有可能 40 空中还包含同样的信息。比对选项,G 选项中的 mistakes 跟上下文构成同词复现,其中的 fixed 跟后面的三个近义复现词 changing, develop and grow 构成反义词同现关系。

再如,2021 年全国新高考 II 卷第 40 题:

"Always keep a pencil and paper beside you. 40. Note also the facts important for your purpose as well as anything which leads you to further research..."

根据空后的句子结构和并列逻辑关系联系词 also 可知,40 空应该也是祈使句,对照选项,E 选项中的 importance 和后句中的 important 构成同词复现关系。

2. 利用词汇的上下义关系判断

如 2023 年全国新高考 I 卷 37 题:
"In a journal or on a piece of paper, put the heading "Personal strengths." 37. Are you caring? Creative? Generous? A good listener? Fun to be around? They don't have to be world-changing, just aspects of your personality that you're proud of."

根据段落信息主位推进,第一句和最后一句话述位相同,personal strengths 和 personality that you are proud of 属于近义词复现。第二句用多个问号分隔开的几个词,其实是两个述位的下义词,本段属于集中型主位推进模式,37 空中的述位很有可能还是个人优点。B 选项述位中 all the characteristics you like 跟那几个形容词仍是上下义复现。

高考七选五题型中,词汇的显性衔接和代词指代是常见且重要的解题技巧,这些例子非常丰富,这里就不一一列举了。

五、标点符号判断选项

(一) 利用分号判断两个相对独立但又相互关联的观点或事实

例如,2021 年全国甲卷 37 题:
"Invite 5—10 people so you have a nice selection. 37, and there may not be enough things to choose from; more than that, and it becomes uncontrollable."

段落主题句在段首,后面是解释说明。两个句子间以分号隔开,且句型结构平行,说明彼此独立但又相互关联。利用比较照应关系,定位答案为 A 选项 Less people than that。

（二）利用冒号的解释说明功能进行判断

例如，2021年浙江1月卷第33题：

"If there are three lines in the store, delays will happen randomly at different registers. Think about the probability: 33. So it's not just in your mind: Another line probably is moving faster."

本段中的两个冒号都表示解释和引出例证，用于解释前面提到的观点或引导后续的论述。D选项"The chances of your line being the fastest are only one in three."中的three跟前文three构成同词复现，并与后文提到的moving faster在语义上形成对比。

（三）利用问号来判断选项

如前面已经提到的2021年全国乙卷中第38题，利用问号判断平行段落，进而快速锁定答案。

（四）利用引号的特殊功能判断选项

例如，2021年全国甲卷第38题：

"38. They should also prepare plenty of reusable bags to carry their 'new' clothes home."

本段中new加上引号，表示特殊含义，指引号中的词语在具体的语言环境中产生了新的意思。根据语篇的说明对象，这里的new包含两层含义，一是新交换的，另一个是干净的。再加上also表达的并列，帮助锁定正确答案Tell everyone to bring clean clothes in good condition。

六、根据动词时态来判断选项

通过在特定文本中灵活运用动词时态和形态的交替，能有效呈现动作和状态的时间背景，区分过去与现在。这不仅能辅助读者跟踪叙述脉络，还能区分文本中对不同时间场景的描述。对于按时间顺序说明事物或阐述过去情况的说明文,分析动词时态有助于缩小选择范围,更精确地找到正确答案。

例如,2023年全国新高考Ⅱ卷第40题:

"The journey you're on won't follow a straight path. 40. Push through, give it time and put in the effort. You will harvest the rewards of an artistic life."

段落首句以将来时告诉读者未来的路不会平坦,尾句也以将来时描绘艺术生活带来的回报。根据空格后告诉该如何做,40空应该是对前句的具体描述和解释,时态上应该一致。E选项"You'll hit roadblocks, and you'll feel discouraged at times."符合条件。

再如,2020年全国Ⅲ卷第40题:

"Housewarming parties get their name from the fact that a long time ago people would actually bring firewood to a new home as a gift. 40. Now most homes have central heating and don't use fires to keep warm."

本段首句解释"暖房"的来源,时间是a long time ago,时态是过去时。空格后Now回到现在时,那么空格内一定是过去时。只有G选项"This was so that the person could keep their home warm for the winter."时态是过去时,且语义匹配。

动词的时体变化在记叙文中会更明显一些,所以做记叙文类的七选五时更需要关注时态变化。

例如,2021年全国新高考Ⅰ卷,文章介绍作者与丈夫在巴黎一周时间,体会巴黎人的生活方式,感悟巴黎的与众不同。前两段重点介绍两人的巴黎生活,时态是过去时,后面对其生活方式的感悟回到现在时,所以语篇前两段中的第36、37两题首先界定选项是过去时。

"My husband and I just spent a week in Paris. 36 So the first thing we did was rent … It was so tiny that we had to leave …

The place wasn't entirely authentic, though. …, the plumbing worked. 37. Our building even had a tiny lift … That is the only French phrase I mastered, …"

选项中只有C和F是过去时态,然后根据语境上下文匹配答案。

通过上面的所有分析可以看出,段落逻辑与衔接多样,答案角度多元,做题时需综合策略多角度验证答案准确性。

再如,2020年北京卷七选五的第二段:

"① 47. ② People who think positively demonstrate increased life spans, lower rates of depression and anxiety, better physical and psychological health, reduced risks of death from heart problems. ③ Positive thinking also contributes to one's ability to deal with problems and hardships. ④ 48. ⑤ For example, researchers have found that in the case of a crisis accompanied by strong emotions, such as a natural disaster, positive thinking can provide a sort of buffer against depression and anxiety. ⑥ Resilient people who think positively tend to treat every problem as a challenge, a chance for improvement of any kind, or as an opportunity for personal growth. ⑦ Pessimists, on the contrary, tend to perceive problems as a source of additional stress. ⑧ 49."

A. It doesn't cause any severe emotional discomfort, either.

B. Negative self-talk damages self-confidence and decreases self-respect.

C. It helps one to remain clear-headed and confident in difficult situations.

D. Positive thinking has several beneficial effects on the body and the mind.

E. As thinking changes, an individual's behaviour and habits change as well.

F. They often offer a real alternative to the common and regular way of thinking.

G. They often feel discouraged long before trying to solve the problem, even if small.

本段共有八句话,首句设空;第二句话说了积极思维带来的健康益处;第三句 also contribute to 表明跟第二句话平行;第五句以举例的方式,说明人们在伴随巨大情感波动的危机处理时,可以应对压力和焦虑,such as a natural disaster 解释 crisis; 回看第四句应该就是在应激状态下的优点,C选项中的 in difficult situations 跟 crisis 是同义词解释,remain clear-headed and confident 也是优点。第六句话仍然是优点,而第七句话 on the contrary 形成转折,开始说悲观者看问题的角度,由此可知,前六句话都在说乐观者心态的优点。第一句话处在段首,极有可能是主题句,后面几句构成平行关系。D 选项中的 several beneficial effects 刚好跟第二到第六句中的优点构成了上下义关系。前面说了积极心态的优点,对比之下,最后一句就应该是悲观思维带来的坏处,G 选项 "They often feel discouraged long before trying to solve the problem, even if small." 在语义上契合。本段的句际关系以图片形式展示如下:

本节介绍了多种解答七选五题目的策略和方法,但所有策略和技巧都应基于对语篇的全面、准确分析。解题技巧应该在明确文章主题、厘清文章逻辑和结构的基础上使用,任何脱离语篇文本的策略和技巧都如同空中楼阁,难以产生实效。

第五章 议论文文体

英语议论文旨在分析、评论或驳斥某一问题或事件,通过摆事实、讲道理、辨是非、呈数据等手段阐述作者的观点和立场。由于语篇理解难度较高,本章将关注课标要求、高考议论文考查和教材议论文语篇分析,指导读者如何审视观点、分析论据,并进行有力论证。深入阅读和细致分析将帮助读者理解作者意图和论证结构,进而提升批判性思维与书面表达能力。

第一节 课程标准对议论文语篇要求及其结构特征

本节主要介绍课程标准对议论文语篇的学习要求,并讨论议论文语篇特点及其结构特征,帮助学生创建议论文阅读的图式。

一、课程标准对议论文语篇的学习要求

英语学科核心素养中的"思维品质指思维在逻辑性、批判性、创新性等方面所表现出的能力和水平"(中华人民共和国教育部,2020: 5),着重于提升学生英语知识的理解、概括、分析与推理能力,并鼓励学生展开独立思考和创新思维。通过讨论争议性话题并借助多种证据来阐述观点,不仅陈述事实,还鲜明地反映了作者的情感倾向和立场。其常用的"设问、论据支撑、总结归纳"结构,为学生提供了学习批判性思维的宝贵资源。教师在议论文阅读教学中,可以充分利用这一优势,积极

影响学生的心智发展,帮助他们深化思维,同时促进批判性和辩证思维的形成与发展。

课程标准对议论文的要求都是从选择性必修课程开始,本身就说明了议论文的学习难度。课标对普通高中英语课程语篇类型内容要求帮助读者判断辨识哪些类型的语篇属于议论文体裁,便于读者阅读时快速开启议论文的格式图式,比较迅捷地抓住文章结构及中心论点。

另外,根据课程标准对高中阶段的议论文知识内容要求,高中议论文学习重在要求学生能够掌握其写作目的、语篇结构特征、论证方法和语篇标记词的语篇功能及常见用法。

二、议论文的语篇特点及结构特征

议论文是运用逻辑推理和论证技巧来阐述、证明某一观点或看法的文体。其核心目的在于通过正面提出见解或反驳错误观点,从而说服读者接受作者的立场。议论文通常由四个核心部分组成:

在构建议论文时,首先确立论题,指向作者欲探讨和解决的根本问题或议题。论点作为文章的精髓,承载着作者的观点、态度和立场,是整篇文章的导向和灵魂。为了支撑论点,作者会精心挑选和引入论据,这些论据可能源于学术理论、权威人士的观点、经典格言、具体案例或者经过科学验证的数据。论点和论据在议论文中相互映衬,共同构建文章的主体结构。最后,论证环节是将论据巧妙地用于支持论点的过程,通过举例、对比、类比、引用权威以及分析因果关系等多种手法,使论证过程更为有力,从而增强文章的说服力,让读者能够更容易地接纳并赞同作者的观点。

议论文应该观点明确、论据充分、语言精练、论证合理且有严密的逻辑。"议论文的特征是有一个中心观点,其余部分围绕该观点进行说明或论证。"(朱晓燕,2023:201)议论文归属于辩论语体,由于其内容主要是阐明事理的,它的结构就是论点与论点、论点与论据的关系和中心论点论证过程的体现。

议论文文体常采用主张—反主张模式和概括—具体模式两种结构。

主张—反主张模式也可以称为假设—真实模式。在这种模式中,作者首先提出一种普遍认可的主张或观点,然后进行澄清,说明自己的主张、观点,或者提出反主张或真实情况。作者会通过引用规则、法律、定理等来支持自己的论点,这类阅读理解题常会出相关的意图或态度题目。这类语篇的常见的标志词有：just as, like, similar, as, as if, but, however, otherwise, on the one hand, on the other hand, in contrast, although/though, while, even if/though, still, yet, nevertheless, nonetheless, despite, in spite of, regardless of, even so, contrary to 等。

在议论文中,概括—具体模式实质上遵循了演绎法的论证逻辑。首先,文章以概括性的介绍开篇,用以引出主题并明确提出论点。随后,论证部分深入展开,详细论述论点。最后,在总结部分,文章再次强调主要论点,并得出结论,形成完整的总分总结构。作者在论证过程中,通过寻找共同点、揭示规律或趋势,有力支持自己的论点。这种结构不仅有助于作者清晰地组织思路,也使读者能更容易地理解文章内容,把握文章的中心思想。

为了突出写作目的,议论文倾向于开篇直接切入主题,通过首段鲜明地阐述其核心观点,便于读者迅速且明确地把握作者的主要立场和观点。但不是所有的论点都在第一句,特别是要注意 however, yet, but 等转折词,论点往往在其后。

另有一些议论文,开篇时并不阐明观点,作者会先列举一系列相关论据,然后在最后一段或最后几段中呈现出总结性的论点,也就是归纳论证法。这种结构的目的是通过给予读者足够的信息和观点来引导他们逐步接受作者的观点和结论,常用于辩论类、分析类和讨论类议论文中。读归纳论证的议论文需要特别注意文章的尾段,因为尾段是对前面所举事例和分论点的归纳和概括。

除了常规的论证方式外,比较论证法也是议论文常用的论证策略,通常涵盖类比法和对比法,都属于从特定案例到另一特定案例的推理方法。类比法侧重于通过比较在某一属性或特征上相似或相近的不同事物,从而得出相应的结论。对比法则侧重于通过对比在某一特性上相反或对立的不同事物,来强化和证明某个论点,如教材语篇 Back to nature 是就是典型地运用了对比论证方式。此类文章需要注意事物的相同点以及不同点,并由此来把握文章的主旨。

在确立论点后,作者会展开详尽的论证,在论证的结尾,往往会针对论点给予清晰明确的总结,彰显作者的写作意图,同时体现文章承载的现实价值。简言之,议论文遵循着相对固定的逻辑结构,即先提出问题,随后深入分析,最终提供解决方案。结尾段一般包括两个内容:一是概括全文立场,呼应文中提及的分论点;二是展望未来,可以针对论点提出解决问题的措施或预测未来的发展方向。

为了方便教与学的理解和操作,可以把议论文的层次关系总结如下:

(1)总分式:总—分、分—总、总—分—总。

(2)并列式:几个论据之间属于平等并列关系。

(3)递进式:几个论据之间属于递进关系。

(4)对照式:把两种事物加以对比、分析、说明,突出其中一种。

议论文的主要结构简化为以下四种:引入话题—正反两方面观点—作者观点;提出问题—分析问题—解决问题;论点—论证—重申论点;常见观点、主张—作者观点—论证。

另外,高中教科书和高考中都比较常见的书评,作为议论文的一种,其结构比较特殊。跟影评相似,通常会在首段介绍书名以及主要的内容,接下来会介绍作者的情况,随后会介绍故事梗概及主要人物,甚至会从书中摘取书评作者印象深刻的片段,最后是对书的评价。

有时候,在判断语篇类型时,容易混淆说明文和议论文,特别是论说文里因为有说明的部分,更容易被认定为说明文。这也是为什么我们在查阅资料时,有时比较权威的来源也会对同一语篇的语体有不同的界定。细读,两者的区别还是比较明显的。

议论文的核心在于深入剖析事物、系统阐述事理、明确表达意见和坚定提出主张。为了论证观点的合理性与正确性,作者会运用摆事实、讲道理、明辨是非等多种手法,从而增强自己主张的可信度与说服力。其写作目的在于以理服人,阐明作者的主观立场,向读者表达明确的个人感情倾向。

议论文的核心在于深入剖析、系统阐述、明确表达和坚定主张。作者会运用摆事实、讲道理、明辨是非等多种手法,旨在以理服人,展现立场并表达情感倾向。议论文通常包含对立场的直接陈述,批判对立观点,选用鲜明词汇来增强说服力。

说明文的核心在于清晰地解释和阐述,其写作目的在于以知授人。解释客观事物的属性,或者对抽象的概念进行剖析,从而帮助读者全面理解事物的形态、结构、性质、分类、起源、作用以及它们之间的关系。虽然介绍新产品或新观点本身就是一种积极的态度,但说明文本身保持客观中立,不掺杂主观情感,也不使用具有强烈情感色彩的词汇。

议论文不仅需要说明作者自己的观点,还要努力让读者接受自己的观点。因此,在词语表达上除了客观之外,还比较委婉。在遣词造句方面多使用虚拟语气、让步状语从句和 can, may, might, could, would, should 等情态动词,以表达作者诚恳的态度和平等交流的语气。为了辩证推理的条理性和逻辑性,往往较多地使用像 since, now that, therefore, in that case, because, so, but, however, hence 等语篇标志词。

三、常见议论文开头模式

（一）对立式

先引出其他人的不同看法,然后提出自己的看法或者偏向于某一看法,适用于有争议性的主题。

例如,Book 2 Unit 4 *Good book, bad movie* 语篇就是对立式开头：

"They say that 'a picture is worth a thousand words', but the briefest look at books and the movies based on them would have anyone questioning this common saying. All too often, great words end up being turned into cinematic 'turkeys'."

2021 年高考新高考 I 卷 D 篇也属于对立式开篇模式：

"Popularization has in some cases changed the original meaning of emotional intelligence. Many people now misunderstand emotional intelligence ... Research has shown that emotional skills may contribute to some of these qualities, but most of them move far beyond skill-based emotional intelligence."

（二）现象式

引出要剖析的现象或者问题,然后评论。这种开头比较多见。

Book 2 Unit 2 *Time for a change* 的开头是典型的以现象开篇：

"A family dinner is an important tradition to celebrate Spring Festival. Nowadays, some people choose to have the dinner in a restaurant, but not everyone is keen on this idea. What do our readers think?"

Book 1 Unit 4 *Click for a friend* 的开头是以问题开篇，本质上也是对现象的说明：

　　"How would you feel if moving to a new town meant losing track of your friends? What if the only way of getting news from faraway friends was writing letters that took ages to be delivered? ... Thanks to advances in technology, how we make friends and communicate with them has changed significantly."

（三）观点式

　　开门见山，直接提出作者对要讨论的问题的看法。这种开头比较常见。
　　Book 2 Unit 2 *Time for a change* 中的两封信的开头直接亮出作者观点：

　　"We have eaten out for the Spring Festival family dinner for the last three years, and we have enjoyed it no less than eating at home. I don't understand why some people refuse to embrace the change.

　　For this year's Spring Festival family dinner, my son has booked a table at the best restaurant in town, but I'm a bit unhappy about it. For me, it just won't feel like Spring Festival having the dinner out."

（四）引用式

　　以名人名言或者有代表性的看法引出文章要展开论述的观点。
　　Book 3 Unit 1 *Little white lies* 中引用诗歌开头：
　　"Written more than two hundred years ago, these lines by Walter Scott remain one of the most well-known excerpts of Scottish poetry:
　　Oh, what a tangled web we weave,
　　When first we practise to deceive!"
　　选必 1 Unit 2 *We regret to inform you...* 语篇也是这种开头：
　　"'We regret to inform you...' These are the words that every writer dreads receiving, but words every writer knows well."

（五）比较式

通过对比今昔两种不同的倾向或观点，引出文章要讨论的观点。

Book 3 Unit 3 *Franklin's experiment: How much is true*? 语篇就是先从富兰克林实验对孩子们科学探索的重要作用开始，提出相反的观点：这个故事可能是编造的。

"Benjamin Franklin's famous experiment with lightning has introduced generations of children to science. However, new research suggests that the story may be fiction instead of fact."

（六）故事式

以简短的故事吸引读者的兴趣，引出文章的主题。

选必 4 Unit 6 *The call of the Challenger* 以历史事件导入，引发读者的兴趣：

"Ever since Neil Armstrong first set foot on the Moon back on 20 July 1969, people have become accustomed to the notion of space travel. Millions watched that first lunar landing on black and white television sets, their hearts in their mouths, aware of how arduous and hazardous an undertaking it was, and of the many things that could go wrong..."

熟悉以上的几种议论文开篇模式，会比较容易帮助读者判断文体，并能快速找到文章的论点以及语篇的组织模式，便于读者进一步探究语篇的写作目的、主旨大意、语篇结构和论证方法。

第二节 高考议论文考查点及教材议论文分析

高考英语阅读理解中的议论文，因其广泛的选材领域，如科技、环保、品格培养、人际沟通、教育和心理学等，乃至学科间的交融，其信息量尤为丰富。议论文的论述严谨,逻辑紧密,语言正式,常涉及生僻词汇、复杂句式及从句等高级语法结构。因其话题有可能超出学生的知识范畴,特别是在心理和文化方面,无疑提升了学生的理解难度。本节旨在分析高考议论文的考查形式,并通过教材实例深入探讨其语篇特点。

一、高考议论文语篇及考查

全国高考题中的议论文语篇较少,考查的主题语境主要是人与社会,考查的语篇数量在全国卷中逐年下降。虽然其在阅读理解题型中所占比重不大,但整体难度较大,是学生阅读中主要的失分点。

相较于其他体裁,学生在议论文方面更容易失分的原因是他们不仅需要具备良好的语言知识能力,还需要具备强大的思维能力。高考真题中的议论文多选自最新的国外报纸杂志,内容新颖,话题结构复杂且语言较为晦涩,充斥着许多生词甚至专业词汇,这成为学生阅读时主要的失分点之一。

议论文逻辑性强,主要从事实、主旨等方面出题,考查学生的思考和判断能力。从近几年高考题来看,议论文的考查以细节理解题和推理判断题为主,另有少量语篇和段落主旨题目,观点态度题较少,且难度有所增加。做题时必须根据议论文的语篇特点,厘清结构,抓住文章的主线,即论点、论据和论证方法,让自己的判断有理有据。

议论文中的细节理解题多数属于单细节题,因为涉及的内容比较单一,定位答案的大体位置相对简单,主要可以采用原文定位及原词复现方式解答。多细节题的解答在理解整体语篇环境的情况下,可以通过语篇衔接手段中的词汇衔接方式,仔细辨别原文和选项之间的关联,进行解答。

推理判断题形式多样,需根据议论文的客观信息和逻辑关系深入剖析,全面考虑所有相关信息以确保推理准确合理。解题时,应注意细节与原文词句的关联、实词的感情色彩,避免主观臆断,同时结合文体特点和篇章结构推断写作意图或出处。

主旨大意题、语篇来源或写作目的题需要学生通读文章,分析段落间关系,找到文章中的论点、论据和论证方法,引导学生据此去分析文章结构,培养其整体语篇意识,并基于图式精准地判断文章或段落主旨以及写作目的。这种题目通常无法从原文中找到原句,需要根据论点、论据进行归纳总结。

下面以最近三年高考题中的议论文为例,粗略分析议论文解读。

针对 2022 年全国乙卷 B 篇,首先识别首尾线索判断为书评,从而解答 27 题。通过书评结构图及题干关键词定位答案段落,运用阅读技巧进行细节比对和合理推断,解答其他题目(图 5-1)。

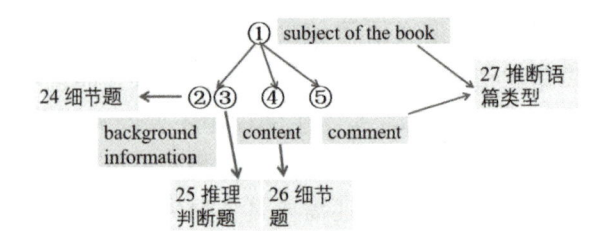

图 5-1 书评估结构图

2021 新高考 I 卷 D 篇,首先指出情商普及导致的误解,即视其为完美品质。作者随后界定情商,并举例论述。第二段强调情商普及的正面影响,第四段提及研究不足。最后,文章呼吁更科学、专业的情商研究,期待科技带来新视角。整体遵循"引入话题—分析问题—提出观点"的框架,指出研究局限并寄予厚望(图 5-2)。

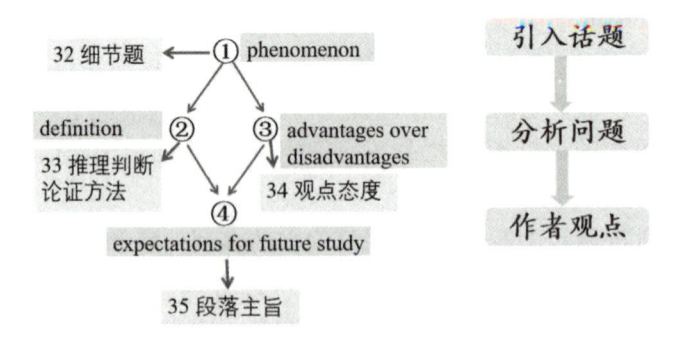

图 5-2 整体框架

2021 年全国甲卷 D 篇开篇两段设问引出论点,第三、四段分析过去天才标准排除多样人群的现象,特别以女孩为例。第五段全球交流背景下,现在不再以性别、种族和阶层等社会因素定义天才,而是提出新标准,回应开篇论点(图 5-3)。整篇遵循"提出问题—分析问题—解决问题"思路,主旨为 Geniuses take many forms。

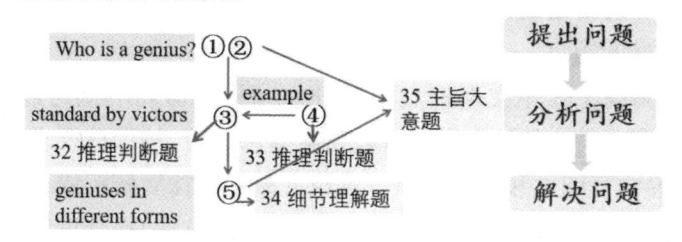

图 5-3 整篇思路分析

总之,议论文教学首先应该培养学生的整体语篇意识,理顺首尾段和其他段落的首句,紧扣议论文结构和段落间关系构建议论文的语篇结构图,从而迅速把握文章的话题、主旨要义和观点等重要内容,将题目和段落匹配,缩小答案范围。

根据上面的几个结构图可以看出,这些重要内容中的大部分是能力考查的命题点,需要给予足够重视。

二、教材议论文设题

根据课程标准对议论文语篇类型的界定,虽然高考中的语篇以说明文和记叙文为主,但外研版教材中的议论文语篇数量并不少,主要包括 10 篇论说文、1 篇科普类论说文、5 篇专题讨论、3 篇书评、2 篇议论文和 5 篇专栏或杂志文章。议论文语篇在选择性必修课程中占多数,难度递增,有利于学生渐进式学习。

针对议论文语篇主旨和结构的角度,教材语篇中出现过多种形式的设题,包括写作目的、解释文章题目或给文章重起题目、语篇来源、匹配段落主旨、语篇结构图等。其设题与高考题相似,考查能力点重合。

从论点角度,设置了观点和事实辨识题。辨识观点和事实是学生议论文学习中的一个难点,经常把事实当成观点,或者将自己的理解代入到原文语篇中,忽视作者的观点。

教材 Book 2 Unit 2 中明确给出了事实和观点的定义:事实是存在或已经发生的事件,或者是可以由证据证明的说法;观点是总体或个人的观点、信念或印象,更多是主观的判断,可以由标志词 feel, believe 或 think 等辨识。简言之,论点就是论题和对论题的评价的结合。

从论证方法角度,教材设题中出现过例证、对比和因果关系等论证方法。

从推理判断题的角度看,教材设题中出现了归纳观点并从语篇中寻找支撑信息的题目。

教材和高考议论文考查点相近,再次证明:教材和高考题是一标两用的教与评手段。教学中应重视教材素材和练习,按课标要求,采用合适策略,培养语言能力和思维品质。议论文教学需深度解析语篇,引导学生剖析论点、论据、论证,激发思考,促进高阶思维发展,提升思维品质。

三、教材议论文分析

本小节以外研版教材 Book 1 Unit 4 *Click for a friend?* 为例进行语篇分析。该语篇是一篇论说文,文章结构清晰,作者的观点陈述和论证层层展开。语篇的结构图式如图 5-4 所示。

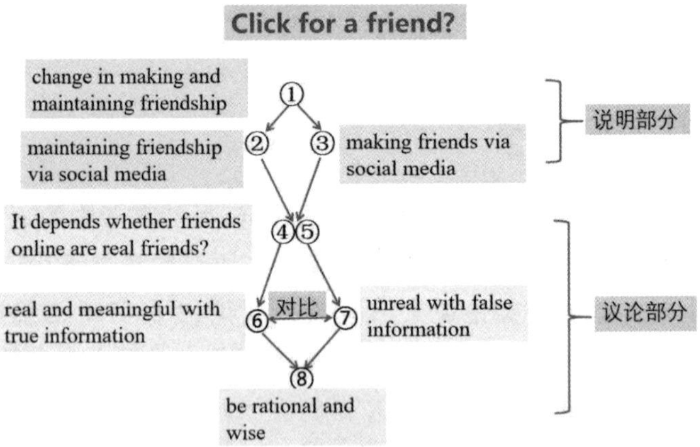

Click for a friend?

- change in making and maintaining friendship ①
- maintaining friendship via social media ② ③ making friends via social media —— 说明部分
- It depends whether friends online are real friends? ④⑤
- real and meaningful with true information ⑥ 对比 ⑦ unreal with false information —— 议论部分
- ⑧ be rational and wise

图 5-4　语篇的结构图式

语篇开篇以设问的方式,引出在结交新友和维护友谊的方式发生了改变。在说明部分,作者以派生型信息推进方式展开说明,分别就第一段中提到的结交新友和维护友谊方面,说明网络为我们提供了便利。

在议论部分,作者仍然以设问的方式,提出了论点:网上交的朋友未必是真朋友。论证部分,以对比的方式从两个角度展开论证,启发读者思考社交媒体这一快捷的交友工具可能存在的弊端,最后得出结论:我们不能因噎废食,可以网上交友。并以亚里士多德的名言结尾,使论证更具说服力。如果接下来还要继续写的话,应该就要从正面给出网上交友的建议了。

作者在文章的推进过程中,采用了先扬后抑的方式。在说明部分说明网络对结交新友和维护友谊的优点,议论部分强调网上交友可能存在的问题,最后得出自己的结论。整个语篇遵循着"引入话题—正反两方面观点—作者观点"的模式,论证层层推进,非常具有说服力。

以上是笔者备课过程中对语篇的整体解构,在教学实践中,我们需要遵循着"学习理解,应用实践,迁移创新"的思路,以问题链的形式,循着课标中的语篇分析结构框架,由浅入深逐渐引领学生探究语篇的主题意义。

问题链的设计,可以参照梁美珍老师(2011)提出的问题类型(表5-1):

表5-1 问题类型及其认知复杂性

问题类型	展示型		参阅型		评估型	
认知层次	识记	理解	应用	分析	综合	评价
提问者对答案的预知程度	强		中		弱	
作答者对文本的依赖程度	强		中		弱	

梁老师将问题划分为展示型、参阅型和评估型三类。

展示型问题旨在帮助学生记忆和理解文本信息,在回答时往往需参照教材内容,比较并识别文中的细节,进而分析这些细节之间的关联性,从而直接在文中找到答案。

参阅型问题是在学生已经理解并掌握了文本中的事实性信息后,教师为了深化学生对文本的理解而提出的。通常围绕文本中的关键点和可延伸的内容设计,答案并不直接出现在课文中。学生在回答时需要分析文章的信息、梳理其发展脉络、把握作者的情感,并结合自己的理解提出创新观点。学生对教材的依赖程度适中,而教师对学生答案的预知程度也处于中等水平。

评估型问题出现在文本处理的最后阶段,旨在加深学生对话题的理解,帮助他们培养有效解决问题的能力和积极态度。问题的答案需要学生基于整体阅读的理解,结合个人生活经验,进行思考和解答。学生在回答评估型问题时,较少依赖教材,且由于问题的开放性和深度,教师往往难以预先知道学生的具体答案。

下面是笔者基于教材内容,参考梁美珍老师的问题类型,为该语篇设计的问题链:

读前预测:

Q1. Based on the picture and the title, predict what the passage talks about.

根据图片和一般疑问形式的题目,学生能比较顺利地猜到语篇的话题。疑问句做题目,其功能通常用来提出一个普遍存在的问题或观点,鼓励读者思考或讨论该问题,其答案通常是主观的,取决于每个人的看法和经验。

导入环节:

Q2. How do you usually make friends?

Q3. What do you do to maintain your friendship?

这两个铺垫型问题用来了解学生的交友和维护友情的方式,同时帮助学生更好地理解和思考相关课文内容,构建话题与自身生活的关联,为课文学习作好铺垫。

阅读环节:

阅读过程遵循着语篇分析框架的 what, how, why 的顺序进行设问,主要从 read for content, structure and attitude, read for approach, read for purpose, read for thought 等方面进行设问。

Q4. Read the passage to get the main idea of each paragraph and construct the whole passage.

Q5. What's the author's attitude towards online friendship? Give your reason(s) by using supporting details in the text.

Q6. Find out the advantage(s) social media can bring us in making and maintaining friendship.

以上三个展示型问题针对文本内容理解,考查的是学生对文本的理解和结构的抓取,以及了解作者对网络交友的态度,并进一步细读,找到支撑结论的细节。

Q7. What's the purpose of the two questions in Para.1?

Q8. How does the author present his/her attitude towards online friendship?

Q9. Why did the author quote Aristotle in the last paragraph?

这三个问题偏重于参阅型,针对语篇的写作手法及论证方式,引导学生理解作者如何逐步论证自己的观点和态度。

Q10. Why does the author say "But this doesn't mean that we should throw the baby out with the bathwater"? Are there any similar sayings in Chinese?

Q11. What's your opinion on making friends online?

Q12. Someone wants to "friend" your best friend online, and he/she comes for your advice. Please give your ideas.

这三个开放式的问题偏重于评估型,主要是启发学生深入思考,运用课堂学过的知识创造性地探究主题意义。

教师在准备议论文教学时,应深入研读教材语篇,明确语篇的核心论点,梳理各部分之间的逻辑关联,并绘制出清晰的思维导图以辅助理解。基于思维导图和对学生学习能力的预判,设计层次分明、条理清晰的问题序列。阅读中指导学生采用个体独立解决或者合作学习的方法逐步解答问题,进而提升知识掌握水平,强化其问题探究与解决能力。"问题链不仅可以帮助学生进行推论理解,还可以为评鉴理解提供支撑。"(钱剑英等,2015:67)经过这样的学习和训练,学生能有效掌握学习议论文的方法,并能有条理、有策略地理解遇到的议论文语篇。

第六章 阅读中的词汇教学

对于英语学科而言,阅读是进行所有学习任务的前提和基础,而词汇是理解语篇的基础,依托文本而存在,是构成语篇的最基本单位。语篇则提供了语言运用的情境供学生学习词汇。在高中英语学习中,词汇量的多少在一定程度上决定了英语水平的高下。然而,实际学习过程中,很多学生最大的问题是词汇量不够,导致阅读理解困难,写作能力不强。英语学习中,并不要求学生全面掌握所有词汇的音、形、意、用。很多词汇属于阅读词汇,能通过阅读理解文章内容,并能够抓住文章的主题、情感态度和价值观等就足够了;而对于核心的写作词汇,则必须全面掌握,并能够根据交际目的正确运用。

第一节 高中学生英语词汇学习的挑战与应对

本节主要分析高中生词汇学习方面存在的问题,以及可以采用的学习策略。

一、高中学生在词汇学习方面存在的问题

一个人的词汇量直接影响着他们的交流能力和语言表达能力。学生在词汇学习中存在的困难可以归结为以下几种。

（一）部分学生发音不准确

这种不准确妨碍了他们将音、形、义有效结合，不仅使学生难以理解词汇的含义，还妨碍了单词拼写与意义的关联。这是学习新词汇时常见的问题。准确发音对于理解语音、语法规则至关重要，影响自然拼读法的应用，并关乎人际交流的效果。

（二）构词法知识掌握不足

学生若未掌握构词法知识，即创造新词的规则与方法，将难以理解和记忆新词汇。在阅读中，他们无法利用构词法推测词义，可能导致因个别核心词汇理解障碍而影响整体理解。逐个字母记词汇不仅效率低下，且记忆难以持久，使学生不得不花费大量时间重复记忆，却收效甚微。面对课程标准要求的数千个词汇和短语，学生往往感到难以应对，产生畏难情绪。

（三）缺乏有效的学习策略，脱离语境、一视同仁地记忆所有教材中或词汇书中的词汇

很多教师仍采用脱离语境的词汇教学方法，试图在开始单元教学前消除词汇障碍。然而，这种方法忽略了词汇的实际应用语境，导致学生难以在阅读中自然习得词汇。缺乏上下文的理解，学生难以在口头和书面表达中准确运用所学词汇。

阅读和表达对词汇的需求各不相同。对于表达中常用的词汇，学生应在语境中全面掌握其音、形、义；而对于阅读词汇，重点应确保不影响阅读理解。特别是高中低年级的学生，主要任务是快速适应难度较大的阅读材料，而不是全面记忆词汇拼写。过高的词汇记忆要求可能会打击学生学习英语的积极性。因此，教师应筛选词汇，降低记忆难度和数量，学生也应根据实际需要选择性记忆。

词汇在语境中的理解和运用能力对评估学习者的整体词汇能力起着决定性作用。然而，在当前的教学模式中，教师常采用默写这一形式来检验学生的词汇学习成果。尽管默写可以检验词汇的拼写和发音，但它无法全面反映学生在实际语境中理解和运用词汇的能力。这种脱离

语境的检测方式不仅使学生陷入低效的死记硬背,而且难以保证词汇的长期记忆和实际应用。

(四)高考难度提升,其中词汇量的增长尤为显著

除了规定的少量超纲词汇,还新增了由派生或转化形成的词汇,且未附带汉语释义。同时,阅读材料难度提升,内容常超出学生认知和个人经验。这些变化导致学生需要掌握的内容增多,出现习得性无助,对词汇学习的动机减弱,内生动力不足。

(五)部分学生主要依赖课本学习语言,课外阅读量偏低

课外阅读量不足限制了他们接触词汇的多样性和数量,进而影响词汇的丰富度。课外阅读是学生深入理解和应用词汇的关键,通过多样化文本和语境,学生可以更好地掌握同一词汇的不同用法。课外阅读量不足会削弱学生对词汇的深入理解和应用能力,并可能影响对文章整体结构和逻辑推理的理解,导致词汇运用不够准确。因此,根据高中英语课程标准,教师应积极创造条件,满足学生的课外阅读需求。

(六)学生往往缺乏在表达中主动运用新学词汇的意愿

准确使用词汇需要全面考量语境、词义以及写作技巧,尤其在面对多义词时,其意义会因语境而变化。害怕出错的心理在一定程度上抑制了学生使用新词的意愿。记忆词汇是一个与实践紧密结合的过程,频繁地运用所学词汇进行阅读、听力、口语和书写等活动,有助于加深记忆并巩固学习效果。相反,被动学到的知识更容易随时间流逝而遗忘。

二、词汇学习的策略与方法

词汇离不开语篇,词汇学习离不开阅读。在阅读教学中如果缺乏对词汇的处理,会给阅读造成障碍和困扰。在以语篇为本的教学模式下,教师必须采取有效的词汇学习策略来帮助学生理解、记忆、运用词汇,才能确保学生的词汇量和阅读能力都能得到提高。

课程标准提出了几种学习策略,包括元认知策略、认知策略、交际策略和情感策略。这些策略可以运用到英语学习的方方面面,具体到词汇学习,我们可以采用有效方法帮助学生提升学习效率,并创造机会让学生运用元认知策略计划、安排、监控、调整、评价自己的学习进度和方向。

(一)确定明确的词汇学习目标

英语词汇学习旨在实现识记、领会、运用和交际四个递进的目标,从基础的拼写、发音、词义开始,逐步深化到对词性的理解和用法的掌握,进而在多种情境中准确应用词汇,并最终达到自如地运用词汇进行有效交际。在这一过程中,学生需要通过不断地学习和实践来深化对词汇的理解和吸收。教师应明确词汇教学目标,结合阅读教学进行词汇教学,确保学生专注于核心内容的学习。

在阅读过程中,处理的词汇并非仅限于单元生词,而应基于文本内容、教师的深度解读以及学生的学情进行选择。这些词汇应有助于文本理解,能结合学生已有认知图式在特定情境中有效处理,并通过梯度性任务促进词汇学习的循环和提升。重点关注三类词汇:与阅读核心内容紧密相关的词汇、阻碍学生理解的词汇,以及在特定语境中具有特殊含义的词汇。对于各类词汇的学习要求,应遵循课程标准,避免过度扩展或缩减学习范围。

(二)引入图式理论能显著提升词汇学习效率

图式理论认为,人们通过构建和激活知识网络来理解和记忆信息。在词汇学习中,该理论鼓励学生建立词汇间的联系,以加强记忆。学习新单词时,学生可以将其与相关的词汇、主题、情景等形成词汇网络,利用已有的语境知识、词汇联想等来帮助记忆。教师可以利用图式理论的特性,指导学生拆解词汇结构,重新组合,以此增强词汇记忆效果。以 subject 这个词为例,可以将其拆分为 sub- 和 ject,然后跟其他前缀、后缀分别组成新的词,如 subway, sub-Saharan, submit, reject, inject, project 和 object 等,构建词汇记忆图式,降低学生的背诵难度,提高背诵兴趣。

(三) 重视学生的语音知识学习

义教版课程标准（2022）中对语音知识内容要求包括语音、语调、节奏等。

语音和语义密不可分，语言依靠语音实现其社会交际功能。要重视学生的语音学习。课程标准对语音教学有这样的提示："高中阶段的语音知识……，侧重通过实践增强学生的语感，体会语音知识的表意功能，帮助学生建构语音意识和语音能力。……使学生学会逐步借助语音知识有效地理解说话人的态度、意图和情感，同时表达自己所希望传递的意义、意图、观点和态度。……帮助学生形成一定的语感、提高表达的自信心和流畅性。"（中华人民共和国教育部，2020：20-21）

(四) 强调学生在语境中的识词、记忆词汇

课程标准对词汇教学有明确的提示"词汇学习不是单纯的词语记忆，也不是独立的词语操练，而是结合具体语境、在特定语境下开展的综合性语言实践活动……，感知、理解相关主题意义，使用词语表达相关话题的信息和意义。……构建不同词汇语义网，积累词块，扩大词汇量，并在大量的语言学习活动中，强化语感，迁移词语运用能力，最终做到词语内化。"（中华人民共和国教育部，2020：22）

词汇学习已经超越单纯的词语记忆，而是涵盖了特定模式、语法规则，适用于各种环境并承载特定意义的语言单元。充分利用语篇语境记忆单词，体现了王初明教授在其"英语学对用好歌"中所说的："伴语境，不可缺，语境丰，语感强。英美人，真语境，与互动，话地道。"强调了语境的重要性，指出丰富的语境能增强语感。词汇学习与语篇语境密不可分，词本无意，皆由境生。教师应引导学生以语用为目标，在情境中学习词汇，并在上下文中理解和演练。不建议学生课前预先查找生词或预习篇章，而是鼓励他们通过阅读技巧处理生词，提高真实的阅读技能。词汇处理服务于阅读，但需注意词汇的语篇敏感性，即在不同语境中可能有不同含义。因此，课堂活动中应巧妙融入目标词汇，确保词汇处理不影响阅读进度，同时保持与文本的紧密联系，避免随意拓展。

在词汇教学中，教师应精准控制每堂课的词汇学习量，避免过量或

过于细化地学习导致学生产生学习压力,进而影响其兴趣和信心。在阅读教学中,应紧密围绕教学目标和语篇主题,设计富有层次和目的的词汇学习任务,使词汇教学与上下文语境自然结合,帮助学生通过实际语境理解词汇含义。

在阅读的导入阶段,对于可能阻碍阅读的新词汇,教师可以采用结构图、构词法、图表、多媒体等多种教学手段,有效增加学生的语言知识储备,提升其对文本主旨的理解能力,并为进一步的目标词汇学习奠定基础。

阅读过程中,学生应在文本的脉络和语境中自然感知和理解词汇,避免脱离文本主题的过度拓展。对于频繁出现的词汇,教师应引导学生进行适当的归纳和总结,帮助他们形成词汇间的联系和记忆网络。

阅读后,教师可以设计情境化的学习任务,让学生在真实的语境中运用所学词汇,达到深度掌握的目的。同时,鼓励学生进行群文阅读,接触多样化的语篇和语境,通过上下文推测词汇意义,理解词汇的多样性和灵活性,提升词汇学习的效率和质量。

在词汇教学中,教师应注重词汇的语义网络和短语搭配,引导学生构建词汇间的逻辑联系。通过分析语篇中的词汇重复和词汇间的搭配关系,不断拓展学生的词汇认知,形成结构化、情境化的词汇知识体系,增强对词汇的记忆和应用能力,进而提高学生的整体语言素养。

(五)利用词块学习提升词汇学习效率

词块是一种综合了语法、语篇、语言功能等语言要素的一种语言结构。词块理论认为,无论是学习记忆,还是使用输出,人们都是通过固定或半固定的结构完成的。"Michal Lewis 认为词块分为四种:单词和短语、高频搭配的单词、惯用话语、句子框架。"(转引自高宝光,2022)词块学习就像运用预制板盖楼,不需要经过特别分析,可以直接记忆,且随时能够调用。

高中英语课程标准要求词汇学习是"重点是在语境中培养学生的词块意识,并通过广泛阅读,进一步扩大词汇量,提高运用词汇准确理解和确切表达意义的能力。"(中华人民共和国教育部,2020:21)

课程标准着重强调动词、介词、名词、形容词和副词词组在习惯搭配和表达上的学习。通过学习和记忆词块,可以显著减轻记忆负担,深入理解词汇在特定语境下的运用和含义,从而避免孤立记忆单个词汇的局限,使记忆过程变得更为高效和便捷。此外,词块中的词汇相互关联,通过它们的共同特点、语义联系或语法关系形成一个整体,有助于建立词汇之间的联想记忆。一旦能够迅速识别和表达常见的词块,我们的语言表达将更为自然流畅,减少停顿,实现更加连贯的沟通。"在主题意义引领下的词块学习能够有效提高学生准确理解和确切表达意义的能力,有助于学生深度理解语篇,并影响学生的思维发展和语言学习成效。"(徐国辉等,2023)

(六)加强重复

语言学与心理学中提到的"七次复习法"是基于"序列记忆效应"的一种理论。它主张要成功记住一个词语,需进行多次复习,每次复习都强化了该词汇在记忆中的位置。特别是首尾的信息更易被记住,而中间的信息则较易遗忘。实践这一方法时,关键在于分散,即多次复习,而非一次性重复七次。尽管次数不必严格限定为七次,但频繁复习对于巩固长期记忆至关重要。虽然此方法尚缺乏确凿科学依据,但根据实践经验,它确实能有效提升记忆效果。

(七)优化词汇检测方式

为了提高词汇检测的全面性和有效性,教师应结合语境来设计检测活动。这样做不仅能评估学生猜测词义和运用词汇的能力,还能促进他们的阅读能力、逻辑思考和推理等多元能力的发展。此外,语境下的词汇检测方法多样,如同义词替换练习、句子翻译以及交际任务等,这些方法有助于学生积累词汇、提升英汉双语切换能力,并在实践中调整词汇学习策略。

在词汇检测过程中,教师应确保以下几点:检测内容与学习目标紧密相连,题目设计需融入有效的语境,同时检测形式应多样化、层次化,以确保检测的科学性和有效性。

（八）教师要努力增加自身的词汇量

教师在教学活动中用词的丰富程度对学生词汇量的增长有着至关重要的影响。本身词汇量不太大的教师，可能无法准确理解和解释生词或复杂词汇，无法给学生提供丰富的词汇背景知识，限制了学生对文章内容的理解和积累词汇的能力。

相反，当教师采用多样化且丰富的词汇进行教学时，能明显促进学生词汇量的快速增长。这种教学方式不仅使课堂内容生动有趣，引发学生的情感共鸣和学习热情，还使学生在不断挑战中深入理解单词的意义、用法和搭配，进而有效扩大词汇量，并提升阅读理解和交际表达能力。在教学实践中，教师应避免因为学生暂时的困惑而减少英语使用或过度依赖汉语解释，以确保学生获得更多直接接触英语的机会，并防止学生养成惰性。

（九）培养学生查词典的习惯，准确把握词汇音、形、义、用

"工欲善其事，必先利其器"。要想学好英语，一本好的英汉双解词典是手头必备的工具，当然对于水平高的学生，也可以一步到位，直接使用英英词典。在我们缺乏语言运用情境的前提下，只有常常向不说话的老师请教，我们才能真正在写作中写出地道的语言。

那么，究竟怎么查、查什么却是需要我们思考的。

三、利用词典帮助学生学习地道英语

第一，要深入了解词汇的基本信息。我们要掌握词的发音、拼写及词性。对于动词，需要辨别是及物动词还是不及物动词，是规则动词还是不规则动词，熟悉第三人称单数及过去式、过去分词的拼写。若是形容词，需要了解是用作表语还是定语，掌握形容词的比较级和最高级。对于副词，则要区分它是修饰整个句子还是仅针对动词，等等。这些基本信息的掌握是词汇学习的关键，应通过查阅词典中的例句来准确判断和应用。

第二，通过英语解释了解确切词义非常重要。世界上没有任何两种

语言是完全对等的,汉语解释很多时候并不能准确传递英语单词的确切含义。学生在语言运用中的错误,往往源于对词汇确切意思的缺乏理解。要准确把握某些词汇的细微差别,查阅英语解释是关键。比如,我们曾做过一个完形填空,里面有这样一句话:

When we practice, our teacher will watch to choose who will dance in the performances. She picks girls with graceful leg and hand ____.

这个题的答案是 movements,但学生们多数选 gestures。

朗文词典给出两个词的解释分别是:

Movement: an act of moving your body, or the way someone moves their body

Gesture: a movement of part of your body, esp. your hands or head, to show what you mean or how you feel

查完词典后,学生会明白,因为原题中提到了 leg,所以 movements 比 gestures 更适合。

同一篇文章中还有一处:…then colors her feet and fingertips red. The red marks help the audience to see what we are doing and make the gestures look very beautiful. 对照英语解释,这里的 gestures 显然用得不合适,学生们也能立马看出问题所在。在这个过程中,他们既学会了批判性思维,又学会了词的确切用法,交际中就能避免同样的问题。

学生曾做过一篇阅读,有这样的一段:In 1795, Napolcon Bonaparte offered a reward to whoever could develop a safe food preservation method for his traveling army. Nicholas Appert took on the challenge, and about 15 years later introduced a method that involved heat—processing food in glass jars with wire and sealing them with wax. His second technique is similar to the one some people still use sealing jars with paraffin wax—a method, FYI, which is no longer considered safe.

学生做完题目之后,给他们提出一个问题:Guess the meaning of the word "technique"。因为在上下文中,method 同词复现三次,还有 ones 的替代功能,给足了猜词的提示。但是,有学生反过来问,怎么能确定 1810 年 Nicholas 第一次提出的方法呢? 这里涉及 introduce 的确切含义。根据朗文词典给出的英语解释,无论哪个词条,共性都是

for the first time 或者 start。针对这个语境,词典如此解释: to bring a plan, system, or product into use for the first time。这解决了学生的困惑,也让他们意识到序列的表达不一定全靠数字呈现。

同样的例子出现在 2016 年全国高考 I 卷的阅读 A 篇,介绍四位各行业中的女性开拓者。当时问题较多的是 24 小题,很多人选不出正确答案 C:

24. What can we infer about the women mentioned in the text?

   A. They are highly educated.   B. They are truly creative.
   C. They are pioneers.   D. They are peace-lovers.

错因主要在于对词汇的理解不到位。首先,很多学生不知道 pioneer 的确切含义: someone who is important in the early devel-opment of something, and whose work or ideas are later developed by other people。其次,在原文中没有关注到表示"发起""开创"等意思的词汇。对 Jane Addams(1860—1935),原文直接表述"Addams became the first American woman to win the Nobel Peace Prize."这个表述很直接;对 Rachel Carson(1907—1964),原文给出的是虚拟语气的句子,强调 Carson 的开创性:"If it weren't for Rachel Carson, the environmental movement might not exist today." 对 Sandra Day O'Connor(1930—present),原文表述为 the first woman to join the U. S. Supreme Court;而对 Rosa Parks(1913—2005),原文是这样表述的:"But it also set off the Montgomery bus boycott. It lasted for more than a year, and kicked off the civil-rights movement."这里有两个 off 短语都能说明问题, set off 英语解释里有这样的一条: to make something start happening, esp. when you do not intend to do so,也就是汉意的"引起,激发";而 kick off 的本意是 starts a football game, a meeting or an event。如果学生能确切知道这些核心句型或短语的解释,这个题目就迎刃而解了。

学生应用文习作中,经常会在结尾处写出这样的句子: "I appreciate you for your help." 典型的汉语式英语。学生经过查词典,得到了这个词的几种确切用法。其中,在他们常用的表达"感激"这个意思时,词典解释为: used to thank someone in a polite way or to say that you are grateful for something they have done. 朗文词典给出了三个例子:

Thanks ever so much for your help, I really appreciate it.
I appreciate your concern, but honestly, I'm fine.

I'd appreciate it if you let me get on with my job.

这些例句非常好地解决了学生使用过程中的问题。一个是 appreciate 表达感谢的意思时,后面跟 something;另外,如果跟宾语从句,需要加 it 作形式宾语。这种用法是很多学生在写求职信或求助信等应用文时结尾句常错的点,总是漏掉 it。

第三,要看词的情感色彩。学过的词要尽可能创造语境运用,才会内化为自己的东西,但一定要利用词典来确保词汇的准确理解和运用。

在学生学了 terribly 这个词之后,在他们的作文中出现不少这样的句子,"I'm terribly eager to get your help." 作文反馈时,笔者让学生观察并查了词典,反馈回来一组实例:

I'm terribly sorry—did I hurt you ?

It's terribly important for parents to be consistent.

They suffered terribly when their son was killed.

The experiment went terribly wrong.

The team played terribly.

通过观察这些句子,能看出这个词的情感色彩,很多学生在这个词的英语解释 very, extremely 的基础上,给出了同义词 badly, desperately, terrifically 等,通过进一步查词典看例句,了解其情感色彩。这样的词汇积累一方面保证了交际用词的多样化,另一方面确保语用准确。

学生习作过程中,表达"坚持"这个词褒义用法时经常会用到短语 insist on。在查过词典之后,学生了解了这个短语的确切用法:to keep doing something, especially something that is inconvenient or annoying,朗文词典给出的例句是:"She will insist on washing her hair just when I want to have a bath."

随后,笔者给学生提供了 persevere 和 persist in doing 两个替代词汇。查过之后,学生清楚地明白如果要表扬某人坚持的话,最好用 persevere。因为朗文词典对这两种表达的解释分别是:to continue trying to do something in a very determined way in spite of difficulties—use this to show approval; to continue to do something, although this is difficult, or other people oppose it,分别给出不同的例句:

It can be tricky at first, but persevere.

He persevered with his task until he had succeeded in collecting an armful of firewood.

He persisted in his refusal to admit responsibility.

She persisted with her studies in spite of financial problem.

从两种表达的词条解释和例句可以看出，persevere 是纯粹的褒义词，而 persist 是中性词，可褒可贬。所以，使用时一定要仔细斟酌，用对这几种表达的感情色彩。

第四，要查词汇的使用频率。查词典时，应关注词汇的使用频率，这有助于确定对词汇的理解及掌握程度的要求。教学中，我们应紧密围绕课程标准，聚焦核心词汇的学习与掌握，确保学生对其有深入的理解和恰当的运用。但在写作实践中，部分学生倾向于使用所谓的"高大上"的超纲词汇，往往因使用不当降低了表达的准确性。我们可以引导学生参考词典中标注的高频词汇，鼓励他们使用核心词汇来表达，避免选择过于生僻或不易理解的词汇。教师应强调使用核心词汇的重要性，避免学生追求超出读者认知范围的词汇，一方面因为学生可能对这些词汇的用法不够熟悉，容易出现错误；另一方面，晦涩难懂的文字难以抓住读者的心。

第五，查词典时要注意英语和美语的不同。随着英语的全球化趋势，可以说一千个说英语的人，有一千种英语发音，所以我们不必强求自己或学生一定要说美式英语还是英式英语，只要是语用准确，哪种都可以。但有些词汇在英式英语和美式英语中是有差异的，有一些如果单凭经验而不去查词典会认为是错误的，如"在周末"，英语和美语有不同的表述，可以说 at weekends，也可以用 on the weekend，这些只要翻翻词典都能掌握。查词典有助于学生准确理解词汇意思，提升语言表达能力，培养批判性思维，确保提供准确的语料。

近几年高考真题的各个题型，甚至是听力中，都出现了大量熟词新义的用法，这就要求学生要多读原版的文字，学地道的表达，同时遇到这种熟词生义一定要查词典。积累多了，语言的表达能力也就提高了。

对词汇学习，教师必须有明确的学习和教学目标，采用各种策略，以语篇为依托，以语篇整体学习为导向，对词汇进行从学习理解、实践运用和创新迁移等三个层面的学习。逐渐培养学生的自主学习能力，开展自主、合作与探究式学习，形成良好的学习习惯和有效的英语学习策略，扩大学生词汇量的基础上，提升阅读理解能力。

第二节　利用高考真题探求阅读猜词技巧

在阅读语篇文本过程中，除了陌生词汇，还有很多在新语境中的"熟词新义"，也会影响学生对文本的解读。尤其是考试中，即便掌握了语篇的结构特征，学生也不能完全理解阅读中的生词，更何况还有熟词生义的情况。所以，语境中的猜词是应用英语的重要能力。本节主要利用过去五年全国高考真题，探讨阅读文本中的猜词技巧。

高中新课程标准中对词汇的理解，提出了根据主题语境、语篇、构词法以及词典的应用等理解词汇的要求。因为在两种语言之间，没有任何一个词语的内涵和外延是完全对等的。

高考题中的猜词，答案出处具备足够的上下文线索，以便考生进行推理时参考分析。答题线索多数在词汇猜测题考点的前后句，有的在段内上下文语境中，还有需要从宏观上了解语篇结构和大意的。考点所在的信息是语篇的核心信息，可能是词汇或短语，词汇可能是熟词生义或者生词含义，短语可以是名词短语或动词短语，近几年很少出现句子意思的推测分析。

例1（2023全国甲卷阅读B篇）"Terri Bolton is a dab hand when it comes to DIY（do-it-yourself）. Skilled at putting up shelves and piecing together furniture, she never pays someone else to do a job she can do herself."

4. Which is closest in meaning to "a dab hand" in paragraph 1?
A. An artist.　B. A winner.　C. A specialist.　D. A pioneer.

【思维过程】根据下文 Skilled at ..., she never pays someone else to do a job ... 可知 Terri Bolton 是 DIY 高手，对应选项 C。

例2（2019年浙江6月卷B篇）"Money with no strings attached ... a board went up with dollar bills attached to it with pins and a sign that read, 'Give What You Can, Take What you Need.'"

24. What does the expression "money with no strings attached" in Paragraph 1 mean?

A. Money spent without hesitation.　　B. Money not legally made.

C. Money offered without conditions.　D. Money not tied together.

【思维过程】根据板上的 Give What You Can, Take What you Need, 人们可以"没有限制条件地"捐出或者拿走钱,对应选项 C。

例 3（2022 年新高考全国 Ⅱ 卷 C 篇）"We need something on the books that can change people's behavior," ... If the Textalyzer bill becomes law, he said, "people are going to be more afraid to put their hands on the cell phone."

10. What does the underlined word "something" in the last paragraph refer to?

A. Advice.　B. Data.　C. Tests.　D. Laws.

【思维过程】根据下文的 "If the Textalyzer bill becomes law... people are going to be more afraid to put their hands on the cell phone" 可知,当 Textalyzer 法案成为法律人的行为才会发生改变。法律的约束和惩罚,才能让司机在开车时放下手机,所以 something 指代的是法律。

本节会分别从语篇分析的衔接手段、段落和句间关系、构词法、标点符号等几个方面理解词义的途径,探求阅读过程中的猜词技巧。

一、从语篇的宏观结构猜测词义

大多数词汇都有多个词性和多种语义,只有在具体的语境中,才能准确判断。虽说语篇中猜词的手段有很多,但大多数都属于语篇分析的微观层面,但有时需要根据语篇的宏观结构来猜词义。

（一）根据文章结构图式猜测词义

例如,2015 广东卷 C 篇。该语篇是议论文,其结构是总分总,同一篇章中"总"的部分内容一致,虽然词汇选择不同,但都是文章主旨部分,可以互相对应,彼此解释。

...We tend to blame TV, he says, for problems it doesn't really cause, overlooking our own roles in shaping children's minds.

...

... However, by showing that television promotes none of the dangerous effects as conventionally believed, Anderson suggests that television cannot be condemned without considering other influences.

【思维过程】第一段中出现"we tend to blame TV for problems it doesn't really cause, ..."最后一段重新阐述主旨,"... television cannot be condemned without considering other influences."两句中的 blame 和 condemn 可以互为解释。虽然当时这个地方没有设题,但是可以作为学生阅读中碰到生词时的理解手段。

(二)根据段落间逻辑关系猜测词义

段落间的逻辑关系可以有效地帮助我们理解段落内细节。例如,2016年全国甲卷 B 篇利用了转折关系猜测词义。

"... Here was an exceptionally creative mind at work. His presence meant that I had an unexpected teaching assistant in class whose creativity would infect other students.

Encouraging this kind of thinking has a downside. I ran the risk of losing those students who had a different style of thinking. Without fail one would declare, 'But I'm just not creative.'"

7. What does the underlined word "downside" in Paragraph 4 probably mean?

   A. Mistake.　B. Drawback.　C. Difficulty.　D. Burden.

【思维过程】划线词汇的上一段,用了很多的褒义词来表明作为老师的作者对有创意的孩子的喜欢,exceptionally creative mind, unexpected teaching assistant, whose creativity would infect...。但是画线所在句子的后面 ran the risk of losing those...who had a different style of thinking, without fail, not creative 跟上文形成转折,也就是段落间是转折关系。downside 的含义应该是 drawback。两段采用了先扬后抑的方式,说明了这样一个有创意的孩子的存在也有其不利的一面。

二、从语篇的显性衔接手段判断词义

（一）代词回指

语法衔接手段中的代词回指功能帮助我们理解语篇细节和词义。
例如：2023 全国新高考卷 Ⅱ 阅读 C 篇：

"…In artists' representations of books and reading, we see moments of shared humanity that go beyond culture and time.

In this 'book of books', artworks are selected and arranged in a way that emphasizes these connections between different eras and cultures. … These scenes may have been painted hundreds of years ago, but they record moments we can all relate to."

10. What do the underlined words "relate to" in paragraph 2 mean?
    A. Understand.　B. Paint.　C. Seize.　D. Transform.

【思维过程】根据上一段中的最后一句，书中展现了超越文化和时代的共有的人性。划线词所处段落的第一句话中的 these connections 以及划线词所处的句子 These scenes 都运用了 these 的回指功能，指代书籍是人类之间相互联系和理解的纽带，所以选择 A，与 understand 意思最接近。

2018 年浙江卷 B 篇也用到了 these 的回指功能和比较照应：

"Americans use more than 100 billion film plastic bags every year. … The bags are prohibited in some 90 cities in California, including Los Angeles. Eyeing these headwinds, plastic-bag makers are hiring scientists like Stein to make the case that their products are not as bad for the planet as most people assume."

25. What does the word "headwinds" in paragraph 2 refer to?
    A. Bans on plastic bags　　　B. Effects of city development
    C. Headaches caused by garbage　D. Plastic bags hung in trees

【思维过程】划线词 these headwinds 指代上文中提到的 growing number of cities do not allow them at checkouts 和 The bags are prohibited in some 90 cities in California, including Los Angeles 两种情况，都是关于禁止使用塑料袋的。另外，下文的比较照应 not as bad for the planet as 是作为 eyeing these headwinds 所采取的措施，也是希望人们会继续使用塑料袋。两者结合判断，答案选 A。

（二）定冠词的回指功能

语篇中，定冠词的回指功能也能帮我们理解词义。如 2021 年浙江 1 月卷 C 篇：

"…, the animals do not appear to use their voices intentionally to communicate messages. This was a significant difference between calls and gestures, Dr Hobaiter said.

…

… 'Moreover, the meanings seem to not go beyond what other animals convey with non-verbal communication. So, it seems the gulf remains.'"

29. What does the underlined word "gulf" in the last paragraph mean?
A. Difference.　B. Conflict.　C. Balance.　D. Connection.

【思维过程】这是一篇研究报告类的说明文，第三段中提到 a significant difference between calls and gestures 来表明大猩猩和猴子可以明白来自同伴的复杂信息，却不能有意识地运用声音传递信息。最后一段表明 the vagueness of the gesture meaning 的几种解释，得到结论 It seems that the gulf remains。通过篇章理解以及定冠词 the 的回指功能，前文一定提及 gulf 的同义词，通过分析首尾段的呼应，只有 difference 可以解释 gulf，答案选 A。

另外，2017 年全国 I 卷 D 篇也用到了定冠词 the 的回指功能：

"To construct a working still, use a sharp stick or rock to dig a hole four feet across and three feet deep. Try to make the hole in a damp area to increase the water catcher's productivity."

33. What does the underlined phrase "the water catcher" in paragraph 2 refer to?
A. The tube.　B. The still.　C. The hole.　D. The cup.

【思维过程】段首 To construct a working still, … 和划线词所在句

to increase the water catcher's productivity 中的"定冠词 the+n"指代前文的 working still,答案选 B。

三、利用词汇衔接手段判断词义

阅读中的猜词最常用的手段就是词汇衔接手段,包括词汇的重现和复现。

（一）利用同义重现判断词义

例如,2023 全国乙卷阅读 D 篇:

"If you want to tell the history of the whole world, a history that does not privilege one part of humanity, you cannot do it through texts alone, because only some of the world has ever had texts, while most of the world, for most of the time, has not. ...

...

In addition to the problem of miscomprehension from both sides, there are victories accidentally or deliberately twisted, especially when only the victors know how to write. ... If we are to find the other half of that conversation, we have to read not just the texts, but the objects."

34. What does the underlined word "conversation" in paragraph 3 refer to?

A. Problem.　B. History.　C. Voice.　D. Society.

【思维过程】本文开篇的一句话,就已经提示了语篇主题"a history that does not privilege one part of humanity, you cannot do it through texts alone, ..."另外,划线单词所在段落先提出观点,历史有时是扭曲的,证明方式主要集中在失败者书写历史的方式上。结合划线词所在句可知,如果我们想要了解历史的另一半,不仅要读文本也要读物品。所以,conversation 指的是"历史"。上下文中运用了多处同义重现,如 history, texts, writing, stories, accounts; recorded, tell, speak to, gives them back a voice, dialogue, conversation 等,答案选 B。

2022 年全国新高考 I 卷 C 篇也运用了同义复现的手段作为猜词提示:

"There are now 700 elderly people looking after hens..., and the charity has been given financial support to roll it out countrywide.

Wendy Wilson, ..., one of the first to embark on the project, said: 'Residents really welcome the idea of the project and the creative sessions. We are looking forward to the benefits and fun the project can bring to people here.'"

30. What do the underlined words "embark on" mean in paragraph 7?

A. Improve.　B. Oppose.　C. Begin.　D. Evaluate.

【思维过程】根据划线词上一段的 roll it out（开始），以及划线处前的 one of the first 可知 Wendy Wilson 是最早开始这项工程的人员之一，所以，embark on, roll out 和 begin 属于同义词复现，故选 C。

2022 年新高考全国Ⅱ卷 B 篇也有类似的例子：

"We journalists live in a new age of storytelling, with many new multimedia tools. Many young people don't even realize it's new. For them, it's just normal.

This hit home for me as I was sitting with my 2-year-old grandson on a sofa over the Spring Festival holiday. ...

Picture this: my grandson sitting on my lap as I hold the book in front so he can see the pictures. As I read, he reaches out and pokes（戳）the page with his finger.

...

Then I realized what was happening. He was actually a stranger to books... He thought my storybook was like that."

4. What do the underlined words "hit home for me" mean in paragraph 2?

A. Provided shelter for me.　　B. Became very clear to me.

C. Took the pressure off me.　　D. Worked quite well on me.

【思维过程】根据第一段"Many young people don't even realize it's new. For them, it's just normal."以及划线词后文"as I was sitting with my 2-year-old grandson on a sofa over the Spring Festival holiday."可知，作者意识到了年轻人对多媒体习以为常。同时，在文章最后一段还有一句话提示"Then I realize what was happening."综合文章的首尾，realize 和 hit home 同义，答案选 B。

另外，2019 江苏卷 B 篇也利用同义词复现解释词义：

"Just at this time NASA decided to test some new highaltitude cameras by taking photographs of Yellowstone. A thoughtful official passed on some of the copies to the park authorities on the assumption that they might make a nice blowup for one of the visitors' centers."

60. What does the underlined word "blowup" in the last paragraph most probably mean?

  A. Hotair balloon. B. Digital camera.
  C. Big photograph. D. Bird's view.

【思维过程】根据段落内第一句"... by taking photographs of Yellow-stone."及划线词所在句中的 pass on some of the copies 可知，blow up 是跟照片有关，下一句话中的 saw the photos，确定了 blow-up 就是 photograph，这几个词属于同义词复现。至于 big，一方面可以从 blow-up 的意象"吹大"判断，另一方面在游客中心张贴的照片根据常识，一定是要放大的，故答案选 C。

同义词复现还出现在另外一种情况中。即同一语篇中，接续相同宾语的动词近义或同义，同样，同一动词接续的不同名词也有可能同义。如下面两张图所示：

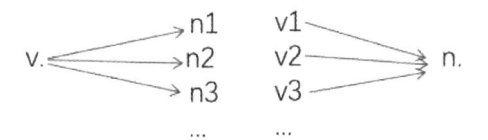

$$v. \begin{array}{l} \rightarrow n_1 \\ \rightarrow n_2 \\ \rightarrow n_3 \\ \cdots \end{array} \qquad \begin{array}{l} v_1 \\ v_2 \\ v_3 \\ \cdots \end{array} \rightarrow n.$$

利用词语的同现关系，同一语篇内，第一个图中同一动词接续几个名词，这几个名词基本可以理解为同义或近义；第二个图中几个动词搭配同一名词，基本可以判断它们为近义词或同义词。

例如，2020 全国 3 卷 B 篇：

"One non-profit organization, which monitors the treatment of animals in filmed entertainment, is keeping tabs on more than 2,000 productions this year.

There are questions about the films made outside the States, which sometimes are not monitored as closely as productions filmed in the States."

26. What does the underlined phrase "keeping tabs on" in paragraph 3 probably mean?

  A. Listing completely. B. Directing professionally.

C. Promoting successfully.　D. Watching carefully.

【思维过程】原文第三段 keeping tabs on 后面接续了 productions 这个名词。在文章的最后一段出现了 monitored... productions 这样的结构。所以，keeping tabs on 的词义等同于 monitor，又经过了同义解释 watch，故选择 D。

同样的规则也出现在 2015 四川 E 篇阅读中：

"The most popular view is that Egyptian workers slid the blocks along smooth paths. ... To make the work easier, workers may have lubricated the paths either with wet clay or with the fat from cattle. Bonn has now tested this idea by building small sleds and dragging heavy objects over sand.

...

West hasn't tested his idea on larger blocks, but he thinks rolling has clear advantages over sliding. At least, workers wouldn't have needed to carry cattle fat or water to smooth the paths."

47. The underlined part "lubricated the paths" in Paragraph 4 means___.

A.made the path wet　　B.made the path hard

C.made the path wide　　D.made the path slippery

【思维过程】除了在 lubricated the paths 所处段落的第一句话中的 slid the blocks along smooth paths 的提示以外，lubricated the paths 后面有 either with wet clay or with the fat from cattle 这样的信息，下文中有 workers wouldn't have needed to carry cattle fat or water to smooth the paths，lubricate 和 smooth 两个动词都接续了名词 paths，而且有 cattle fat 进一步佐证，所以 lubricate 和 smooth 属于同义词复现，经过进一步的同义解释，答案选 D。

（二）利用反义词同现线索猜测词义

例如，2023 新高考 I 卷 C 篇，同时利用了同义词复现和反义词同现手段猜词：

"Part one concludes by introducing my suggested method for adopting this philosophy: the digital declutter. This process requires you to step away from optional online activities for thirty days. At the end of the thirty days, you will then add back a small number of carefully chosen online activities that you believe will provide massive benefits to the things you value."

29. What does the underlined word "declutter" in paragraph 3 mean?
 A. Clear-up. B. Add-on. C. Check-in. D. Take-over.

【思维过程】根据划线词下文 step away from 和 add back 这一对反义短语同现，declutter 必然跟 take away from 一样属于同义复现，加上 de- 前缀本身就有 away from 这个含义，所以 declutter 的意思最接近答案 A。

再如，2013 北京卷 A 篇也用到了反义词对比的方式进行释义：

"The advanced EP also heats the room evenly, wall to wall and floor to ceiling. It comfortably covers an area up to 350 square feet. Other heaters heat rooms unevenly with most of the heat concentrated to the center of the room. And they only heat an area a few feet around the heater. With the EP, the temperature will not vary in any part of the room."

58. The underlined word "evenly" in paragraph 4 probably means _____.

 A. continuously B. separately C. quickly D. equally

【思维过程】原文中对 evenly 的解释是 wall to wall and floor to ceiling，下文用到了反义词 unevenly 的解释 with most of the heat concentrated to the center of the room. And they only heat an area a few feet around the heater。段尾用了 the temperature will not vary in any part of the room 来回应第一句话中的 evenly。整个段落全部都在解释 heat the room evenly 这一个功能，故答案选 D。

（三）利用语义场内词汇同现关系猜测词义

例如，2017 全国Ⅲ卷 C 篇利用了同一语义场的词汇链猜测词义：

"Gray wolves once were seen here and there in the Yellowstone area and much of the continental United States, but they were gradually displaced by human development. By the 1920s, wolves had practically disappeared from the Yellowstone area. They went farther north into the deep forests of Canada, where there were fewer humans around.

The disappearance of the wolves had many unexpected results."

29. What does the underlined word "displaced" in paragraph 2 mean?

A. Tested.　B. Separated.　C. Forced out.　D. Tracked down.

【思维过程】在划线单词的句子开头一句话表明灰狼在美国的分布非常广,下文 had practically disappeared 和 disappearance of the wolves 这一对同词复现来说明美国已实际上没有灰狼。但它们并非被杀死了,而是 went further north into the deep forests of Canada, displaced 跟 driven away 近义,所以灰狼是被 forced out,故答案选 C。

再如,2013 年江西卷 A 篇,根据段内语义场词汇和虚拟语气的句子猜测词义:

"The light from the campfire brightened the darkness, but it could not prevent the damp cold of Dennis's Swamp creeping into their bones. It was a strange place. Martin and Tom wished that they had not accepted Jack's dare. They liked camping, but not near this swamp."

56. The underlined word "dare" in Paragraph 1 is closed in meaning to _____.

A. courage　B. assistance　C. instruction　D. challenge

【思维过程】段落内 could not prevent, damp cold creeping into, strange 等词都是同一语义场中的同现,情绪消极,而且后面的虚拟语气表明了 dare 的情感倾向,也应该是消极情绪的词,四个选项中只有 D 符合语义。

四、根据句子间逻辑关系猜测词义

句子间主要的逻辑关系有:因果、转折、并列、解释、顺序、递进、对比、条件等,看懂这些内在的逻辑会帮助解决具体的词句理解问题。

例 1. 2021 年全国新高考 I 卷 C 篇可以利用上下文的信息对比和解释说明两种逻辑关系猜测词义:

"When the explorers first set foot upon the continent of North America, the skies and lands were alive with an astonishing variety of wildlife. ... Unfortunately, it took the explorers and the settlers who followed only a few decades to decimate a large part of these resources. Millions of waterfowl were killed... Millions of acres of wetlands were dried..., greatly reducing waterfowl habitat."

29. What does the underlined word "decimate" mean in the first paragraph?

A. Acquire.　B. Export.　C. Destroy.　D. Distribute.

【思维过程】根据段首句中的 the skies and lands were alive with an astonishing variety of wildlife. 和前一句"Native Americans had taken care of these precious natural resources wisely." 可知,北美的土著人把这些珍贵的自然资源保护得很合理,本句中的 Unfortunately 与上一句形成了转折,阐述殖民者破坏了自然资源,故划线词义是"破坏"。下文的两个并列句子解释说明了破坏的原因,从整个段落的逻辑可以判断 C 选项为正确选项。

例 2. 2021 全国新高考 Ⅱ 卷 B 篇可用句间因果关系和不定式表结果猜测词义:

"As they grew more mobile, …, but when we were asleep we had to contain them in a large room, otherwise they'd get up to mischief. We'd come down in the morning to find they'd turned the room upside down, and left it look like a zoo."

25. What do the underlined words "get up to mischief" mean in paragraph 3?

A. Behave badly.　　B. Lose their way.
C. Sleep soundly.　　D. Miss their mom.

【思维过程】划线短语所在句跟下一句话本身构成因果关系,下一句话中的不定式表结果 to find they'd turned the room upside down, and left it look like a zoo 跟 A 选项近义,故答案选 A.

例 3. 2022 年北京卷 D 篇可用句间的因果关系和词汇的感情色彩猜测词义:

"As quantum computing attracts more attention and funding, researchers may mislead…, worst of all, themselves about their work's potential. If researchers can't keep their promises, excitement might give way to doubt, disappointment and anger, Johnson warns. Lots of other technologies have gone through stages of excitement. But something about quantum computing makes it specially prone to hype, Johnson suggests, ..."

13. What does the underlined word "prone" in Paragraph 3 most probably mean?

A. Open.　B. Cool.　C. Useful.　D. Resistant.

【思维过程】自段首开始,段落内出现了很多消极的词汇 mislead, worst of all, give way to doubt, disappointment and anger,出现了一个 excitement,后面还跟上了转折 but,所以 prone 也一定是消极意义的词汇。加上后面的因果关系,因为大家不懂,所以更容易被过度宣传,语义类似于 vulnerable 和 sensitive,故答案选 A。

例 4. 2019 年北京卷 D 篇可用句子间的转折和因果关系猜测词义:

"Phytoplankton live at the ocean surface, where they pull carbon dioxide into the ocean while giving off oxygen. ..., an important process that helps to regulate the global climate. But phytoplankton are vulnerable to the ocean's warming trend. Warming changes key characteristics of the ocean and can affect phytoplankton growth, since they need not only sunlight and carbon dioxide to grow, but also nutrients."

43. What does the underlined word "vulnerable" in Paragraph 3 probably mean?

A. Sensitive.　B. Beneficial.　C. Significant.　D. Unnoticeable.

【思维过程】由划线词上一句中的 an important process that helps to regulate the global climate 可知,phytoplankton 对调节全球气候的正向作用。But 让情况发生转折,特别是段落最后一句中的因果关系表明,温度变化对 phytoplankton 有很大的影响,且是负面的。由此推断,phytoplankton 对海洋的温度很敏感,故选 A。

例 5. 2017 年江苏卷 B 篇可用段内句间的转折和递进猜测词义:

"Before birth, babies can tell the difference between loud sounds and voices. They can even distinguish their mother's voice from that of a female stranger. But when it comes to embryonic learning, birds could rule the roost. As recently reported in The Auk: Ornithological Advances, some mother birds may teach their young to sing even before they hatch. New-born chicks can then imitate their mom's call within a few days of entering the world."

The underlined phrase in Paragraph 1 means_____.

A. be the worst B. be the best C. be the as bad D. be just as good

【思维过程】段首以人类宝宝具备的两种辨别声音的能力铺垫，然后 But 进行了转折，并用下文的研究 may teach their young to sing even before they hatch 和 "New-born chicks can then imitate their mom's call within a few days of entering the world." 进一步表明，鸟类对于声音的敏感和能力远超人类，所以选 B。

例6. 2017江苏卷D篇可用段落内因果、转折等多种逻辑关系来猜词：

"When it comes to adaptation, it is important to understand that climate change is a process. We are therefore not talking about adapting to a new standard, but to a constantly shifting set of conditions. This is why, in part at least, the US National Climate Assessment says that: 'There is no 'one-size fits all' adaptation.'"

65. The underlined part in Paragraph 2 implies_____.

A. adaptation is an ever-changing process

B. the cost of adaptation varies with time

C. global warming affects adaptation forms

D. adaptation to climate change is challenging

【思维过程】段落中的第一句话就点明 climate change is a process，第二句话利用了因果关系和 not...but 进一步强调这个过程是 a constantly shifting set of conditions，故答案选 A。

例7. 2019年全国Ⅱ卷阅读B篇可以利用句间的解释关系猜测词义：

"You can use me as a last resort, and if nobody else volunteers, then I'll do it."...

... She may just need a little persuading. So I try again and tug at the heartstrings. I mention the single parent with four kids running the show and I talk about the dad coaching a team that his kids aren't even on... At this point the unwilling parent speaks up, "Alright. Yes, I'll do it."

25. What does the underlined phrase "tug at the heartstrings" in paragraph 2 mean?

A. Encourage team work. B. Appeal to feelings.

C. Promote good deeds.　　D. Provide advice.

【思维过程】第一段开头一句话 You can use me as a last resort… 是对作者的拒绝,第二段作者试着从对方的角度来解释拒绝的原因,想到 She may just need a little persuading，随后在划线短语所在句后面,举例解释划线短语的意思,说明如何从情感方面打动对方,故答案选 B。

上面几个例子都是利用句间的逻辑来猜测词义。连接词也可以显示句子内部的逻辑关系。

例1. 2020年全国新高考Ⅰ卷B篇利用了让步状语和比较照应来猜测词义：

"But I imagine that, while money is indeed wonderful and necessary, rereading an author's work is the highest currency a reader can pay them. The best books are the ones that open further as time passes."

26. What does the underlined word "currency" in paragraph 4 refer to?

A. Debt.　B. Reward.　C. Allowance.　D. Face value.

【思维过程】while 表示让步，money is indeed wonderful and necessary,钱很好很有必要,但是 rereading an author's work is the highest currency。此处 currency 属于熟词新义,前有最高级修饰,重读一本书对作者来说比钱更重要,这是对作者最高的奖赏或敬意,故答案选 B。

例2. 2022浙江6月卷C篇利用了句间对比关系来猜测词义：

"How long we stay on the clock and how we spend that time are under careful examination in many workplaces. The young banker who eats lunch at his desk is probably seen as a go-getter, while his colleagues who chat over a relaxed conference-room meal get dirty looks from the corner office…"

28. The underlined word "go-getter" in Paragraph 3 refers to someone who_____.

A. is good at handling pressure

B. works hard to become successful

C. Has a natural talent for his job

D. Gets on well with his co-workers

【思维过程】根据划线词的前文 who eats lunch at his desk 的界定,与后半部分 while 构成对比 who chat over a relaxed conference-room meal get dirty looks from the corner office,两种不同的就餐方式被领导认为是两种不同的工作态度,后者要受领导白眼,故答案选 B。

例 8. 2020 年全国 Ⅱ 卷 C 篇也可以利用句内因果关系猜测词义:

"The fur trade kept nutria in check for decades, but when the market for nutria collapsed in the late 1980s, the cat-sized animals multiplied like crazy."

30. What does the underlined word "collapsed" in paragraph 5 probably mean?

A. Boomed.　B. Became mature.　C. Remained stable.　D. Crashed.

【思维过程】划线所在句子的前后两部分之间构成了因果关系,前者是因,后者是果 the cat-sized animal multiplied like crazy,故答案选 D。这个题的难点还在于不少人不知道 A 选项 boomed 的意思,可能错选 A。

例 9. 同样运用举例法的还有 2018 全国 Ⅰ 卷 C 篇:

"Soon afterwards, ..., and their languages too became more settled and fewer in number. In recent centuries, ..., all have caused many languages to disappear, and dominant languages such as English, Spanish and Chinese are increasingly taking over."

29. Which of the following best explains "dominant" underlined in paragraph 2?

A. Complex.　B. Advanced.　C. Powerful.　D. Modern.

【思维过程】本段前半部分说了很多语言消失或使用者减少的原因,and 表示转折,以几种联合国官方语言为例来说明这几种语言强大,越来越占主导地位,故答案选 C。

五、利用标点符号猜测词义

标点符号功能强大,不仅可以分隔句子和段落,帮助读者理解文本的结构和意义,还能帮我们理解文本和传达意思。不同的标点符号在词汇学习方面发挥着积极作用。

例 1. 2021 年全国乙卷 B 篇可利用破折号的解释功能猜测词义:

"Of those Australians who still have a landline, a third concede that it's not really necessary and they're keeping it as a security blanket—19 percent say they never use it while a further 13 percent keep it in case of emergencies."

25. What does the underlined word "concede" in paragraph 3 mean?

A. Admit.　B. Argue.　C. Remember.　D. Remark.

【思维过程】家里虽然留有电话座机,但是划线词 concede 后面的内容是 not really necessary, keeping it as a security blanket,破折号进一步解释作为 security blanket 的使用现状和目的,这些都表明 landline 的用途其实并不大,也就是这 1/3 的人承认的事实,故答案选 A。

例 2. 2019 全国Ⅲ卷 B 篇同样可利用破折号的解释功能猜测词义:

"... Chinese women are not just consumers of fashion—they are central to its movement... not only are today's top Western designers being influenced by China—some of the best designers of contemporary fashion are themselves Chinese. 'Vera Wang, Alexander Wang, Jason Wu are taking on Galiano, Albaz, Marc Jacobs—and beating them hands down in design and sales,' adds Hill."

26. What do the underlined words "taking on" in paragraph 4 mean?

A. learning from　B. looking down on

C. working with　D. competing against

【思维过程】上文中 ...are not just consumers of fashion—they are central to its movement,说明中国模特在时尚方面的地位,接下来继续用破折号进行解释 some of the best designers of contemporary fashion are themselves Chinese,划线短语的前后是一些中国名字和西方名字的对比,下文破折号进一步解释说明 and beating them hands down in design and sales,时尚界的中国力量确实强大到跟西方力量对抗时完胜,故答案选 D。

例 3. 2019 全国Ⅰ卷 B 篇用到了省略号作为释义手段:

"But he's nervous. 'I'm here to tell you today why you should ... should ...' Chris trips on the 'ld', ... '... Vote for ... me ...' Except for some stumbles. Chris is doing amazingly well."

What does the underlined word "stumbles" in Paragraph 2 refer to?

A. Improper pauses.　B. Bad manners.

C. Spelling mistakes.　D. Silly jokes.

【思维过程】段首交代了 Chris 的心理状况 But he's nervous,后面用省略号和词汇重复表明 Chris 的演讲不流畅,停顿不合理。这些表现与划线词后 Chris is doing amazingly well 构成转折关系。这与礼貌和演讲内容无关,跟心态和表现有关,故答案选 A。

例 4. 2017 年天津卷 C 篇利用了冒号的解释功能释义:

"The proposal attempts to deal with what some call the 'death valley' of autonomous vehicles: the grey area between semi-autonomous and fully driverless cars that could delay the driverless future."

46. What does the phrase "death valley" in Paragraph 2 refer to?

A. A place where cars often break down.

B. A case where passing a law is impossible.

C. An area where no driving is permitted.

D. A situation where drivers' role is not clear.

【思维过程】利用冒号的功能解释,death valley 的意思是 the grey area…,跟选项 D 吻合。

六、运用多种方法猜测词义

语境中的猜词,即在很多情况下,上下文中会出现不止一种提示,我们在阅读中要尽可能多地找到这些"路标"进行词义的判定,从最大程度上确保正确理解。

例 1. 2022 全国乙卷 C 篇的猜词可用代词指代及同词、同义词复现猜测词义:

"… The more regularly they can be inspected, the more railway safety, reliability and on-time performance will be improved. Costs would be cut and operations would be more efficient across the board.

That includes huge savings in maintenance costs and better protection of railway personnel safety. It is calculated that European railways alone spend approximately 20 billion euros a year on maintenance, including sending maintenance staff, often at night, to inspect and repair the rail infrastructure. That can be dangerous work that could be avoided with drones assisting the crews' efforts."

29. What does "maintenance" underlined in paragraph 3 refer to?

A. Personnel safety.　　　　B. Assistance from drones.

C. Inspection and repair.　D. Construction of infrastructure.

【思维过程】划线单词所在句子开头的 that 属于承接上段最后一句话的同义指代，含有 cost 的降低和 operation 的高效两个方面。在划线单词所在段落的下文中出现了同词复现，另外，还有 personnel 和 staff 同义词复现，下文以 including 的形式举例说明，maintenance staff ... to inspect and repair rail infrastructure，由此可知，maintenance 包括 inspection 和 repair 两个方面，故答案选 C。

例 2. 2021 年全国甲卷 C 篇可以利用段落内信息推进模式和破折号的解释功能猜测词义：

"... We spoke our own language. And my favorite：Safe. Safe meant cool. It meant hello. It meant don't worry about it. Once, when trying a certain trick on the beam, I fell onto the stones, damaging a nerve in my hand, and Toby came over, helping me up：Safe, man. Safe. A few minutes later, when I landed the trick, my friends beat their boards loud, shouting：'Safe! Safe! Safe!' And that's what mattered—landing tricks, being a good skater."

9. What do the underlined words "Safe! Safe! Safe!" probably mean?
A. Be careful!　B. Well done!　C. No way!　D. Don't worry!

【思维过程】画线部分前文已经用了下定义的方式说明 cool 的几层含义"Safe meant cool. It meant hello. It meant don't worry about it." 紧接着以派生型的信息推进模式对不同的意思举例说明运用场合。划线部分后面运用破折号的解释功能，重要的事情是 landing tricks, being a good skater, 也就是上文提到的 safe 的第一个意思 cool, 故答案选 B。

例 3. 2020 年全国新高考 Ⅱ 卷 B 篇可以利用段落间的提示、破折号和原因状语从句猜测词义：

"My imaginary Grandma's Box worked like magic that spring, and later. Sometimes, students would ask me to describe all the things I had in it. Then I would try to remember the different possessions I supposedly had taken away—since I seldom actually kept them. Usually the offender would appear at the end of the day, and I would return the belonging.

The years went by, and my first grandchild Gordon was born. I shared my joy with that year's class. Then someone said, 'Now you can use your Grandma's Box.' From then on instead of coming to ask their possessions back, the students would say, 'That's okay. Put it in your Grandma's Box for Gordon.'"

5. What do the underlined words "the offender" in paragraph 8 refer to?

A. The student's parent.　　B. The maker of the Grandma's Box.
C. The author's grandchild　　D. The owner of the forbidden fruit.

【思维过程】划线词所在段落和下一段形成了对比，前者 the offender 会在一天结束时取走 the belonging—since I seldom actually kept them，利用了破折号和 since 原因状语从句的解释功能。利用 the 的回指功能，在第一段中找到回指的对象 students，下一段中作者当了奶奶之后，"instead of coming to ask their possessions back, the students would say..." 说明前文的 offender 就是学生，拿玩具去学校的学生，故答案选 D。

例 4. 2021 天津卷 B 篇可利用类比和词汇复现猜测词义：

"The poignancy（酸楚）of Jordan retiring from his beloved basketball ... took me by surprise. As I watched him take off his basketball uniform and replace it with a baseball uniform, I saw him leaving behind the layer that no longer served him, just as our lizard had. ... I realized that we have to learn to leave the past behind.

Humans do not shed skin as easily as other animals. The beginning of change is upsetting. The process is tiring. Damage changes us before we are ready. I see our lizard, raw and nearly new."

43. The underlined part "leaving behind the layer" in Paragraph 8 can be understood as_____.

A. letting go of the past　　B. looking for a new job
C. getting rid of a bad habit　　D. giving up an opportunity

【思维过程】划线短语上一句有提到 take off his basketball uniform and replace it with a baseball uniform，划线短语后面 just as our lizard had 进行表层意思的类比，本段最后一句 ... to learn to leave the past behind 中 leave...behind 跟画线部分同词复现，跟 let go of 同义，而 the layer 跟 the past 同义。另外，下一段先抑后扬，用到了不少消极情感的

词汇 not as easily as, upsetting, tiring, damage 等。但同时表达了乐观:"I see our lizard, raw and nearly new."故答案选 A。

词汇在阅读和理解中占据核心地位,与语境紧密相连。词汇在各自的环境中传达着独特的意义和情感,失去语境,它们便失去生命力。在猜词时,需依赖上下文语境,确保词义与文章主题相契合,而非主观臆断。这里主要强调的是上下文语境,而情景和文化语境则较为次要。阅读时,应首先把握文章主旨,再逐步深入到各个层次进行分析。通过语法、词汇、连接词、信息推进模式、构词法、标点符号等宏观和微观的线索来学习词汇。若常规方法失效,还可以从选项中反向推测词义,特别要注意词汇的情感色彩,从中寻找线索,理解其在语境中的真正含义。

阅读猜词技巧不仅适用于考试场景,同样有助于日常阅读中处理与记忆生词。整体输入式阅读能够深化对词汇内涵和外延的理解,同时培养我们的思维方式和模式,从而提升思维品质。针对高考词汇量增加的趋势,教师在教授词汇时,应引导学生通过增加听力输入来更好地掌握词汇,以便在口头和书面表达中灵活运用。

第三节 教材中常见介词的用法介绍

本节先整体介绍介词的功能和用法,然后介绍教材中最活跃的几个介词及其主要用法,所用例句大部分都来自高中外研版教材。

一、介词

介词虽然是虚词,不能独立作为句子元素,却是英语中最活跃的八大词类之一,是连接词、短语或句子的重要手段,可以说,英语句子几乎离不开介词的使用。有的学者甚至把英语称为介词的语言,或者可以说,看一个人的英语地不地道,功力深不深厚,看介词学得如何就能窥见一斑。介词总数虽然不多,但个个万般能耐,十八般武艺。张道真先生曾把介词比作螺丝钉,体积虽小,却处处用得着,没有它们,英语这台机器就无法运转。它们本身就有很多词义,跟其他词搭配,词义更多。不掌握介词的用法就不可能掌握英语,甚至会造成语篇解读困难。例如,"Let's have a talk over a cup of coffee.(让我们一边喝咖啡一边聊聊天。)"如果不知道 over 可以表示跨越一段时间的用法,这个句子就无法理解。

介词可以分为三类,在语言表达中各有其独特的价值和功能。首先,直接的单一介词,如 about, at, between, over 等。其次,由两个或多个单词组成的合成介词,传达更为复杂或特定的位置或关系,如 inside, onto, within 等。最后,短语介词,通常用于表达更为详细或具体的含义,比如 according to, along with, apart from 等。正是因为有了介词的存在,英语才变得更丰富,表达也更简化。

英语中介词如此活跃,跟英语的表达方式有关。按照连淑能教授的说法,"英语的动词使用受到形态变化规则的严格限制。一个句子结构通常只用一个谓语动词,大量原来应该由动词表达的概念,除了用非谓语动词来表达外,必须借助动词以外的词类,其中主要是名词和介词。名词可以由动词派生或转化而来,由于比较不受形态变化规则的约束,因而使用起来灵活、方便,这就导致了名词的广泛使用。介词与名词密切相关,因而介词也得以广泛使用。名词与介词的优势不仅降低了动词出现的频率,而且削弱了动词表达的意义,产生了动词的弱化与虚化。名词优势于动词的特点使英语的表达呈现静态倾向。"(连淑能,2010:154)

也就是说,英语中名词的广泛使用导致了介词的广泛使用。介词常前置于名词或名词性词语,二者结合加剧了英语的静态倾向。英语中经常会用介词短语取代动词短语,也就是以"静"代"动"。例如:

I was frightened at the sight of the test paper.=I was frightened when I saw the test paper.

As this artwork is rarely on display, people have sometimes queued up to six hours for a chance to see it. =As this artwork is rarely shown, people...

Upon arrival, give him the letter. =As soon as you arrive, give him the letter.

The math problem is beyond me. =The math problem is too

difficult for me to work out.

The problem is under discussion. =The problem is being discussed.

…and that this government of the people, by the people, for the people, shall not perish from the earth. =…and this government belonging to the people, ruled by the people and serving the people, …

以上例句可以看出,介词的使用使句子表达更加简洁、更有表现力,特别是最后这一句林肯在葛底斯堡的演说,正是介词的简洁和排比,使这个演讲更具感召力。

虽然有时介词可以省略,但不是可有可无的,如"He has trouble (in) understanding his English teacher at first."整体而言,介词在英语中有不可替代的作用。而且,大多数介词都有与之同样活跃的同形副词,后面的例子中会捎带着介绍副词的重点用法。

二、介词宾语

介词作为虚词,必须结合宾语组成介词短语后才能作为句子的成分。介词的宾语主要是名词、名词短语和名词从句,但还可以接续不定式、形容词、介词短语等。

接不定式作宾语:

But with an increasing number of problems and worries popping up this year, which were caused by my poor physical health, I came to realize that there was no choice but to work out.

Sitting back in my seat, I can't quite believe that I'm about to travel along the railway that many foreign experts claimed was "impossible".

接介词作宾语:

He jumped out from behind the door.

另有类似的例子,如 from under the table, from behind the curtain, for over two years 等。

接形容词作宾语:

It's far from satisfactory.

At the time, however, she (the Titanic) was not only the largest ship that had ever been built, but was regarded as unsinkable, for she had sixteen watertight compartments.

接副词作宾语：

He has been back from abroad for two years.

还有一些常见的短语，如 from here/there, from now (then), till now (then), for long, by far 等都属于这种现象。

接动名词作宾语：

I don't feel like studying today.

He succeeded in solving the problem.

Give me a call before leaving home.

接分词作宾语：

Spoiled kids always take it for granted that their parents should do everything for them.

I consider the problem as settled.

We have finished the work as scheduled.

这一类过去分词常常跟前面的介词一起构成常用短语。

接从句作宾语：

But I was surprised at how good I looked after the makeover!

He differs from us in that he dislikes most games.In that 常作固定短语用，很少拆分。

You can do everything except that you can't open that door. Except that 也常用作固定短语。

I worry about whether I can pass the exam.

The book for which you have been looking has been found.

介词是用于名词之间的媒介，常常跟名词一起构成介词短语。介词短语在句中能够充当的成分很多。

作主语：

Between nine and ten will be OK with me. 介词短语实际是定语，省略了隐含的真正主语 the time。

From words to deeds is a great space. 介词短语实际是定语，省略了隐含的真正主语 the distance。

作宾语：

Peter jumped out from behind the tree.

作表语：

The solution to the mystery of the monarch's amazing ability comes at a time when it is in serious trouble.

作定语：

However, the increase in the amount and variety of art produced has also raised questions over its overall quality.

The young man in question, Charles Darwin, was a geologist and naturalist, fascinated by rocks, plants and animals.

作状语：

With water falling off its thick, brown hair, the bear stared back at me.

In the quiet courtyards of Xi San Suo behind the high walls of the Forbidden City, time ticks at its own pace.

作补语：

We elected him as president.

I found everything in good condition.

三、教材中的几个最活跃的介词

英语介词很多，但是在教材中活跃度表现不一。下面重点介绍几个教材中课文里最活跃的介词，如 at, in, on, off, over, through, up 等。为了让学生能更直观地感受介词的活跃度，并借助各种例句指导他们在表达中准确地使用介词，以下例句集纳了外研版教材中大多数含有相关介词的句子。分类未必完全合理，主要是方便理解和记忆。

（一）介词 at

介词 at 的用法非常多，但核心用法主打"点"的概念，可以用来表示时间点、地点、速度、距离、温度、年龄等。可以说，凡是可以用各种"刻度"表述的概念，都可以用 at 表达。另外，at 还经常跟动词搭配，表示动作的目标等。这里重点把教材中的课文用法进行归类。

1. 表示地点

这里汇总了所有表示地点的介词用法，不做更细致的划分。

At the information desk **at** the entrance, I asked a lady where the shoe section was.

A table and two chairs **at** front centre. Grandfather and Father, seated **at** the table, are playing chess.

The letters told wonderful stories about Father Christmas's life and adventures **at** the North Pole.

For this year's Spring Festival family dinner, my son has booked a table **at** the best restaurant in town, but I'm a bit unhappy about it.

He was even shocked **at** their wedding when he saw how the Chinese ate almost every part of an animal.

Now, **at** the top of these stone stairs...get a load of that!

While waiting **at** the gate, Han Gan used a stick to draw pictures in the dirt and was seen by the poet himself.

He found inspiration where others could not, in simple, everyday scenes, such as a man buying oranges **at** the local grocery store, or a woman riding home on the graffiti-covered subway.

As an official in the Eastern Jin Dynasty, Tao felt conflicted over life **at** court.

Dating from 405 AD to 1002 AD, these hidden treasures give us a picture of Dunhuang when it was **at** the very centre of the Silk Road trade.

By 700 AD, Maya civilisation was **at** its peak.

2. 表示时间点

可以用来指某个时刻、时候或时期。

At that moment, he was no longer an athlete aiming for a medal——he was just a brother.

Many animals move from one place to another **at** certain times of the year.

It can be quite stressful **at** times, though, which in turn makes me feel anxious.

We see a woman swimming **at** night in a dark sea.

At one point, the host asked people in the audience to stand up if Nicholas Winton had saved their lives.

Nothing like this has been invented yet and I'd say we're a long way from an invention like that **at** the moment!

I have often thought it would be a blessing if each human being were stricken blind and deaf for a few days **at** some time during his early adult life.

At midnight, permanent night would close in on me again.

He probably didn't realise it **at** the time, but it was where he learnt to be creative and flexible as a player.

I would like to have more freedom with money and no doubt I will be getting a credit card **at** some point, but I currently don't have a steady income, ...

Never have I viewed my ugliness as **at** the present moment.

With these words ringing in their ears, Allied soldiers prepared for what would become known as D-Day **at** dawn on 6 June, thousands landed by parachute behind enemy lines in northern France.

The biggest challenge **at** the initial phase was to persuade people to work for me, which was totally outside my experience.

Everything was difficult **at** the beginning, and it was so painful that I wanted to give up many times.

3. 表示其他 "点"

（1）表示速度

经常跟三个表示速度的词 speed, pace, rate 搭配。

Despite a weight of up to 300 kilograms, they can run **at** a speed of around 64 kilometres per hour and are also excellent swimmers.

Unable to distinguish between blue sky and glass, birds crash into windows **at** speeds of about 30 miles per hour.

In the quiet courtyards of Xi San Suo behind the high walls of the Forbidden City, time ticks **at** its own pace.

They seem totally unaware that we are speeding past **at** over 100 kilometres an hour.

It is expanding **at** such a rate that we can only imagine what it will comprise in the future.

Maya civilisation began to collapse **at** different rates in different places.

Imagine bone-white-coral 6,000 metres below the ocean's surface growing **at** the rate of only one or two millimetres per year.

（2）表示年龄

Nicholas Winton passed away on 1 July 2015, **at** the age of 106.

I became interested in languages **at** a young age.

（3）表示距离

The solar rays shone through the watery mass easily, and consumed all colour, and I clearly distinguished objects **at** a distance of a hundred and fifty yards.

（4）表示深度

Shall I be believed when I say that, **at** the depth of thirty feet, I could see as if I was in broad daylight?

However, we are only beginning to overcome the challenges of pressure, darkness and extreme cold **at** vast depths.

In addition, China's underwater vessels, such as the Jiaolong and Shenhai Yongshi, have been exploring waters **at** depths of thousands of metres.

（5）表示高度

Located **at** over 5,000 metres above sea level, this is the highest railway station in the world.

（6）表示价格

This wealth of ways of sharing is a response to our increasing demand for quality goods and services **at** competitive prices, all delivered at the click of a button.

4. 表示某个方面

也可以理解为"在某个点上"。

Throughout my entire life, I've had my brother trying to beat me **at** everything I do.

Until a few years ago I was a chef, and a happy one **at** that, but I wanted more out of life.

I'm crazy about basketball, and pretty good **at** it too, which is probably why I was so mad when we lost our last match.

5. 表示"朝,向"

常常表示动作的目标。

With water falling off its thick, brown hair, the bear stared back **at** me.

"Do you have pigs' ears?" "No," the butcher said, pulling **at** his own ears, "just these ordinary ones."

He looked across the classroom **at** the drinking fountain.

One moment she seems to be laughing **at** me, but then again I catch a sense of sadness in her smile.

Only shots perfectly aimed **at** its centre went into the heavy, thick basket.

Life throws many alternatives **at** us on a daily basis.

When the Challenger space shuttle took off on 28 January 1986, the world seemed to have lost its wonder **at** the amazing achievements of the astronauts involved.

Our power to investigate and thus understand space changed dramatically when the first telescope was angled **at** the night sky, increasing as it did the power of the human eye and enabling us to understand that the universe is far larger than was previously imaginable.

We will view stars and galaxies billions of light years away and look back **at** a past that was billions of years ago.

6. 表示原因

表示引起某种情绪或动作的原因,常常跟在形容词、过去分词或动词之后。

You also have to wonder **at** the unique madness of a language in which a house can burn up as it burns down, in which you fill in a form by filling it out, and in which an alarm is only heard once it goes off!

But I was surprised **at** how good I looked after the makeover!

7. 表示状态

指处于某种状态或进行某种活动,经常跟名词一起构成短语。

People say that one man's meat is another man's poison, but I feel **at home** with food from both my cultures.

By the end of the run, all my stress has disappeared and I'm ready to face the next day **at work**!

With new technological tools **at our fingertips**, more and more people are exploring their creative sides.

A group of Tibetan antelopes is moving under the bridge, with some stopping to eat grass **at their leisure**.

With the country **at war**, students at Lianda were not going to shirk their duty.

Nearly every job is potentially **at risk** in the long run.

In today's modern world, their ideas about living simply and **being at ease with** nature may take us a step closer to attaining personal well-being and fulfilment.

8. 表示行为、方式、环境等

常跟其他名词一起构成短语。

In the 1960s and 1970s, the greatest fear was that the human race, and possibly all advanced life forms on the planet, could be wiped out by nuclear missiles, just **at the push of** a button.

This wealth of ways of sharing is a response to our increasing demand for quality goods and services at competitive prices, all delivered **at the click of** a button.

These are among the 669 children, most of them Jewish, that Nicholas Winton will go on to save from death **at the hands of** the Nazis.

At a glance I can distinguish China from Arizona. If one gets lost in the night, such knowledge is valuable.

I have seen them intimately, close **at hand**.

They are people in whose lives slight fall of snow is an event, even **at the risk of** appearing to this fair and witty reviewer as another Mr Woodhouse, I must insist that last night's fall of snow here was an event.

Some companies are taking unfair advantage of this situation to expand their share of the market, often **at the expense of** more traditional and established companies.

9. 其他一些固定短语

（1）at first

这个短语经常跟 but, but soon 这样的词语搭配，表示前后情况的转变和对比。但学生经常把这个短语跟表示序列时的 first 混淆。教材中这个短语的例子有很多。

At first, I kept running just to see my name in the top five. **Soon**, I found that I was not alone.

At first, I was really sad, **but later** I realized that I joined the team for the love of the sport.

At first, I thought what I heard was a violin, **but later** I learnt that it was an instrument with two strings called jinghu.

At first, I only regarded it as a hobby, **but** companies started paying me to take photos and publish them.

At first, Ryan was nervous, **but** soon a great warmth filled him.

At first, I was pleased we could stay at home, **but soon** it got really tough.

It felt bizarre **at first**. I didn't like being reviewed from head to toe.

（2）at all

经常用于否定或疑问句中。

And should I say anything **at all** to my teammate?

Whenever I met one of them who seemed to me **at all** clear-sighted, I tried the experiment of showing him my Drawing Number One, which I have always kept.

We also need to consider that some of these so-called "urban animals" have never moved **at all**—it's we humans who have moved into their territory.

（3）at the same time

If you go to university and play music **at the same time**, you will have two options for your future.

At the same time, a friend of Ryan's mother helped make his story go public.

（4）at last

In Uganda, Ryan **at last** saw the finished well with his own eyes.

At last, showing a strong will and the steeliest nerves, they played a close match against Serbia to seize gold in the final.

（5）at one

It is my great pleasure to give a lecture here on behalf of the Be **at one** with Nature Association.

（6）keep...at bay（=to prevent something dangerous or unpleasant from happening or from coming too close）

A tear swam in the eye of Quasimodo, but did not fall. He seemed to make it a point of honour to **keep it at bay**.

（二）介词 in

介词 in 是三维的，主打意思是"内，里面"。适用于有边界的立体时空或者抽象的时空概念，或其他抽象概念。In 的用法特别多，多数都是跟其他词一起组成短语，下面的分类很粗，也未必科学，却足以看出 in 的诸多用法。

1. 在空间范围内

And there we see the Chinese players embracing, with tears of happiness **in** their eyes...

The Chinese women's volleyball team holds a very special place **in** the nation's heart.

Living **in the open air**, we became breakfast, lunch and dinner for the mosquitos.

Goals were hung **in the air**.

While we're doing all this traveling, we can get seasick at sea, airsick **in** the air and carsick **in** a car, but we don't get homesick when we get back home.

Here are some of our favourites, to remind us that some of the English we learn in the classroom is rather different from the English **in** the outside world!

But there weren't any errors **in** my paper.

An eagle flew over the snow-capped mountains, which were reflected **in** the still lake below.

My most frightening but magical experience was now captured forever **in** a single image.

Firstly, there are few large, flat areas of land **in** the region.

At one point, the host asked people **in the audience** to stand up if Nicholas Winton had saved their lives.

Millions watched that first lunar landing on black and white television sets, their hearts **in** their mouths, aware of how arduous and hazardous an undertaking it was, and of the many things that could go wrong.

有时有"进""到……里面"的意思,跟 into 差不多。

The man whispered something **in** the lion's ear, after which the lion shook its head and walked away unhappily.

2. 表示抽象空间、位置

Alistair pushed himself towards the finish line **in** the burning heat, but as he came round the corner, he saw his brother about to fall onto the track.

The move put Jonny **in** second place and Alistair himself **in** third.

With just 700 metres to go, Alistair Brownlee was **in** third place and his younger brother, Jonny, was **in** the lead.

At first, I kept running just to see my name **in** the top five.

One of the most wonderful migrations **in** nature is that of the North American monarch butterfly.

The more we know about this lovely creature, the greater the chance it will survive and keep its place **in** the natural world for a long time to come.

These two pieces of information—the time of day and the point where the sun is **in** the sky—allow the butterfly to determine the way to go.

But despite the wind and the rain, I still enjoy working outside **in** the wild.

Playing **in** a band is not a job.

If you spend more than eight minutes **in** a shower, you'll use as much water as **in** a bath—about 50 litres of water.

When reading The Road Not Taken, one cannot help but see **in** one's mind images of a peaceful wood deep within the countryside.

Because of this, Chinese literary works really strike a chord **in the hearts of** Egyptian readers.

Given our limited knowledge, it is perhaps no surprise that exploration of the oceans continues to lead to discoveries **in** various scientific fields.

After I had pictured it over and over again **in** my mind, the big day finally arrived.

With this **in mind**, are the benefits of climbing Qomolangma worth the risks?

But we need to keep **in mind** that what we see on social media is often not the whole truth about a person.

Shall I be believed when I say that, at the depth of thirty feet, I could see as if I was **in** broad daylight?

3. 在时间范围内

In the 1980s, the team burst onto the international volleyball scene with several major world titles, and an amazing three-set victory over the United States in the final of the 1984 Los Angeles Olympics.

Going back to Walter Scott's lines, we may find even white lies have results we cannot know **in** advance.

In December 1938, a friend asked Winton to come to Prague to aid people who were escaping from the Nazis.

This was no doubt the reason behind the invention of the wheel **in** ancient times, which much later developed into the car.

Night-Shining White, now kept in New York's Metropolitan Museum of Art, is regarded as one of the most significant horse paintings **in** the history of Chinese art.

Born into a poor family **in** the early Tang Dynasty, the young Han Gan had to help support his family by working **in** a local wine shop. 前一个 in 表时间，后一个表地点。

Our street turned into a river **in** seconds.

For example, **in** our free time we can sculpt a sculpture and paint a painting, but we take a photo.

Its population has crashed by as much as 90 per cent **in** the last few years.

Imagine mountains wrapped **in** silver water, shining **in** the spring sun. During autumn, these same mountains are gold, and **in** winter they are covered **in** sheets of white frost. 句中的 in 有表示时间的，也有表示状态的。

Starting **in** the Yuan Dynasty, work on the terraces took hundreds of years, until its completion **in** the early Qing Dynasty.

So you have to trust that the dots will somehow connect **in** your future.

有时表示"在(某一段时间)末尾",常用在将来时中,表示"……后"。

We figured that **in** twenty years each of us ought to have our destiny worked out and our fortunes made, whatever they were going to be.

What will we be doing **in** ten years' time?

4. 在其他抽象概念中

(1) in+ 抽象名词表示情感状态

Some children, though, don't feel like laughing, especially if they're **in pain**.

I woke up early and rushed out of the door **in my eagerness** to get to know my new school.

Maybe I'll fall **in love** with stinky tofu—someday.

I looked at them **in panic**.

In desperation, Doyle killed off the famous detective in a novel published in 1893 so that he could focus on his "serious" writing.

(2) In+ 抽象名词短语表述情况或状态

These sights **set** Hofman's idea for Floating Fish **in motion**.

Can a video of someone slicing a tomato played **in slow motion** really be called "art"?

It is understandable **in that situation**, but we should always think before we speak.

In Prague, Winton saw people living **in terrible conditions** and whose lives were **in danger**.

They are captured and taken inside the submarine, where they meet the man **in charge**, Captain Nemo.

A regular character in the letters was Polar Bear, who once climbed the North Pole (an actual pole **in this case**) and fell through the roof of Father Christmas's house.

I only joined my local athletics club because my doctor told me that **in my particular case** exercise could improve how my lungs work.

In some cases, local produce might have used more energy and produced more greenhouse gases than produce grown a long way away—even taking into account its transport.

Once we make a decision, **in** most circumstances, there is no going back.

So, if you are a runner with a story to tell, get **in touch**—we'd love to hear from you!

Nowadays, we can move around the world and still stay **in touch** with the people that we want to remain friends with.

His brother was **in trouble**.

But perhaps what is most significant is the way in which people have worked **in harmony with** nature to make these terraces and grow rice.

Devices **in this mode** still use power, and older devices in stand-by mode can use even more.

As many of us already know, having plans **in place** for the future is no guarantee that they will become reality.

Here are the Happiness of the Blue Sky, who, of course, is dressed **in** blue, and the Happiness of the Forest: you will see him every time you go to the window...

She resists instinctively; and, **in their hesitation**, the DOVE escapes and flies away.

Move over here where you can see it **in more detail**.

（3）In 单独使用或与名词搭配，都可以表示"在……方面"

Zhu Ting, named Most Valuable Player at the Rio Olympics, also identified this as the special ingredient **in** the team's success.

However, the increase **in** the amount and variety of art produced has also raised questions over its overall quality.

Despite his father's successful career, Stephen was thought by many people, including his high school teammates and coaches, to be too short, too thin and too weak to follow **in his father**'s **footsteps**.

The bumps and rocks that lined the road under the basket caused the ball to bounce **in all directions**.

But he is equally well known for his witty remarks **in** his everyday interactions with people.

He returned to Britain in 1931, where he worked **in business**.

For example, advances **in** virtual reality and wearable tech, as well as the flexible battery, mean we should soon be seeing further developments.

What's more, huge advances **in** solar technology mean it can be eco-friendly, too.

Its artist, Han Gan, is known for his skill **in** capturing not only the physical features of the animal, but also its inner spirit and strength.

It is still not known if he succeeded **in** reaching the top of Qomolangma before it took his life.

It lists your performance against other runners **in** your social network.

I want to focus on my band and have a career **in** music when I leave school.

Thanks to advances **in** technology, how we make friends and communicate with them has changed significantly.

In this respect, some people are more fortunate than others, as can be illustrated by comparing the lives of two famous authors, born 40 years apart.

To succeed **in** business, you need more than a good idea, hard work and determination.

（4）in 介词短语表示方式

In this way, practising day in and day out helped Stephen sharpen his skills.

A recent project used technology and data **in** the same way that Rembrandt used his paints and brushes.

After receiving the Most Valuable Player award for two years **in** a row, Stephen explained his philosophy.

If you feel one of your teammates isn't pulling their weight, then raise your concerns **in** a professional way with your team coach.

Captain Nemo walked **in** front, one of his men following some steps behind.

What if, **in** choosing one, we are unknowingly turning down other future opportunities?

5. In 介词短语表示动作

相当于实义动词的用法。

They migrate to find food, seek a partner, or **in search of** warmer weather.

Can we become the person we really want to be? **In the face of** such questions, how should we approach the future?

Like Zhang, they present their ideas **in the hope of** getting investment and advice, and they have the same passion and devotion.

The 500-metre dish of the "Eye of Heaven" as it is known, is being used **in the search for** dark matter, thought to be composed of subatomic particles invisible to ordinary telescopes.

6. 其他一些固定短语

Seeing their daughter so much happier has **in turn** made Lara's parents more relaxed.

It can be quite stressful at times, though, which **in turn** makes me feel anxious.

Perhaps the overall prize for perseverance should go to three sisters from Victorian England who dreamt of seeing their words **in print**.

Inspiring others to **believe in** themselves, Stephen Curry is living proof that what other people think of you does not have to influence what you become.

"Nothing **in particular**," she replied.

Is there anything else **in particular** that you'd like to share with us?

In addition, important advances have been made in medicine and environmental science thanks to increasing computer power.

In addition, publishing houses tend to look to other countries to see which Chinese works have sold well there, I've so far translated the writings of Han Han, and I am now working on those of Xu Zechen.

In terms of the environment, it is now possible to create an intelligent walking house.

Thankfully, Smartie came home just **in time**.

In my opinion, what or where we eat on Spring Festival Eve really doesn't matter.

With butterflies in my stomach, I breathed deeply.

You also have to wonder at the unique madness of a language in which you **fill in** a form by filling it out.

He told us that Maggie couldn't teach that day COZ she **had a frog in her throat**.

But **in the end**, you just advised me to think carefully.

With the majority of attempts to climb Qomolangma **resulting either in** total success or failure, is there also a scientific reason behind this risk-taking?

Of course, the greatest dilemmas arise from moral problems, when we are uncertain which choice **results in** doing the right thing.

Some research seems to indicate that Maya people themselves may have **played a part in** their downfall.

But this was going to be no ordinary excursion, and millions of people **tuned in** to witness the take-off on TV.

In reality, humans can see very little of the night sky with the naked eye.

To see even further into the universe, many countries **are now engaged in** building ever more advanced telescopes.

When she received her first rejection letter, she decided that it meant she now **had something in common with** her favourite writers, and stuck it on her kitchen wall.

I think Egypt and China are closely connected and both have a lot **in common**.

（三）介词 off

介词 off 的本意就是"离开,脱离（原本的位置）",引申义为"离……（在有某一距离的地方),在（某条街）旁边"。大多数由 off 构成的短语基本是这两层意思。

1. 离开，脱离（原本的位置）

With water falling **off** its thick, brown hair, the bear stared back at me.

It breaks down walls and brings people together on and **off** the field.

To make sure your appliance is in fact **off**, remove the plug from its power supply.

One very hot summer, the sun reflected **off** it and melted cars parked below! Will this happen again today?

2. 离……（在有某一距离的地方），在（某条街）旁边

Located **off** the coast of North-east Australia, the Great Barrier Reef is the largest living thing on the planet.

One such find is the ancient Roman city of Neapolis, discovered **off** the coast of Tunisia.

3. off 短语

You also have to wonder at the unique madness of a language in which an alarm is only heard once it **goes off**!

When we **turn off** a device, such as television, it goes into stand-by mode.

This happens because electricity continues to leak from the device, even when it is **turned "off"**.

Each runner receives a gorilla suit and **off** they **go**!

When my muscles got sore, the cold wind hit my face and the sweat **poured off** my forehead.

Finning is a type of fishing where sharks are caught and their fins **cut off**.

Those who saw Han Gan's horse paintings all sang high praises for his unique skill, saying that his horses "could **gallop off the paper**".

I was sitting in my room with my cat, Smartie, on my lap, when the roof just **flew off**.

Well, when I **take off** my wig and my red nose, I'm still wearing a big smile, as I remember all the fun and laughter of the day.

The sharing economy is **taking off** in all sorts of areas.

When the Challenger space shuttle **took off** on 28 January 1986, the world seemed to have lost its wonder at the amazing achievements of the astronauts involved.

He hardly ever **took a day off** and not once stayed home sick.

I speak with the on-duty nurse, who tells me that Lara's parents rushed her to the hospital after she **fell off** her bicycle.

With this little joke, Lin was able to make people laugh, while gently **telling off** the president.

Their perseverance **paid off** with an epic comeback against the defending champion Brazil in the quarter-finals.

Lang is only too aware that as soon as a team **steps off** the victory podium, they need to start from zero to prepare for new challenges ahead.

In desperation, Doyle **killed off** the famous detective in a novel published in 1893 so that he could focus on his "serious" writing.

(四)介词 on

On 做副词的时候用法比较单一,经常表示"继续""穿戴上"或"开着"等意思。例如:

It was **from then on** that his grandchildren started to be in control of what to do with the money they receive: spend, save, invest, or give?

It is for us, the living, rather to be dedicated here to the unfinished work which they have, thus far, so nobly **carried on**.

He looked thicker and stubbier with his spacesuit **on**, but he could handle the lunar gravity as no Earth-born human being could.

介词 on 属于二维平面,主要的意思是"在其上",强调在平面上。

引申意思很多,如支撑、依靠、承担、借助、关于、启动、进行中等意义。

1. 在(平面)上,在(一条线)上,到……上面

And when we are traveling we say that we are in the car or the taxi, but **on** the train or bus!

She said that it was **on** the first floor.

But we need to keep in mind that what we see **on** social media is often not the whole truth about a person.

On social media sites, people tend to post only positive updates that make them appear happy and friendly.

Whatever our hobbies, the Internet can connect us with others who also enjoy doing them, even if they live **on** the other side of the world.

Like Twain, but **on** the other side of the world, Lin Yutang was soon to become famous for his unique brand of humour.

Then, seeing the main characters come **on** stage, I was surprised!

We started from Vancouver, where we picked up our vehicle for the trip—a home **on** wheels.

I should probably put my flat **on** the market and buy a boat.

Stepping out of the station with a heavy heart, I suddenly feel a fresh wind **on** my face.

I was sitting in my room with my cat, Smartie, **on** my lap, when the roof just flew off.

All we had left were the clothes **on** our backs.

More than 25 million years old, the Great Barrier Reef is made up of living coral growing **on** dead coral.

In the afternoon I should take a long walk in the woods and intoxicate my eyes **on** the beauties of the world of nature.

We are met here **on** a great battlefield of that war.

But there are so many important places not yet **on** this list.

In the very deepest ocean trenches that are more than 8,000 metres below the surface, the pressure is equivalent to 50 aeroplanes stacked one **on** top of another.

2. 常与动词构成其他短语,可用于引申意义

I tried to **turn on** my brain but the engine just wouldn't start.

Looking back on my high school life, the most important advice I'd give is these wonderful words from the writer Maya Angelou.

How will we **look back on** our lives?

I want to **focus on** my band and have a career in music when I leave school.

You really have to **focus on** the one reason that's most important and unique to you.

This lack of self-interest and promotion kept Cunningham **focused on** his craft, enabling him to capture New York's unique street style.

While I was **concentrating on** photographing this amazing scene, I suddenly had a feeling that I was being watched.

Embarrassed and ashamed, I can't **concentrate on** anything.

While the doctor **concentrates on** examining Lara's ankle, I get her attention by doing a magic trick.

These terraces also provide a perfect environment for birds and fish, some of which **feed on** insects that can harm the rice crops.

They say that "a picture is worth a thousand words", but the briefest look at books and the movies **based on** them would have anyone questioning this common saying.

It **depends on** how long you spend in the shower and how large your bath is.

While these same jokes might not be as funny to us now as they were then, their authors understood that humour could not only entertain but also **throw new light on** sensitive or emotive issues.

Thinking on his feet, Lin started to tell a story about a cruel Roman emperor who tried to feed a man to wild animals.

Rowling had spent years **surviving on** little money, spending all her time writing.

Even when serving in the US Army during the Second World War, he carried six chapters of The Catcher in the Rye with him and **worked on** the novel throughout his war service.

Given the complexity of the work and the lack of necessary materials, this means that each expert can **work on** a maximum of two large pieces a year.

With the detox finished, they've **switched on** their devices and they're back online.

Casey encouraged us to share our ideas and comments **on** the books, by writing them on a large board in one corner of the store.

Following in the footsteps of his own teacher all those years ago, Mr Wang has now **passed on** his skills to the new members, who will **take on** many of the future repairs.

Today, the action of sharing **takes on** extra meaning.

One thing I think we all **agree on**, though, is that saying "My AI did it" won't be any excuse for illegal or immoral behaviour!

Enter NEIGHBOUR BERLINGOT, a little old woman **leaning on** a stick.

It was the most disastrous space accident ever, and it **cast a shadow on** people's hearts.

Life throws many alternatives at us **on** a daily basis.

His writing had a profound effect **on** me, and I have this to thank for my passion for Chinese literature.

I also keep a close eye **on** what's being self-published online by new, young authors—they have some good ideas.

What's more, sharing encourages us to reuse items, thereby **cutting down on** waste.

Ever since Neil Armstrong first **set foot on** the Moon back on 20 July 1969, people have become accustomed to the notion of space travel.

3. 表示时间,某一天或某一天的上、下午或晚上

The short story "After Twenty Years" is set in New York **on** a cold, dark night.

I've also been taking driving lessons, and in fact I will be taking my driving test **on** the very day I turn 18.

On a typical day, we spend our time cheering up patients, their families, and more often than not, the hospital staff, too!

On the first day, I should want to see the people whose kindness and gentleness and companionship have made my life worth living.

4. 当……时,在……后(引起时间状语)

(1)跟动名词,表示"一……就"

On leaving school, Winton worked in banks in Germany and France.

On receiving a Kare bag, one woman said, "You make me feel like a human being."

On leaving high school, he joined a local Kansas newspaper as a trainee reporter.

On discovering that Morrie is being weakened by severe illness, Mitch starts visiting him at his house on Tuesdays.

(2)跟表示动作的名词

The horses, whether resting or **on the move**, offered him plenty of inspiration.

But **on reflection**, I can see how much of my time had been occupied with checking my phone.

5. 与其他词构成短语作状语,说明活动的性质或目的

To celebrate, we went **on a boat trip** yesterday.

For instance, while **on** a lecturing tour of the United States, Twain went into a barber's shop to get a haircut and a shave.

6. 与其他词构成短语,常作表语,说明状态、特征、处境等

But, in fact, I was **on the edge of** my seat!

For two years, two months and two days, he lived in a cottage in the forest **on the edge of** Walden Pond, **focusing on** himself and his writing.

It breaks down walls and brings people together **on and off** the field.

Florentijn Hofman is a Dutch artist, whose large sculptures are **on display** all over the world.

Tragically, she never returned to her classroom as the shuttle exploded just over a minute after taking off in Florida, and all seven astronauts **on board** were killed.

Once, having been invited to dinner at a university, he was **put on the spot** when the president suddenly asked him to give a speech.

In 2014, Macquarie Island was declared pest-free and the island's ecology is finally **on the road to** recovery.

7. 表示"关于""对于"

The research **on** the monarch's behaviour has however led to a greater awareness of this creature.

Starting in the Yuan Dynasty, work **on** the terraces took hundreds of years, until its completion in the early Qing Dynasty.

Surely, if you're old enough to earn a wage and pay taxes, you should be allowed to **have a say on** how the government spends them!

I use my photography to **make an impact on** people, especially when it comes to environmental issues.

I expected to feel instantly different, as if I had closed the door **on** my childhood and stepped into a whole new adult world.

I know I could get a bank loan to pay the deposit **on** my very own apartment, but I don't feel ready to make that kind of commitment.

Recent headlines have seen more and more teens **maxing out** their parents' credit cards **on** games and other online activities.

Last year, hundreds of people **spent** good **money on** an experience that they knew would include crowds, discomfort and danger.

We have to be very sensitive and work closely with the doctors and nurses, who keep us updated **on** each patient.

"We feel that we don't know the central character well enough" was the criticism he received **on** his manuscript for *The Catcher in the Rye*.

Darwin explained this theory in his book, **On** the Origin of Species.

I was one of the people who came from all parts of China to **work on** this railway.

What's worse, I then spent so much time **catching up on** news, I almost missed the party.

I was told that the community had decided to **work** together **on** a campaign to save the Rainbow Bookstore.

Maisy, a retired public health official from Darwin, Australia, whose local team of volunteers educated people **on** preventing infection.

But, although the death rate is very high, we will never **give up on** a patient, and our efforts do sometimes end in miracles.

It can be an expression of our personalities, helping us **make a** good and positive **impression on** others.

Surely, if you're old enough to earn a wage and pay taxes, you should be allowed to **have a say on** how the government spends them!

By imagining a world without birds, she aimed to alert not only the scientific community but also the general public to the damaging effects of human activity **on** natural ecosystems—in particular, to the harmful use of pesticides, such as DDT.

The weekly conversations between Mitch and Morrie result in series of lessons **on** the meaning of life and how best to live it.

Morrie's reflections **on** love and friendship made me think about my life and all the good friends that I've lost touch with along the way.

8. 其他 on 短语

When I saw the tragic scenes **on the news**, I felt it was my duty as a doctor to go there and offer my help.

It is my great pleasure to give a lecture here **on behalf of** the Be at

One with Nature Association.

Professors and students alike in the three universities made an epic journey over a distance of more than 2,000 kilometres, most of them **on foot**.

Still, do think that developments in AI will **on the whole** make doing day-to-day things a lot easier.

On the whole, I do have to admit that here, people's knowledge of Chinese literature is rather limited.

On top of all this was an achievement unique in the Americas at that time: a true writing system.

（五）介词 over

介词 over 主要的意思是"跨越"，可以指空间上"从上方跨过"，也可以指时间上的跨越，还有"在……上面或外面""多于"等。引申义有"对于，关于""渡过（困难），逾越（障碍）"等。

1. 空间上的"从上方跨过"

Alistair then pushed his brother **over** the line.

An eagle flew **over** the snow-capped mountains, which were reflected in the still lake below.

Nothing in history has allowed us to see so much **over** such great distances, from enormous clouds of gas where stars are being born, to huge black holes, and even to new planets where we might conceivably find life.

The first landmark to catch my eye is the splendid Qingshuihe Bridge, the world's longest bridge built **over** permafrost.

So then I chose another profession, and learned to pilot airplanes I have flown a little **over** all parts of the world...

Nearby, customers were pouring **over** shelves selling stationery, posters and other best-seller-themed gifts.

Professors and students alike in the three universities made an epic journey **over** a distance of more than 2,000 kilometres, most of them on foot.

Zhang Changning serves. **Over** the net, Popovic dives for the ball.

With foxes in London mountain lions in San Francisco and wild pigs in Hong Kong: it is almost as if our cities are being **taken over** by wild animals.

Today, however, environmental problems have **taken over** as the greatest risk to life on Earth.

2. 时间上的"跨越(一段时间)"

The letters were Tolkien's way of keeping Father Christmas alive for his four children, **over** a period of more than twenty years.

Over time, this could make her a danger to people living in the area.

The history of the game goes back **over** two thousand years to Ancient China.

Dating back to the 18th century, Peking Opera has **over** two hundred years of history.

Over time, it had slowly evolved into many new species.

Encouraged by discoveries **over** the years, space agencies of various countries are planning manned missions to Mars that could take place within the next 25 years.

However, despite the immense hardships and the daunting challenges, it was right in this place, **over** a period of eight long years, that the nation's intellectual heritage was not only guarded but fortified by the passion and belief of the worthy academics of Lianda.

3. 超过,多于

In the 1980s, the team burst onto the international volleyball scene with several major world titles, and an amazing three-set victory **over** the United States in the final of the 1984 Los Angeles Olympics.

It seems that emojis have clear advantages **over** written language.

4. 关于，就（因为）……某个问题，某事

Despite arguments **over** "stupid things" now and then, Alistair agrees that having a brother is an advantage.

However, the increase in the amount and variety of art produced has also raised questions **over** its overall quality.

I pondered deeply, then, **over** the adventures of the jungle.

You may just send them a string of crying faces to express your sadness **over** your separation.

As an official in the Eastern Jin Dynasty, Tao felt conflicted **over** life at court.

（六）介词 through

介词 through 的用法主要表示"穿过，通过（时间、空间）"，引申义为"经历，经受""通过（途径，方式，方法等）"。

1. 空间上的穿过

Last spring in Yellowstone, I followed a path that took me **through** a dark forest.

How was it possible, I asked myself, to walk for an hour **through** the woods and see nothing worthy of note?

The solar rays shone **through** the watery mass easily, and consumed all colour, and I clearly distinguished objects at a distance of a hundred and fifty yards.

This dazzling carpet, really a reflector, drove away the rays of the sun with wonderful intensity, which accounted for the vibration which passed **through** every atom of liquid.

He was particularly interested in the old story about a fish jumping **through** the "Dragon Gate".

The light that came **through** the windows was very strange, and it made the familiar business of splashing and shaving and brushing and dressing very strange too.

One theory behind this is that these birds have yet to change their migratory routes that take them **through** cities with high-rise buildings.

Walking **through** the seven crimson gates towards his workplace, Wang Jin still regards himself as an ordinary worker in the Palace Museum.

Moving carefully **through** the darkness, she passes row upon row of rose plants.

Swimming **through** these black depths is the barreleye, a strange fish with eyes that can look upwards **through** its transparent forehead. 前一个 through 指通过空间，后一个 through 指通过一种途径。

2. 时间上的贯穿

做此意的时候，常跟 throughout 用法相同。

After that they are not able to move, and they sleep **through** the six months that they need for digestion.

Ultimately, the road ahead—the road **through** our lives—is a mixture of choice and chance.

A box of tissues will be needed to **get through** this book!

Throughout my entire life, I've had my brother trying to beat me at everything I do.

There have been golden ages of invention **throughout** history.

Throughout his life, he made over 90 self-portraits!

Cunningham's passion for photography lasted **throughout** his life.

Throughout history, the great thinkers of the world have often rather romantically referred to their academic struggles as being like "war".

3. 经历，经受

Together, the Chinese women's volleyball team has fought their way **through** ups and downs.

He's at the rocket station, **going through** the tests.

4. 通过(途径、方式、方法等)

This knowledge is passed down **through** families, which means that new generations continue to use ancient methods of agriculture to maintain the terraces.

Hofman's inspiration for Floating Fish came from Chinese folk tales passed down **through** the generations.

A regular character in the letters was Polar Bear, who once climbed the North Pole (an actual pole in this case) and fell **through** the roof of Father Christmas's house.

A flash of lightning hit the kite, and electricity was conducted **through** the string to the key.

Conseil and I remained near each other, as if an exchange of words had been possible **through** our metal cases.

I who cannot see find hundreds of things to interest me **through** mere touch.

I don not know what it is to see into the heart of a friend **through** that "window of the soul", the eye. I can only "see" **through** my fingertips the outline of a face.

Through self-belief, hard work, perseverance and some help from an old hoop, he has shown that anything is possible.

Whatever your opinion, people have been expressing their thoughts and ideas **through** art for thousands of years.

You'll also be asked to promote the islands **through** newspapers, magazines and TV interviews.

After reading the posts on this forum, it seems that something rather than money has also been raised **through** the detox.

Inside the bags are necessities such as toothpaste, soap and socks, bought first with her pocket money and then **through** crowd funding.

The bookstore, which was a legendary fixture in the neighbourhood, was a place where anyone could drop in and connect **through** their love of books.

Through interviews, I was able to discover what "me" means to other people, and how they have learnt to appreciate the beauty in themselves.

Through his fascination with what people were wearing, and not who they were, he opened the doors of fashion to everyone.

But, **through** their painstaking efforts, Mr. Wang and his students do more than repair the clocks—they bring them back to life.

The water is then recycled **through** the building's plumbing system.

This century is bringing the Silk Road to life once more **through** the Belt and Road Initiative.

Through comparison, he found that the locations of the 117 known Maya cities correspond to the positions of the stars.

However, **through** closer international scientific economic and cultural cooperation, we are all becoming part of a global mission to open up our planet's final frontier.

5. 跟动词搭配的 through 短语,意思基本是本义

Looking through my newspaper, I'm shocked by photos showing that a hurricane in Asia has destroyed a town.

I was nearly as excited about it this morning as the children, whom I found all **looking through** the window at the magic outside and talking away as excitedly as if Christmas had suddenly come round again.

Whether I'm at the gym or on the road, my nervous energy **pushes me through** mile one.

Emma spent an hour with me in the staff room **talking me through** the daily routine.

(七)介词 up

up 这个词无论作介词还是副词,第一个基本意都是"向上,上面",第二个意思是"靠近,走近"。教材中的主要用法是副词用法。

1. 表示向上的动作

If you look **up**, you can see the paintings and other artworks that are testimony to how the Silk Road brought East and West together.

Zhang never thought that this was something she would end up doing. Surrounded by roses as she was **growing up**, she paid them little attention.

The slope was a gentle one and even the weight of the spacesuit couldn't keep Jimmy from **racing up** it in a floating hop that made the gravity seem nonexistent.

Her head and arms are missing, but you can imagine her **holding her arms up** high, celebrating the result of an ancient battle.

Picking up a free newspaper at the Tube station, I see the title "Hot! Hot! Hot!".

2. 表示到(高处),来(去),在(高处)

They dance merrily around the CHILDREN, then the one who appears to be the chief **goes up to** TYLTYL with hand outstretched.

And you're really going to love what's **coming up** next.

And now, it's time to get **up** close and personal with one of history's greatest artists—Rembrandt!

So I went **up** to the first floor, but couldn't find any shoes.

He goes **up** to the man and finds he has a scar on his face.

I just spent the days watching the boats going **up and down** the street and looking out for Smartie.

3. 和动词构成短语表示动作的(彻底)完成

After Sherlock Holmes made him a household name, Doyle **gave up** medicine and devoted himself entirely to writing.

That is why, at the age of six, I **gave up** what might have been a magnificent career as a painter.

You may have spent years **giving up** your weekends and free time to write your life's work, yet still this is often not enough.

But, although the death rate is very high, we will never **give up** on a patient, and our efforts do sometimes end in miracles.

However, the reason why the Library Cave was **sealed up** all those years ago remains a mystery.

He finally **ended up** playing college ball at a small, little-known school, Davidson College, not too far from where he lived.

You also have to wonder at the unique madness of a language in which a house can **burn up** as it burns down.

I really don't think it's worth the effort of spending so much time preparing for a single meal, and then another hour **cleaning up** the mess after it's over.

4. 到期,期满,时间到了

He was 87 when he passed away, and had been working right **up** until his last illness.

5. up to 短语

(1) It's up to sb to do 由……决定

It's up to us to find out what is important in our lives and establish our own values.

This could involve saving for university, but it could also mean saving for that special something you've seen in the stores—**it's up to you**.

Now **it was up to** the living to remove not only the divisions between North and South.

(2) 高达

The dark zones of the oceans may contain **up to** 90 per cent of the planet's fish.

As this artwork is rarely on display, people have sometimes

queued **up to** six hours for a chance to see it.

However, making a paper bag uses four times as much energy as making a plastic bag and **up to** three times the amount of water.

Despite a weight of **up to** 300 kilograms, they can run at a speed of around 64 kilometres per hour and are also excellent swimmers.

The cats in consequence turned their attention—and their stomachs—back to the native birds, killing **up to** 60,000 each year.

（3）（口语中）在做秘密的事或不该做的事

By the fifth day, I wondered—was I really missing out by not constantly checking my phone to see what everyone else **was up to**?

Social media tools let us see what our friends **are up to** and maintain friendships.

6. 其他一些 up 短语

Despite its widespread recognition, my first impression was that Tuesdays with Morrie **is just made up of** collection of over-emotional thoughts and messages, many of which are repeated.

More than 25 million years old, the Great Barrier Reef **is made up of** living coral growing on dead coral.

Allied troops **made up** mainly **of** British, Canadian and American soldiers were gathering in large numbers.

Taking it as an object of study, psychologists have published various papers stating that the behaviour of sharing is beneficial to **setting up** positive emotional bonding.

Later, Ryan's experience led him to **set up** a foundation to encourage more people to help.

However, through closer international scientific economic and cultural cooperation, we are all becoming part of a global mission to **open up** our planet's final frontier.

Now, after eight months of endless adjustments, the time has finally come for Mr Wang to **wind up** the gigantic clocks that date back to the time of Emperor Qianlong.

And that is why when I **wind up** my watch, it starts, but when I **wind up** this passage, it ends.

What's more, inspired to follow in his father's footsteps, Mr. Wang's son now has also **taken up** repairing antique clocks.

The Allied forces then prepared to enter Germany, where they would **meet up with** the Soviet military moving in from the east.

Their bed was the dusty road and their roof was the open sky, often **lit up** by exploding Japanese bombs.

The artworks by American artist Janet Echelman look like colourful floating clouds when they are **lit up** at night.

Reading this book made me feel as if I'd been **woken up** from a long sleep and finally opened my eyes to the world!

I **woke up** early and rushed out of the door in my eagerness to get to know my new school.

You go to bed in one kind of world and **wake up** to find yourself in another quite different, and if this is not magic, then where is it to be found?

For unless we do listen to Rachel Carson's warning, one day we may **wake up to** the strange and quiet horror of another silent spring.

I'm now trying to spend less time online and more time **picking up** my hobbies.

We started from Vancouver, where we **picked up** our vehicle for the trip—a home on wheels.

What's worse, I then spent so much time **catching up on** news, I almost missed the party.

I joined Casey, who was **looking up** at the screen on which readers' comments kept **popping up**.

But with an increasing number of problems and worries **popping up** this year, which were caused by my poor physical health, I came to realize that there was no choice but to work out.

To be **caught up** in such a crisis creates powerful bonds between people, not only between carers and patients, but also between all those who have come from different parts of the world and joined together in a common cause.

Experts felt it necessary to **come up with** a plan to remove all the rabbits from the island.

Some have even questioned the story about the apple that fell on Newton's head and led him to **come up with** his theory of gravity.

On a typical day, we spend our time **cheering up** patients, their families, and more often than not, the hospital staff, too!

I can't count how many times I tried to **build up** my body, but tiredness, pain and laziness always prevented me from finishing the race.

All too often, great words **end up** being turned into cinematic "turkeys".

Many people thought she didn't **live up to** Helen's title of "the most beautiful woman in the world", influencing opinions of the movie to some extent.

I came a thousand miles to stand in this door tonight, and it's worth it if my old partner **turns up**.

本节中介绍的每个介词，其用法都远超上面的介绍，这里仅就教材中常见的高频介词进行了归纳。通过这些介绍，我们可以推断出哪些是学生在日常教学中需要熟练掌握的。另外，还有一些介词在高考试题中出现的频率也很高，如 beyond，因此在日常教学中我们需要更加关注、深入理解并正确使用这些介词，努力让学生的表达更地道！

第七章 阅读中的语法学习

在人际交往的语境中,语法作为语言的构造基石,对语言的组织与呈现的精准、达意起到关键作用。课程标准要求语法学习要遵循"形式—意义—使用"统一的三维动态语法观。本章会重点聚焦阅读中的语法学习,其中包括很多人会忽略的标点符号的用法。

第一节 小标点,大用途

标点符号看似很小,作用却很大。高考书面表达的评分标准对标点的使用有明确要求,但很多学生在英语写作中由于对英语标点符号了解不够,使用随意,造成很多的问题。比如,很多学生在写作过程中,经常犯的错误就是用逗号连接两个或几个句子。前面的章节中已经介绍过标点符号在解答七选五题型中的作用,本节重点介绍几种常用标点符号的用法,帮助学生在交际中准确表情达意。

一、语篇题目中的标点符号

现行高中英语外研版教材中,必修和选必修共七本书中,带有标点符号的题目有 15 篇文章。题目本身是语篇的高度概括,加上标点符号,更好地表达作者的态度和更多的内容。

在英语中,感叹号用于表示强烈的感情或惊叹的语气。在三篇带有感叹号的文章中,感叹号都比较强烈地表达了文章中人物的情绪:

从 *Absolute agony*! 这个题目能非常清晰地看到文中人物的愤怒和痛苦。文章由两封书信组成,一封是求助信,描述了同学间相处时出现的问题;另一封是被求助者的回信,针对求助信中的问题给出了建议。

词汇加上感叹号,连续重复三遍,*Hot! Hot! Hot!* 的作者热不可耐的心情跃然纸上,画面感很强!作者以乘坐伦敦地铁的经历生动描写伦敦的酷热,并由报纸上关于飓风的灾害,引发对环境问题的思考。

It's all about me! 用感叹号旗帜鲜明地表明了三位年轻人对自我形象的认知和对内、外在美的不同看法。

十二篇以疑问形式作题目的文章,根据各种疑问句本身的特点和用法,功能和表达的内容各不相同。

特殊疑问句作题目,通常用来引起读者的好奇心,引导读者对某个特定问题进行思考或探索。特殊疑问句的答案通常是具体和明确的,因此也常用于设置悬念或引发争议。

What's really green? 以特殊疑问的形式设置了悬念,介绍了生活中常见的关于环保的误区,并针对问题进行解答:怎样才算是真正环保的做法。

What inspires you? 引起读者兴趣,关注三位著名艺术家对艺术灵感的解读和他们的作品,答案明确直接。

Franklin's experiment: how much is true? 质疑大家相信了多年的富兰克林的风筝实验,问题代表了对这个风筝实验的怀疑,以及由此带来的求证,客观说明实验情况,同时提出作者自己的观点。

而 *Why Shennongjia*? 以省略的特殊疑问形式作演讲的题目,唤起听众的好奇心,进而引导听众了解神农架的神秘独特之处。

选择疑问句作题目,通常用来给出两个或多个选项,让读者在文章中作出选择或判断。选择疑问句的答案通常是简单明了的,因此也常用于引导读者进行思考或权衡利弊。例如, *Sharks: dangerous or endangered*? 以选择性疑问形式引发读者对于鲨鱼的思考。文本解释了人们对于鲨鱼的态度变化,得出了鲨鱼不会对人构成威胁,不是 dangerous 而是 endangered 的结论,提升人们保护鲨鱼的意识。

一般疑问句作题目,通常用来提出一个普遍存在的问题或观点,鼓励读者思考或讨论该问题。一般疑问句的答案通常是主观的,取决于每个人的看法和经验。教材中的七篇以(省略的)一般疑问形式作题目的文章都属于这种情况,但表达观点的主体和文体略有不同:

Click for a friend? 和 *Good book, bad movie*? 都是论说文,引发读者对于题目表达的内容的思考和讨论,最终都给出了作者自己对于题目的态度。前者的结论是:网上可以交友,但必须谨慎。而后者讨论了文学作品改编的电影常不尽如人意的原因,最后提出要在各种作品的类别内进行判断,交叉评判没有意义。

Emojis: a new language? 是说明文,但是题目激发了读者的兴趣,随后作者引领读者逐步了解 emoji 的发展,表明自己的观点。

剩下的四篇 *Time for a change*? *Climbing Qomolangma: worth the risks*? *Plan B: life on Mars*? *Artificial intelligence: a real threat*? 基本属于专栏文章或杂志文章,通常发起问题的人不展示自己的观点,给予读者以充分的自由,思考问题,表达观点。而对问题的答案,往往出现对立的现象,孰优孰劣,由读者自行评判。

总之,不同类型的疑问句在充当英语文章的题目时具有不同的含义和用法。作者通常会根据文章的主题、内容和目的选择合适的疑问句类型来吸引读者的注意力并引导他们进行思考。

英语中的标点符号与汉语标点符号在形式上稍有不同。例如,英语中的句号是一个点,汉语中的句号是个小圆圈;英语中的省略号是三个点,汉语中的省略号是六个点;英语中没有书名号,通常采用斜体加首字母大写的方式标记文学作品的书名。有的书名使用斜体加首字母大写,有的用正体加首字母大写,有的用引号,有的不用,有的书名使用斜体,等等。

除了这几种形式上的不同,其他的标点符号在英汉两种语言中基本通用。用法上虽然存在一些差异,但大部分差别不大。以下介绍几个英语中常用且比较重要的标点符号。

二、逗号的用法

逗号在英语中,用于分隔句子中的独立子句,也可以用于列举项目或列举事物的属性,其用法非常多变,在学习中需要特别注意。

(1)在三个或三个以上的项目并列时,在最后一项前使用连词,其余各项用逗号隔开。这种逗号通常被称为并列逗号。

My goal is to help my students develop awareness of their strengths, weaknesses, and learning needs, and to enable them to learn throughout their lives.

Each volume in the set explores a wide range of material, explains the basic concepts of major applications of digital systems, and discusses the influences they have on everyday life.

（2）插入语通常与整个句子的意思没有多大关联，通常要自带逗号，也就是前后都需要用逗号与主句隔开。

Jimmy, expert though he was, couldn't outrace Robutt, who didn't need spacesuit, and had four legs and tendons of steel.

用作呼语的名字或头衔做插入语时，也要用逗号隔开。

Hi, Stephen, guess who I saw at the city library? Andy Clarkes — the leading actor in The Good Lawyer— the famous TV series.

Today I'm joined by a former student of our school, Lisa Osborne.

非限制性定语从句不起定义或限制的作用，只是单纯地增添一些补充内容，也可视为插入语，因此需要添加逗号。例如：

This knowledge is passed down through families, which means that new generations continue to use ancient methods of agriculture to maintain the terraces.

（3）日期通常含有插入的词或数字，按如下方式加标点：

Wednesday, November 27, 2023

注意，当日期按以下格式书写时，按照习惯省略逗号。这种形式是书写日期的最佳方式，单词夹在两个数字中间，一目了然：

1 January 2024

（4）在语法上起同位语作用的引语或作动词的直接宾语的引语前，通常要加逗号，并将引语放在引号内。例如：

People say, "Well begun, half done."

There is an old American saying, "Loose lips sink ships."

As the Chinese saying goes, "A kind-hearted person lives a long life."

In the words of Mark Twain, "Humor is mankind's greatest blessing".

（5）但是，当引语后面有限定性短语的时候，逗号应该放在引号内：

"Nice to know we share the same name," said my new teacher.

"Obviously, when your older brother is doing it, you think it's a cool thing to do," says Johnny.

（6）对话中对人的称呼需要跟后面的内容以逗号隔开；非正式书信

或邮件的称呼语后也要用逗号。

Lisa, thank you for coming to share your suggestions for high school with us.

Dad, can we talk?

Dear Agony Aunt,

I'm in a total mess here—hope you can help me out!

Dear Ben,

There is an old American saying, "Loose lips sink ships."

（7）当主句前有短语或从句时,须用逗号将两部分隔开。例如:

A well-known bilingual writer, Lin brought the concept of humour to modern Chinese literature.

To cheer her up, we went to a typical Quebec restaurant for lunch.

（8）在引导独立从句的连词前加逗号。

While we're doing all this traveling, we can get seasick at sea, airsick in the air and carsick in a car, but we don't get homesick when we get back home.

两个语法结构完整的句子,且中间没有连词连接的情况下,组成复合句时,一定不能用逗号连接(学生写作中的常见错误)。但是如果有连词连接,则可用逗号。

I was just letting off steam really, because I was so angry, but then my friend went and told everyone else what I'd said.

The painting is a lot smaller than you would expect, and is protected by glass.

（9）"如果句子由两个分句组成,且第二个分句由as（表示"因为"）,for,or,nor或while（表示"与此同时"）等连词引导时,同样需要在连词前加逗号。"（威廉·斯特伦克,2016:10）例如:

The world will little note, nor long remember, what we say here, but can never forget what they did here.

With this little joke, Lin was able to make people laugh, while gently telling off the president.

（10）"如果一个从句或一个须用逗号隔开的引导性短语位于第二个独立分句前,则连词后不需要逗号。"（威廉·斯特伦克,2016:10）例如:

You go to bed in one kind of world and wake up to find yourself in another quite different, and if this is not magic, then where is it to be found?

（11）"当两个分句的主语相同，且主语仅出现一次时，如果连词为but,则应该加逗号；如果连词是and且两句关系紧密，则不用逗号。"(威廉·斯特伦克,2016:10)例如：

As the world's first national park, Yellowstone is famous for the variety of its wildlife, but it is probably best known for its bears.

It takes hundreds of years for plastic to break down, but much less time for paper.

It seems like common sense: eating local food should be better for the environment, because it does not need to be transported long distances and kept cold during transport.

It looks like she has just flown down out of the sky and is standing on a ship.

（12）逗号可以用来代替文本中的省略部分，使句子更加简洁有力。

And the stage was really simple: a decorated whip represented a horse, and a screen with Chinese characters, a study. 逗号部分省略了动词 represented。

It turns out, it's just math working against you; chances are, the other line really is faster. 两个逗号处都省略了引导词 that。

（13）逗号可以用来指明宾语的位置。

Take, for example, "When the cat's away, the mice will play"…

Take, for example, the epic movie Troy, which is in part based on Homer's The Iliad and was met with mixed reviews from the audience.

这两个句子都是因为宾语太长，以逗号补位，宾语放在后面。

（14）但是如果分句十分短小且形式相近，或句子语气轻松、口语化，需要用逗号。特别是在一些成语或谚语中。例如：

Well begun, half done.

Take a deep breath, calm down, and always remember: think first, speak later.

（15）逗号还可以用来分开两个同等重要的形容词。

Firstly, there are few large, flat areas of land in the region.

Xiao long bao (soup dumplings), …, encasing hot, tasty soup and sweet, fresh meat, are far and away my favorite Chinese street food.

三、分号的用法

分号在英语中用于分隔两个并列的句子。

（1）分号通常用于表达两个相对独立但又相互关联的观点或事实。例如：

A young person could be old; a woman could be a man; we could even be sharing our information with criminals.

On the mornings that had once throbbed with the dawn chorus of ..., and scores of other bird voices there was now no sound; only silence lay over the fields and woods and marsh.

（2）两个语法结构完整的句子，且中间没有连词连接的情况下，组成复合句时，用分号连接。例如：

This new generation of artisans will not only help preserve traditional skills; the innovation they bring to the craft will also ensure that the art of clock repairing stands the test of time.

（3）如果两个分句由副词连接而不是连词引导，如 accordingly（相应地，从而），besides（此外），moreover（另外），however（然而），nevertheless（仍然，然而），then（那么，然后），therefore（因此），thus（这样，因而）等，仍需要使用分号隔开。例如：

You don't need expensive equipment; even the ball doesn't have to cost much money.

四、冒号的用法

冒号在英语中用于引出下文或解释之前的内容。在独立分句之后用冒号引导一系列具体事物、同位语、解释或起例证作用的引语。

（1）冒号前后的内容紧密相关。冒号比逗号效果更好，分隔的作用比分号弱，比破折号正式。例如：

And the stage was really simple: a decorated whip represented a horse, and a screen with Chinese characters, a study.

As a photographer, I love the bright light and amazing colours:

red rocks, green plants, blue-green waters and blue skies.

With us long believing that talking plants are fantasy, new research has revealed something amazing: it appears that plants can communicate after all.

The only thing I don't like is that my mom wants to know every part of my life: Becky, what are you doing tomorrow? Where? With whom?

（2）如果两个独立分句中第二个分句阐释、详述了第一个分句的含义，则需要用冒号连接两个句子。（威廉·斯特伦克，2016：16）例如：

Watched by millions, the ending to the race has divided opinions: should the brothers have been disqualified or highly praised for their actions?

What's more, football has become one of the best ways for people to communicate: it does not require words, but everyone understands it.

It seems like common sense: eating local food should be better for the environment, because it does not need to be transported long distances and kept cold during transport.

（3）冒号也可以用于补充前句的引语。例如：

But for Alistair, this decision was easy to explain: "Mum wouldn't have been happy if I'd left Jonny behind."

If you're in any doubt about this, take a moment to reflect on this line from The Secret Garden: "Where you tend a rose...A thistle cannot grow."

（4）冒号还有一些形式功能：在正式信函的称呼后面可用；表示时间时用于分隔小时和分钟；隔开书名和副标题。例如：

I am writing to invite you to attend our program "Talk and Talk" in our school broadcasting station at 7:00 pm. next Friday.

Eric Weiner's *The Socrates Express: In search of Life Lessons from Dead Philosophers* reawakened my love for philosophy.

Hence this book, *Chasing the Sea: Lost Among the Ghosts of Empire in Central Asia*, which talks about a road trip from Tashkent to Karakalpakstan, where millions of lives have been destroyed by the slow drying up of the sea.

五、破折号的用法

破折号(—)主要用于表示补充说明、解释或强调。"在英语中表示突然的停顿或中断、引导较长的同位语或总结性语句。破折号功能相当于强化版的逗号,但比逗号分隔作用强,却不及冒号正式,也不如括号严谨。"(威廉·斯特伦克,2016:17)

(1)表示解释或补充说明,通常可以看作对主句的附加信息。例如:

I just wanted you to be happy, and an engineer——a happy engineer.

The letters were also beautifully illustrated——each must have taken its true author, Tolkien, a long time to complete.

Growing up in England with a British father and a Chinese mother, I've enjoyed food from both countries ever since I was able to hold a knife and fork——and chopsticks!

The majority of us of course don't tell the truth——we lie and say that the food is "delicious".

(2)用于强调语气。通过破折号的使用,作者可以强调某个观点、想法或语句,使之在整个句子中更加突出和重要。例如:

Treated this way, you're sure to feel hurt——we should always be able to trust those closest to us, and it hurts even more when we find we can't.

Think of your first draft as a patch cut out of the jungle——as part of an exploration, not as a complete highway.

Maybe I'll fall in love with stinky tofu——someday.

So, if you are a runner with a story to tell, get in touch——we'd love to hear from you!

(3)破折号在某些情况下可以表示对比或转折。例如:

In some cases, local produce might have used more energy and produced more greenhouse gases than produce grown a long way away——even taking into account its transport.

Having seen quite a few productions of Hamlet and read the play many times, I was full of confidence——until the Peking Opera came to town!

总体说来,英语和汉语的标点符号虽然有差异,但用法在很多方面有相似或共同之处。这一节主要是根据教材中的例句,解释了常用的一些功能比较丰富的标点符号,希望通过这些例句,可以帮助我们更好地理解和运用标点符号,从而在书面表达中准确表达思想。

第二节　阅读中的语法学习

语法学习是语言学习的重要内容,直接影响学生综合语言运用能力,语法教学也一直是教学的重点。本节主要围绕语法内涵及其在语言学习中的作用、课标要求、高考对语法的考查变化以及语法学习策略方面进行分析,最后以情态动词为例,说明笔者对语法教学的实践。

一、语法的内涵及在语言学习中的作用

"语法作为有理据的语言体系,既是表达人际意义的交际手段,又是实现交际目的的语言资源。"(张艳君,2009)语法是规范语言使用的基石,掌握它有助于我们准确、得体、有效地表达思想,并促进学习和交流,避免形式错误。

语言学对语法的分类角度很多,包括历史角度、描写对象、描写方法、描写目的等方面。中学学习的语法是专为教学设计的,称为教学语法,涵盖基础、常用规则,是英语教材中的实用教学材料。陈力博士对教学语法和语言学语法有清晰的比对(表7-1)和阐释。

表7-1　教学语法和语言学语法对比

	语言学语法	教学语法
目标	明理的语法	致用的语法
分类	要求有概括性和排他性	要求不十分严格,以说明用途为主
举例	以例子说明类别	力求翔实,例子本身是学习材料
对象	语言的研究者,学术兴趣	语言学习者,学习条件不尽相同

"教学语法应该是"表达的工具",而不是"规则的描述"。它是用来

帮助学习的,而不是学习的目的本身。学生应该以应用为目的学习语法,而不是要把自己训练成为语言学家。外语教学中的语法应该是不同于理论语法的教学语法,它是基于语用和意义表达,以促进学习者言语技能为目的,对某些规律性语言结构形式的适当关注。"(陈力,2011)

语法教学是英语学习的基础,帮助学生理解语言规则,提高交际能力,这是提升英语应用能力的重要一环。对于中国学生而言,特别需要在教师的指导下,深入学习和掌握英语语法规则,并培养中英两种语言的对比意识,以免出现理解和表达方面的偏差,影响交际能力的发展。没有语法知识,就无从谈起听、说、读、看、写等几种能力。语法知识是英语学习的重要内容,是学习语言知识和语言技能的基石,它确保我们在表达时能够选择恰当、准确的语言形式。实际上,语法既是知识的积累,也是能力的体现,更是我们准确、有效地传达思想和情感的基础。

英语学习对于中国人来说,属于外语学习。我们缺乏习得英语的自然环境,所以我们对英语的掌握要靠学得而非习得,仅仅靠模仿、操练对绝大多数人来说不可能学会,必须在教师引导下刻意学习。认知心理学和二语习得研究都认为注意力是导致习得发生的必要条件,学习语言时,学习者需主动感知语言输入以促成内化,觉知与习得紧密相连。

另外,正如连淑能教授分析的那样,由于文化环境、思维方式等的不同,英汉两种语言在语言与文化方面存在着很多不同,如汉语重意合,英语重形合,两种语言的表达方式差异很大。"英语造句常用各种形式手段连接词、语、分句或从句,注重显性衔接,注重句子形式,注重结构完整,注重以形显义。英语是重形式的语法型语言。"(连淑能,2010:74)"汉语造句少用甚至不用形式连接手段,注重隐性连贯,注重时间和事理顺序,注重功能、意义,注重以意役形。汉语是重意会的语义型语言。"(连淑能,2010:78)英语语法体现了西方演绎法逻辑思维的刚性,汉语语法体现了中国理性思维的灵活性。在语言的结构图式方面,两者有很大的差异。按照二语习得理论,语法教学中注意汉英对比,有助于提高教学的针对性,促进学生的母语正迁移,预防负迁移。

学习外语能够锻炼学习者的逻辑思维和批判性思维能力。"英语表达方式比较严谨、精确,模糊性较小,歧义现象较少,用词造句遵守严格的词法和句法,造句成章也服从某种逻辑规则,适合于科学思维和理性思维。"(连淑能,2010:6)

思维方式的差异本质上是文化差异的表现,是沟通文化的桥梁。英语语法学习的过程一定程度上也是对西方文化的学习和理解,有助于理解和掌握英语语言文化,培养文化意识,而这本身也是课标要求的英语核心素养的一个重要目标。学习过程中要避免带着民族或文化偏见,否则容易产生文化冲击,也会影响语言学习的效果。

语法知识学习对于促进语言综合能力发展非常重要,它不仅是交际能力的基础,也是其中的一个重要组成部分。外语语法教学与培养语言运用能力并不矛盾。强调运用能力并不意味着要淡化语法的重要性,而是要专注研究和探索如何改进语法教学的内容和形式,从而更有效地促进学生语言能力的发展。

二、课程标准对于语法学习的要求

英语学习活动观六要素中的两个要素是语言知识和语言技能。语言知识中包含语法知识,语言技能包括听、说、读、看、写等方面的技能。而语法知识全面渗透在这些语言技能中,没有语法知识就无法确切地运用语言。

课程标准认为,"语法参与传递语篇的基本意义,语法形式的选择取决于具体语境中所表达的语用意义。据此,语法知识的使用不仅需要做到准确和达意,还要做到得体,因为语法形式的准确并不等同于语言使用的有效,有效的语言使用还涉及说话人的意图、情感态度及其对具体语境下参与人角色和身份的理解,这些都离不开语用意识和相关的语用知识。"(中华人民共和国教育部,2020:25-26)

从课程标准出发,教授语法的真正意义是其作为发展学生语言实践能力的有效方法。教学的最终目标是帮助学生将语言的形式、意义及交际功能融合为一体。通过在实际语境中的体验和应用,学生能够内化语言规则,从而准确、有效地进行语言交流。这也是语法学习的核心目的。

三、高考语法考查形式

语法知识在高考中的体现在听说、阅读、语法填空和写作等各个环节,而所有这些环节的考查都是以语篇形式进行的。

对比单句型的单项选择题,"语法填空考查的都是核心语法,更多的是从语言运用的角度考查,考查'形式—意义—运用'的结合,考查综合语言运用能力。"（陈新忠，2020）语篇型语法填空能从语篇层次考查考生对所学语法知识的运用，更符合语言学习过程中应尽量使用真实情境的要求。对语言产出性技能兼顾词法知识和句法知识，能够有效考查学生在语篇背景下的知识运用能力，更契合语言实际运用的要求。语法填空同时涉及对语篇意义理解能力的考查，需要首先关注文本意义，做到意义先行。一方面，这体现了语法规则的灵活性；另一方面，该题型基本上规避了考生通过乱蒙得分的可能性，测试信度相对较高。

在写作板块中，"应用了较多的语法结构和词汇"是英语写作评价标准之一。这里的"语法结构"更侧重句子和语篇的层面的丰富性，如果学生作文中的语言表达地道、丰富且能够体现多样性，势必能打动读者，获得认可。好的作文要求学生熟练掌握动词时态、情态动词、被动语态和虚拟语气等语法知识来表达情感和态度，并灵活运用不同类型的句子结构以增强语气和调整思维节奏，从而促进思维的成长。

语篇的显性衔接手段，多数都是语法方面的内容。甚至在阅读理解题目中，语法知识也起到了重要的作用。第四章第二节中给出过高考题的例子，而2023年泰安二模卷D篇第12题也可以运用语法知识解题。它对应的语篇内容如下：

…In the past, such desires appeared to be impossible. Our personalities were thought to be formed in childhood and to remain fixed throughout lives. Recent research, however, suggests that with the right psychological strategies and enough effort, people can successfully mould their core traits into the shape they desire. That is what psychology professor Nathan Hudson and his colleagues have shown with studies.

12. What can we learn from the text?

A. Personality remains fixed in life.

B. Personality change is possible.

C. Personality keeps changing with age.

D. Personality varies from person to person.

这个题目的解答，首先看题目中的四个选项，全都是一般现在时，体现的是规律性的东西。原文中对应段落的前半截是一般过去时，跟现在毫无关系，这是一般过去时的核心意义。所以，题目的答案应该从recent research往下寻找，people can successfully mould their core traits into the shape they desire 说明答案选 B。我们应该同时联想到，动作发生在过去，想要跟现在有关，需要运用现在完成时，这也是为什么应用文写作中的活动收获和感悟最好用现在完成时表达。

语法的学习不仅是一个形式的问题，而是如何在合适的语境下使用恰当的结构，才能表达确切的意义。语篇解读中，师生只有通过逐步挖掘、深度解读文本（这里就包含语法内容的解读）才能获取文本意义，而文本意义的构建有助于学生思维品质和文化意识的提升，同时也是学生对语言学以致用的过程。

四、语法教学的问题

目前高中语法教学中存在着一些与课程标准倡导的以语言运用为导向的三维动态语法观契合度不高的理念和做法。

首先是理念方面的偏差。陈力博士在《中学英语语法教学的内容、原则和方法》一文中提到，近二十年对语法教学的片面认识大致涉及两方面问题：一是语法知识与语言能力的关系问题，二是中小学英语课程的属性和目标问题。第二个问题目前已经达成共识："语法是我国中小学英语教学不可或缺的重要内容，'不是要不要教语法的问题，而是教什么样的语法和怎样教语法的问题'。"（陈力，2011）。对于第一个问题，实际上，"知识学习可以促进能力发展，语法能力本身也是交际能力的基础和构成要素，外语语法教学与培养语言运用能力并不矛盾。交际法和任务型语言教学也不排斥语法教学，不过是更强调语言的交际功能，强调'用语言做事'罢了。强调运用能力不意味着就要淡化语法，而是要研究探索如何改进语法教学的内容和形式，以便更有效地促进学生语言能力的发展"（陈力，2023）。

针对高中英语教师在语法教学方面的做法，存在两种截然不同的倾向。一方面，有的教师误解了新课改中的"淡化语法教学"，认为这意味着完全忽略语法教学，仅让学生通过主题、语篇和活动自行发现语言规律，对于学生难以理解的基础和必要的语法现象也不予讲解。这种做法割裂了知识与能力的关系，导致学生未能系统掌握语法知识，进而影响语言交际的准确性。另一方面，部分教师过于强调语法知识的讲授，脱离语境和意义，仅教授语法规则，以应对考试和练习为主，导致学生的学习重心偏向记忆语法理论，忽视了在真实语境中提升语法的应用能力。

其实这两种倾向都太绝对,教师应以折中的方式在教语法,既不过分注重语法规则的系统化,也不是完全不讲语法。但近些年学生的语法不成体系也是不争的事实,语法教学该不该系统讲或讲到什么程度,认识并不统一,教学活动随之产生差异。

首先,语法教学内容的取舍随意性较大。

面对教材语法项目时,部分教师因对其重视程度和理解不足,倾向于追求系统性,从而补充完整相应语法项目的所有规则。然而,教材中的语法内容是基于课程标准,强调在真实语境中通过理解和表达语篇意义来进行教学,避免孤立教授语法形式。同时,教材不仅以主题意义为单元编排,还融入单元教学理念,语法内容既在特定教学板块呈现,也贯穿于听、说、读、看、写等各项语言活动中。此外,教师可利用教参中的语法教学指导作为参考,并研究高考真题,以明确语法考查的重点,从而在教学中有针对性地选择和侧重。

人教社陈力博士曾谈过教材中教学语法内容的编写原则,其中有几条我们需要特别注意:"(1)教学语法是折中的,不是只依靠某一个特定学派,哪个学派对某个语法项目的解释最容易让学生接受就采用哪个学派;(2)教学语法不把语法看成静态的规则系统,而是把它看成动态关联的系统;(3)教学语法项目的选择不过分追求系统性,内容取舍主要是根据学生的水平和需要,内容的组织则要按照由浅入深、由易到难、由近及远的原则;(4)教学语法应该是和母语语法相对比的,重点放在形式、意义和语用与母语语法不同或似同实异的语法项目上;(5)教学语法的编写需要与学习者错误分析密切结合,讲解我国学生易犯的错误,提高学生对易犯错误点的警觉性。"(陈力,2023)

教师在实践中,可以给学生补充课本以外的内容,但一定要保质、限量,同时要考虑学生的认知,不能超纲。毕竟,课程标准对于语法项目的学习有明确的阶段性要求,要由浅入深、由易到难。初中英语语法是基础,高中英语是对语法结构更深层次的探索和学习,语法教学对提高外语学习者的准确性起着积极的作用。学生进入高中时,对大部分语法都不是一无所知。语法教学中,除了根据教材编排的语法内容,更重要的是要根据学生的既有水平进行内容的筛选,可以采用刻意练习的形式,重点解决学生的实际问题,让教学更有针对性。

其次,刻板追求语法规则,轻语言功能及意义。

有些教师对语法规则的记忆仍停留在自身的学习经历,严格刻板,难以在特定的场合及情境中理解和运用语言形式实现交际目的。一方面，语言本身是动态的变化体系，语法规则也在随时变动，原本认为错误的语法规则有可能已经被广泛接纳；另一方面，语法规则多具普遍性，但也有特例，且语境多样导致语言表达多变。"有些语句或表达是否可以被接受，很大程度上取决于语境，而不完全取决于句子本身是否符合语法规则。因此，在语法教学中，教师要特别注意所讲语法知识的适用性，所举例句在不同语境下的意义和可接受性。"（程晓堂，2020）

教师在教授语法时，要向学生传递这样的信息：语法学习要根据语境的意义表达，灵活掌握，而不能刻板认定特定场合下的特殊用法是错误的，要培养学生主动运用语法的意识和能力，而不是死记硬背孤立的语法规则。

再次，教学方式单一，不能根据内容选取合适的方法。

语法教学不仅要注意创设情景，而且要注意情景的真实性以及情景与所教语法项目的契合度。但很多情况下，"教师孤立地讲解语法知识，既没有主题引领，也没有语境支撑，导致学生对语法知识的学习只停留在对零碎知识点的记忆上，所学的语言知识不能直接服务于在特定语境下对相关主题内容的理解与表达。"（张献臣，2022）

有时所用例句来源不权威，导致呈现的语言不够真实、地道和典型。学生处于被动接受状态，对英语学习毫无兴趣可言，难以实现自主性、探究性学习，学习效率低下，且长期不重视语法和句法的学习，学生很难有较高的综合语言运用能力。

五、语法教学的策略和方法

从上面的分析可知，语法需要教，但是如何教，教到什么程度，陈力博士的二十四字口诀对高中学生来说就是最好的策略："'意义领先、先例后法、提醒注意、点到为止、随遇随点、适时归纳'。也就是反对离开语境和意义讲语法规则，不主张离开意义背口诀；反对将语法知识点搞得支离破碎，主张适时归纳，但也反对没有足够感性积累的情况下过早归纳；语法规则的归纳反对教师灌输，提倡教师提供典型实例，学生或师生共同总结归纳；反对不切实际地让学生去探究发现他们很难归纳出来的规律，也反对不顾学生需要和接受能力过分地追求系统全面。"（陈力，2011）

根据新课标倡导的理念,教师在教学中应改变过多讲解语法知识的做法,将传统的讲述式语法教学,转变为英语学习活动观指导下的动态运用式的教学。刘道义老师在语法教学中的观点与陈力老师的观点异曲同工:"新课程的课堂教学中,可以采用'呈现—发现—归纳—演绎—实践—活用'的教学步骤来优化语法课堂教学。"(刘道义,2011;转引自李宝荣,2016: 64-65)

新课程理念下的语法教学赋予了语法交际的意义,从语用的角度学习语法,通过设置明确的任务目标和创设符合语言交际的真实情境的课堂环境,将语法规则放入有意义的交际情境中进行教学。通过各种连续的、非连续的、书面的、口头的语篇形式呈现语法内容或进行操练,逐渐培养学生的语感和有效的学习策略,以实现语言功能的表达和实现特定话题的目的。

研究表明,语言形式与不同语境的有机结合是使用语言的关键。教师在教授语法时,应侧重于在语境中介绍新知识,引导学生观察语法项目的表达形式、基本意义及语用功能。鉴于教材中语法讲解的简化与分散,教师应引导学生在实际学习中先在语境中感知语法现象,体会其应用,以培养对语言形式与意义之间关系的敏感度,但需避免过度拓展。待学生获得足够的直观认识后,鼓励他们自主总结,并在教师引导下明确语法的用法和差异。随后,通过各类语境练习,特别是情景和文化语境,加深理解和应用能力。教师应引导学生反思错误原因,吸取教训,明确薄弱环节,并据此进行有针对性地学习补充。在语境中运用语法有助于学生将所学知识有效应用于实际语言交流中。

六、以情态动词为例开展的语法学习实践

有效的语法学习直接影响着学生语言理解、表达的准确性和得体性,因此教师在教材学习时,应将语用含义作为重要的思考方向,充分利用教材创设的主题语境、通过开展活动来引导学生挖掘和阐释语用含义,帮助学生深入理解,提高学生的英语学习能力。

情态动词是初中阶段就要求学习掌握的语法项目,但高中教学实践中还是能够看出学生对其的理解和掌握比较刻板、只是知道基本意思,但难以在语境中理解其确切含义和用法。本小节通过对教材和高考题中常见的几个情态动词用法进行讲解,引领学生理解语境中的情态动词,确保语用得体。

（一）情态动词 would 和 must have done

外研版教材必修 2 Unit 2 的语法项目是情态动词,其中语篇 The Real Father Christmas 的第三段 "Every Christmas, an envelope with a North Pole stamp arrived... Who **could** it be from? The children **must have been** very excited as they opened it. Inside, they **would** find a handwritten letter from Father Christmas. The letters were also beautifully illustrated—each **must have taken** its true author, Tolkien, a long time to complete." 中,出现了多个情态动词的不同用法。

Could 表达了疑问中的推测,会是谁从北极给孩子们写信呢? 拆信后, The children must have been very excited. 推测了孩子们收到圣诞老人来信的激动之情,下文中破折号后用了 must have taken...,表达了作者对 Tolkien 的拳拳爱子之心的敬佩和羡慕。同样的表达出现在 Unit 1 的语篇 A child of two cuisines 中：中英混血的作者在去买猪耳朵时,英国卖肉人说没有猪耳朵,同时扯了扯自己的耳朵,作者用了 He must have thought I was joking,比较肯定地推测卖肉人以为自己在开玩笑。生动表达了作者因为自己跟卖肉人不同的饮食而表现出来的忍俊不禁,画面感很强。这两处的 must have done 都表达了语气比较肯定的推测。

在上面提到的段落中,还有一个 Inside, they would find...,这里的 would 表达的是一种过去的习惯,通常要跟过去时间状语连用。本段段首有时间状语 Every Christmas,也就是 Tolkien 每年圣诞节都会以圣诞老人的身份给孩子们写信。

在同一单元的语篇 Time for a change? 中, 第二封信的第二段 "**When I was a little boy**, the dinner on the eve of Spring Festival was what I looked forward to most. ... I **would** run around the house, ... I'd get under my mother's feet in the kitchen, ... **She**'d put tokens in some dumplings：..., all of us **would** sit around the table, ..."

整个段落中,作者连续用了多个 would 回忆自己小时候过年,一家人一起准备过年的场景,充满了对跟家人一起过年时光的回忆和留恋,支撑自己要表达的观点：过年，一家人就要一起在家里准备年夜饭、吃年夜饭。

在这两个文段中，教师可以设置问题"What feelings does the writer want to convey by using the modals in the paragraph?"其目的是让学生体会情态动词表情达意的功能。

选必三 Unit 2 中 Life behind the lens 语篇介绍了摄影师 Bill Cunningham，在说到他成功的原因时，语篇的第四段中有这样的句子"Cunningham would go out onto the streets of New York ... He would even stay outside in a storm，..."第六段中说到他人品正直，"He valued his integrity and would not be bought by anyone，..."其中的 would 也是过去经常性的动作。经过了必修二的学习之后，再次见到会激活学生的记忆，深化他们的理解。

看得多了，学生对其用法就能轻松掌握，在高考题中自然也能很好地进行语用的迁移。Would 的这个用法出现在 2020 年天津高考题中的完形填空题第二段："The lady **would** get a call from a stranger **every morning** who _____（eventually，frequently，previously，occasionally）make her believe that he was her friend... Jones was shocked when she said she didn't actually mind being cheated. 'Otherwise, I **would** never speak to another person for weeks on end,' she said."

该篇主要讲了警察 Jones 为了解决孤独造成的抑郁甚至犯罪问题，在社区设置 Happy benches 供人们闲坐聊天，因其效果显著，被广泛采纳。第二段是 Jones 想法的起因：独居女士被骗取了大笔的钱，可是她不在乎，因为如果没有骗子每天给她打电话，她会连续几周没有人可以说话。

如果考生掌握 would 的这个用法，后面空中的副词就会首先排除 frequently 和 occasionally 两个词，previously 没有语境支持，答案自然选择 eventually。

（二）情态动词 can

在 Book 2 Unit 2 的 *Time for a change*? 中，第一封信的作者软件工程师 Wang Peng 的观点是：在哪儿吃年夜饭不重要，重要的是家人之间的爱保持不变。接受形式的改变，维持节日核心价值的不变。

语篇第二段"**Can**'t they admit that the preparations for the dinner are hard work? ... We work all year, so **why can**'t one day be about spending time with family and relaxing?"

Wang 在段首和段尾两个疑问句中运用 can't 强烈表达了自己不想经受操办年夜饭的辛苦，而要跟家人一起在外面吃年夜饭的态度。这里，可以这样提问学生，"Why does Wang Peng use two questions to show his idea? What kind of feelings are conveyed?" 同时可以探讨、比较在家吃年夜饭和外出吃年饭态度背后的原因，"What do you think are the possible reasons behind the different opinions?"

阅读训练需学生既重文本内容，又了解其在语境中的语用功能，领悟作者的情感态度和价值观。

（三）虚拟语气

课程标准中的语法项目一览表里，虚拟语气是标注三个星号的语法项目，具体要求是：选修（提高类），在语篇中恰当地理解和使用虚拟语气（中华人民共和国教育部，2020：25）。也就是说，虚拟语气不是高考要求，但是虚拟语气的实际运用特别广泛，可用于多种体裁的语篇中，表达情感、意图和想法。

在教材 Book 1 Unit 3 *Just a brother* 的语篇里，Alistair 在铁人三项比赛中，帮助即将倒下的弟弟一起完成比赛。这一做法引发了两种对立的观点：取消哥俩的获奖资格还是大力表扬他们的做法？ Alistair 的回应是"Mum wouldn't have been happy if I'd left Jonny behind." 这个虚拟语气的运用，说明如果他不管弟弟，那么妈妈一定会不开心，是对过去情况的一种虚拟推测。

2023 全国新课标 I 卷的完形填空，也说了一个类似的故事：越野赛场上，选手 Melanie Bailey 背着受伤的 Danielle Lenoue 冲向终点线，并把她送到医疗点。语篇中有两处用了虚拟语气：

故事的点题部分"Melanie Bailey should have finished the course earlier than she did." 和故事的评议部分"She would have struggled ... without Bailey's help." 都运用了对过去情况的虚拟。

第一个 should have finished the course earlier，表明 Bailey 有实

力成绩更好,但她比赛中因为帮助别人而耽误自己的成绩,表达了一点点的遗憾。后者说明如果 Danielle 没有 Bailey 的帮助,会非常痛苦地独自挣扎到医疗点,表明了 Danielle 对 Bailey 的深深感激!

记叙文里常常需要表现主人公的情感变化,除了用动词、副词和名词等各种词汇表达,还可以用虚拟语气非常精准地表达情感的转变。2023 年全国乙卷的 B 篇阅读中,作者记录了自己不畏艰险,到野外拍摄高质量风景照的经历。最后一段中有这样的文字 "…, it was stressful getting lights and cameras set up in the limited time. …, they are some of my best shots though they could have been so much better if I would have been prepared and managed my time wisely." 虚拟语气的使用表现了作者虽然觉得这些照片可以归为自己拍出的最好照片,但仍然遗憾时间紧,否则可以更好地调整灯光和相机,拍出更好的照片。

高考题中的考点,在教材中都能找到相应的语用案例。外研版教材选必二 Unit 2 *Social Media Detox* 中有这样的句子 "The detox was more difficult to tolerate than I had expected. I felt like I had lost an arm! Not eating for two days would have been easier!" 说话人 Anna 戒断手机两天,过程非常难熬,甚至说出了即便两天不吃饭或许比这更容易一些,来衬托出她对手机的上瘾程度和戒断手机的煎熬!

教材选必三 Unit 3 *War and Peace* 中 The D-Day Landings 里 "But even in the depths of war, few could have been prepared for the violence and horror they would experience there." 这样的一句话就足以让人想象到战争的残酷和令人毛骨悚然!

教材选必四 Unit 2 *The road not taken* 里 "Like the writer, all we can do is look backwards 'with a sigh' and imagine what could have been." 其中的 could have been 以淡淡的忧伤情绪表达了作者因为没有选择某条路而有的遗憾。

虚拟语气的用法 "情态动词+have done" 是对过去的虚拟,从事件的发生来看,本质上就是一般过去时。例如,烟台 2023 二模第二套题 B 篇第 7 题就是在语境中对该用法的展示:

Most of Browne's works are in private collections. In 2017, the Florence Griswold Museum held Matilda Browne's first exhibition in over eighty years—Idylls of Farm and Garden. It seems that this modern recognition was long overdue.

7. What does the last sentence of the text imply?

A. Browne remains unrecognized as a world-famous artist today.

B. Browne should have been accepted as a celebrated artist much earlier.

C. Few people know Browne was a successful artist in the early 20th century.

D. Female artists in the 20th century deserve to be acknowledged in modern times.

本题是推理判断题，正确选项采用的是同义句型的转换。原文 was long overdue 是过去时，should have been 也是一般过去时，且除了 B 以外的选项都是现在时，故答案选 B。本题考查原文语义的理解，同时时态的判读对该题的理解起着关键作用。

通过多阅读，学生对某一语法现象产生感性认知后，可自主归纳，教师则负责纠偏和补充关键或考点，结合归纳与演绎法，促进学生全面理解。将语法学习融入阅读教学，既有助于理解其在文本中的作用，又为交际中的准确表达提供范例。教师应创建真实语境，让学生有机会内化所学。掌握任何技能都需多次实践，语法学习亦然。学生需经历由控制到半控制练习，直至自由运用的过程，锻炼从习得到归纳、学习的综合应用能力，方能轻松应对高三复习。

语法教学应聚焦于语言运用，确保知识的精确、恰当和得体。教师应根据课程标准和学生情况，精选教学内容，结合词汇教学，实施个性化策略，并指导学生高效学习。通过多样化教学情境，达成教学目标，激发学生兴趣，提升语法应用能力。

参考文献

[1]Masoumeh Akhondi, Faramarz Aziz Malayeri, Arshad Abd Samd. How to teach Expository Text Structure to Facilitate Reading Comprehension[J].The Reading Teacher, 2011（5）：368–372.

[2]Richards, J. C. Beyond Training[M]. Cambridge：Cambridge University Press, 1998.

[3] 曾庆茂,李华平．英语修辞鉴赏与写作 [M].上海：同济大学出版社,2020.

[4] 陈力．小学英语语法教学答问 [J].小学教学设计,2011(5)：4-5.

[5] 陈力．外语教学中的话题、主题与主题意义 [J]．小学教学设计, 2023（21）：1.

[6] 陈琳．英语：选择性必修．第一册到第三册 [M].北京：外语教学与研究出版社,2019.

[7] 陈新忠,李鹏,杨琳,等．2020 年高考英语试题分析与教学策略（上）[J].英语学习,2020（10）：26-38.

[8] 陈新忠,汤青,李静,等．2019 年高考英语试题分析与教学策略（下）[J].英语学习,2019（10）：21.

[9] 程晓堂．基于主题意义探究的英语教学理念与实践 [J]．中小学外语教学(中学篇),2018,41（10）：1-7.

[10] 程晓堂,周宇轩．主题、话题、主题意义概念辨析 [J].中小学外语教学(中学篇),2023（6）：1-5.

[11] 程晓堂．中学英语语法教学中的几个突出问题 [J]．中小学课堂教学研究,2020（4）：3-8.

[12] 程晓堂．基于语篇分析的英语教学设计 [J]．中小学外语教学(中学篇),2020（10）：1-8.

[13] 高宝光. 词块理论在高中英语词汇教学中的应用探究 [J]. 校园英语, 2022,（39）: 16–18.

[14] 葛炳芳. 主题、话题和主题意义的区别及其对基础外语教学的启示 [J]. 英语学习, 2022（10）: 4–9.

[15] 郭华, 徐广华. 素养导向的"教—学—评"一体化何以实现: 基于英语教学评价改革的思考 [J]. 英语学习, 2023（12）: 29–35.

[16] 胡壮麟. 语篇的衔接与连贯 [M]. 上海: 上海外语教育出版社, 1994.

[17] 胡壮麟, 朱永生, 张德禄, 等. 系统功能语言学概论 [M]. 北京: 北京大学出版社, 2008.

[18] 胡壮麟. 语言学教程（第五版中文本）[M]. 北京: 北京大学出版社, 2019.

[19] 黄国文. 语篇分析概要 [M]. 长沙: 湖南教育出版社, 1988.

[20] 黄国文. 功能语篇分析纵横谈 [J]. 外语与外语教学, 2001（12）: 1–19.

[21] 黄国文. 语篇分析的理论与实践——广告语篇研究 [M]. 上海: 上海外语教育出版社, 2001.

[22] 黄国文. 功能语篇分析面面观 [J]. 国外外语教学, 2002（4）: 25–32.

[23] 中华人民共和国教育部教育考试院. 高考试题分析: 2024年版. 英语 [M]. 北京: 语文出版社, 2023.

[24] 李宝荣. 中学英语教学设计优化策略 [M]. 北京: 北京师范大学出版社, 2016.

[25] 李杰, 李若菲. 在英语语篇教学中培养逻辑思维的实践 [J]. 中小学外语教学(中学篇), 2021（8）: 1–6.

[26] 李兴勇. 问题与突破: 高中英语作业设计现状与新理念 [J]. 英语学习, 2023（11）: 4–8.

[27] 连淑能. 英汉对比研究（增订本）[M]. 北京: 高等教育出版社, 2010.

[28] 梁美珍. 高中英语文本处理阶段的问题类型及设计方法 [J]. 中小学外语教学(中学篇), 2011（4）: 1–6.

[29] 刘道义, 郑旺全. 英语（必修第2册）/普通高中教科书 [M]. 北京: 人民教育出版社, 2023.

[30] 龙群力. 激发和培养高中学生英语阅读动机与兴趣的策略探究[J]. 中学生英语(高中版),2012(11):45-49.

[31] 梅德明,王蔷. 普通高中应用课程标准(2017版)解读[M]. 北京:高等教育出版社,2018.

[32] 皮连生. 学与教的心理学(第五版)[M]. 上海:华东师范大学出版社,2009.

[33] 钱剑英,徐钰,杨新辉,等. 英语阅读教学中的信息加工:提取与整合[M]. 杭州:浙江大学出版社,2015.

[34] 苏霍姆林斯基. 给教师的建议[M]. 杜殿坤,译. 北京:教育科学出版社,1984.

[35] 王来民. 高考真题阅读材料辅助高中英语阅读教学的研究[J]. 英语教师,2020(7):31-33.

[36] 王瑞林. 教考衔接,破旧立新——对高考改革中两个热点问题的思考[J]. 中国教育报,2022,9(16):9.

[37] 王燕艳,崔林凤. 核心素养导向的14种英语课型设计框架及课例解读(中学教师版)[M]. 大连:大连理工大学出版社,2023.

[38] 威廉·斯特伦克. 英语写作手册:风格的要素[M]. 北京:外语教学与研究出版社,2016.

[39] 文秋芳. 二语习得重点问题研究[M]. 北京:外语教学与研究出版社,2010.

[40] 武和平. 因文而雅,由文而化——学科核心素养视角下的文化教学[J]. 英语学习,2017(6):7-8.

[41] 武银强,武和平. 以文化人化——文化教学的课标理念与课堂实践[J]. 英语学习,2022(3):4-12.

[42] 徐国辉,杨茜,张金秀,等. 主题意义引领下的高中英语词块教学策略[J]. 中小学课堂教学研究,2023(4):4-8.

[43] 余文森. 核心素养导向的课堂教学[M]. 上海:上海教育出版社,2017.

[44] 张道真. 英语介词用法例解[M]. 北京:外语教学与研究出版社,1985.

[45] 张德禄. 非语言特征的衔接作用[J]. 解放军外国语学院学报,2000(4):22-25.

[46] 张德禄. 论衔接关系化——话语组成机制研究[J]. 外语教学,

2003（1）：1-6

[47] 张德禄,刘汝山.语篇连贯与衔接理论的发展及应用[M].上海：上海外语教育出版社,2003.

[48] 张金秀.主题意义探究引领下的中学英语单元教学策略[J].中小学外语教学(中学篇),2019（7）：1-6.

[49] 张献臣.基于核心素养目标的中学英语语法教学原则和策略[J].中小学外语教学(中学篇),2022（6）：12-17.

[50] 张艳君.语法的语用内涵诠释[J].天津外国语学院学报,2009（6）：9-14.

[51] 赵振才.英语常见问题解答大辞典[M].西安：世界图书出版西安有限公司,2016.

[52] 中国高考报告学术委员会.高考评价体系解读[M].北京：现代教育出版社,2021.

[53] 中国高考报告学术委员会.高考评价体系解读[M].北京：现代教育出版社,2022.

[54] 中华人民共和国教育部.全日制普通高级中学英语教学大纲[M].北京：人民教育出版社,2000.

[55] 中华人民共和国教育部.普通高中英语课程标准(2017年版2020年修订)[M].北京：人民教育出版社,2020.

[56] 中华人民共和国教育部.义务教育英语课程标准(2022年版)[M].北京：北京师范大学出版社,2022.

[57] 教育部考试中心.中国高考评价体系[M].北京：人民教育出版社,2019.

[58] 教育部考试中心.中国高考评价体系说明[M].北京：人民教育出版社,2019.

[59] 钟启泉.核心素养十讲[M].福州：福建教育出版社,2018.

[60] 种秀娟.从文体特征角度备战高考英语阅读[J].英语教师,2015（9）：62-65.

[61] 朱晓燕.英语教学中的语篇分析：汉文、英文[M].北京：外语教学与研究出版社,2023.